Meeting Myself

Beyond Spirit of the Empty Hand

by

STAN SCHMIDT

Editor: Randall G. Hassell

Meeting Myself
Beyond Spirit of the Empty Hand
by Stan Schmidt

Published by: Focus Publications
                P.O. Box 15853
                St. Louis, MO 63114 U.S.A.

© 1997 by Focus Publications
All Rights Reserved
ISBN 0-911921-25-7

Library of Congress Cataloging-in-Publication Data

Schmidt, Stan, date.
    Meeting myself : beyond Spirit of the empty hand / by Stan Schmidt.
    p. cm.
    ISBN 0-911921-25-7 (pbk.)
    1. Karate--Psychological aspects. I. Schmidt, Stan, date- Spirit of the empty hand. II. Title.
GV1114.3.S336   1997
796.815'3'019--dc21   97-26008

First Printing 1997

Printed in the United States of America

To Judy and Lisa
Caryn and Mark
Debbie and Keith
Tia and Clayton
My delightful grandchildren
My Mother
Ray and Joel

Acknowledgments

Thanks to

Dawn Kenmuir
for her tireless and efficient word processing

Randy Hassell
for his constant encouragement and editing

My loyal and faithful instructors and students

Instructors and Staff of Japan Karate Association

Those special people who have shared with me in inspiration, encouragement, sorrows and joys

The Early Birds
(See Appendix for Names of the Early Birds)

TABLE OF CONTENTS

Chapter 1	**Breaking New Ground**	9
	Sorry, We're Full	
Chapter 2	**The Lessons of an Inflated Ego and a Broken Ankle**	15
	From My Backyard to a Dojo in Orange Grove	
Chapter 3	**Orange Grove to Tokyo**	23
	Confusing Days	
	First Grading Attempt	
	Quiet Bank Clerk Can Kill	
Chapter 4	**Kase *Sensei* Through the Back Door**	35
	The Initiation	
	New House - New Dan	
Chapter 5	**Enter Enoeda**	43
	The Warrior Gentleman	
	Happy Hacking Golf - Then Some Serious Confrontation	
	Returning to the Source	
Chapter 6	**The Golden Era of JKA**	55
	Welcomed by Mr. Takagi	
	Meeting 'The Animal'	
Chapter 7	**Confronting the Top Guns**	67
	"Your Whole Body is an Eye"	
	A Head Butt and a Bite	
	Human Beings Emerge	
	Creativity Becomes a Desperate Need	
	Asking the Right Questions	
Chapter 8	**The Third *Dan* Grading**	83
	Closing the Distance Between Self and Reality	
	Loneliness and Then ...	

Chapter 9	**Breaking Bricks and Building Bridges** *Daily Bread* *Nasty, Unwelcome Visitors* *Aching to Return to Japan* *Teacher Becomes Student*	91
Chapter 10	**Heaven & Hell** *The Gates of Heaven* *One Day Zen* *Reading, Wrestling and Ruminating* *Claude Chanu - Ground Worker*	101
Chapter 11	**A Re-Look at the Japanese and Their Unique World** *Musashi Says - Nakayama Does* *Sumo, Keno and Nunchaku* *"I Felt Insecure"* *Healthy Company?* *The Japanese in My Own Back Yard* *"Get The Hospital Truck Ready"*	113
Chapter 12	**The Dan Ranks. Stepping Stones To ...?** *New & Higher Mountains* *Breaking the Chains*	131
Chapter 13	**Tanaka Made an Impact** *Takahashi and a Gemstone* *Nakayama Sensei Visits my New House Dojo* *Only the "Color" of One's Spirit Matters* *"They will Shoot You..."*	137
Chapter 14	**Unforgettable Experiences** *Kill or Be Killed* *Close Down That Dojo* *Sashimi, Tanaka Style* *Unexpected Dan* *In The Empty Hand, The Cure* *"We Kill The Jet Lag"* *Like Dying and Coming To Life Again* *Soul of Karate*	145

Select Your Heroes Carefully
The Movies vs. The Truth

Chapter 15   **Back To Basics, Then .....**   163
Prepare Properly
Zanshin
"What is Mister Stan?"
Seven Significant Things
"Take It With Your Own Hand"

Chapter 16   **The Road to Seventh *Dan***   179
"You Think"
The Golf Drive and The Reverse Punch
1988
Three Important Points
"Too Sharp!"
Specialized Training
"Okay, You Change Flight"

Chapter 17   **Ups and Downs**   193
"Promises, Promises ...."
Deep Depression, Then .....
Back to White Belt
Stress
Injury to the Body of JKA, but the Soul Stays Healthy
Back to Square One Again
The Man With Spirit

Chapter 18   **New Attitude, New Life**   209
Self-Defense Through the Spirit
Milk and Honey
Reunion

Appendix 1   **Black Belt Ranking Standards**   221

Appendix 2   **The Early Birds, Past & Present**   225

1

BREAKING NEW GROUND

Meeting Myself

When I was 10 years old my father died of a burst appendix. He was a senior master at King Edward VII school, which is located in the affluent Johannesburg suburb of Houghton. We lived on the other side of Louis Botha Avenue in the lower middle class suburb of Bellevue, Johannesburg, known as *Egoli* or 'The City of Gold' in South Africa.

My father graduated from Stellenbosch, a University, nestling in the heart of the Cape wine lands. He then joined the police force, mainly for the physical training, and was posted to Grahamstown. After that he accepted a teaching post at a school for black children in the Transkei. I was born in Kokstad, and when I was five, we moved to Johannesburg.

My father's death at the age of 42 came as a great shock to my mother, who worked as a switchboard operator to support the two of us. I had no brothers or sisters.

As an only child I received great affection from my mother, yet I developed a complex and would not allow her to attend any of the school functions in which I participated.

At school, my sporting activity declined from playing in the under-thirteen "A" rugby team in Form I, to being barely selected for the fourth team in my matriculation year. Every year, I just managed to scrape through to the next form. My only saving grace was when I started a body building gym in my mother's back yard, where I pumped iron with a few friends. When I failed my matric exam, I was so shocked that I immediately enrolled at a night school and passed the exam six months later. I was working in a commercial bank at that time. On the day I received my first paycheck, I strolled through Johannesburg city with the 28 pounds burning a hole in my pocket (Pounds Sterling was the currency of South Africa at that time. Now it is termed Rand). I came to a shop glittering with musical instruments. I liked the look of a shining, golden trumpet, so I walked in and bought it. A day later I enrolled at Hymie Baleson's School of Trumpet.

Between my banking, body building, and trumpet practice, I had very little time for girls or other pursuits.

Then came my three-month army call up. With me went the trumpet. I ended up in two squads—a PT squad of 150 specially selected athletes (which would put on a demonstration at the Johannesburg Diamond Jubilee Festival) and in the army band.

When I came out of the army, a school friend of mine, Cyril Vickers, asked me to accompany him playing the drums. We played simple Dixieland tunes. One day during a break, as we relaxed on his front lawn, he invited me to try to wrestle him to the ground. At the time I tipped the scales at 200 pounds. He was a lean, wiry man and weighed about 155 pounds. I tried to push, pull, and trip him up, but to no avail. Then he neatly threw me onto my back. This greatly impressed me, of course, and I asked him how he did it.

"I've been studying judo," he said. "Last week I received my orange belt."

Then he impressed me again by inviting me to hold him down on the ground. Try as I might, he got out every time. He just had a way of twisting and turning and squirming his way out of my seemingly powerful grip. Then he held me down. I couldn't get out. I was both surprised and disillusioned. With all my size and power I couldn't handle little Cyril who had always been a pushover at school. A few weeks later I enrolled at Sebastian Hawkin's judo school, the Kodokan University of Judo, situated then on Eloff Street in the center of Johannesburg.

Now I was really busy. Trumpet practice in the morning, body building at lunch time, and judo every evening. The banking increasingly became a hobby.

Then I met Manny Lubowitz. I saw an ad in the newspaper: *"Looking for trumpet player who digs the blues"*. As I stepped into the Lubowitz home I heard the single note, bluesy piano riding the rhythm of a very steady drum beat. I was drawn in and stood watching Manny on piano and Saul Ozinsky coaxing out the pulse beat. They were so engrossed they only noticed me 10 minutes later as the piece came to a close.

With no more than a nod, Manny indicated that I tune the horn and join them on their jazz journey.

"You're in," he said, as we neared the end of a marathon session.

By that time half of the neighborhood had congregated in the small lounge, some bopping along or watching, while others studiously ignored us.

We began to perform at various types of gigs—weddings, 21st birthday parties, *bar mitzvahs*—and all we played was *blues*. Manny was the first piano player I ever saw who stood up while playing. He was a real madcap and an instant hit with party crowds. But Manny was going one way and I the other. My judo brown belt training was becoming heavy and the band work was not helping my energy level—nor was the body building and the banking. Something had to give. So the trumpet found its way into the back of a cupboard. Manny left for overseas, and I haven't seen him since.

That was around 1960. Some years later a hit song reached the top of our charts. It was *"Do Wa Diddy-Diddy"*, by a new British group, Manfred Mann's Earth Band, none other than Manny Lubowitz from Highlands North. My bluesy piano partner had come a long way. At 23 I had just put my foot on the first rung of the judo ladder and still had a long climb ahead of me.

Sorry, We're Full

At the age of 21, I was quite a big man, six feet, two inches of more than 200 pounds of carefully cultivated muscle, by order of the Reg Park Health Studios. Yet my stomach twinged uncomfortably as I entered the neat reception area of the Kodokan University of Judo on Eloff Street, Johannesburg. This was around 1957. The Registrar showed me into his office and asked me what he could do for me.

"I think I want to take up judo," I said uncertainly.

"Do you know that judo can turn you into a veritable fighting machine?" he claimed.

"Is that so?" I sat forward on my chair. "I will be joining this school," I said.

"Sorry," he replied, pausing, "We're full."

"Oh, no!" I blurted out. "I really want to learn judo. Can't you fit me in?"

A hint of a smile crossed the man's face. He stood up and opened a door leading into a spacious area covered in light green *tatami* mats (straw mats). I caught a glimpse of do*zen*s of white-uniformed individuals throwing other individuals onto the mat.

The registrar returned with two brawny black-belted men, one on either side of him. The first one, an Angus-Bull-of-a-man, was Dr. Sebastian Hawkins, the principal of the school, and the other, with the look of a trained Alsatian, was Jimmy White, the chief instructor.

"This young man very badly wants to learn judo," said the registrar. A picture of Jigoro Kano, the founder of judo, decorated the wall behind him. I was aware of a tense silence and was sure they could hear my heart beating.

Beyond Spirit of the Empty Hand

"What do you think?" asked Dr. Hawkins, looking across at Jimmy White, who had been openly inspecting me from head to foot.

"I reckon he looks pregnant with possibilities," he smiled. "I'll fit him in somewhere."

As a novice white belt, my first instructor was Steve Vermeulen, an extremely patient and well-mannered second *dan*. I learned to fall first. Sideways, backward, forward, overhead rolls, and numerous mat-bashing techniques. The falling routines were a kind of toughening-up process. As we mastered a fall, so we learned the throw that initiated it. For instance, after learning sideways falling, we were taught the leg sweep, *ashi-barai*.

Norman Robinson's older brother, Joe, was well-known for this technique at the time. I had, of course, heard of the famous Robinson family, but I thought that you had to first be a champion black belt to be one of their students.

After about three months of beginners' training I was, together with lean, wiry Jimmy Coker, and short, stocky Dennis Clarke, promoted to Jimmy White's class. Jimmy drove and pushed us. We did incessant repetitions of *uchi-komi* or "entries" as Jimmy called them. Where in the beginners' class we had learned the rudiments of ankle trip, leg throw, hip throw, shoulder throw and so on, we now took only one throw and repeated it endlessly with our partners resisting our efforts to topple them. This was both exhausting and frustrating. What had seemed relatively easy in the beginners' class now became a major problem. In that class we learned form only. Now, with added resistance, we had to develop, in addition to form, two extra qualities—power and coordination.

My colleagues, Jimmy Coker and Dennis Clarke, developed rapidly. Although my power exceeded theirs, their form and coordination put me in third place. By the time I achieved green belt (6th *kyu* level) they were ahead of me with blue. Then came the Johannesburg championships.

I had never won anything in my life, in any sphere, until then. I was certainly not the favorite for the white to green belt section of the tournament. There was a large audience watching. One voice rooted for me as I struggled with my first opponent, and that was all I needed. The hip throw came from nowhere, and my opponent flew overhead. I was awarded my very first *ippon* (full point). With the whole crowd now cheering me on, I became inspired and won the event.

Meeting Myself

It changed me. I had never felt I was good at anything until then. This little win had done something for my self-image. From training three times a week, I upped my training to seven times a week.

2

THE LESSONS OF AN INFLATED EGO AND A BROKEN ANKLE

Meeting Myself

Winning the white to green belt section at the Johannesburg Judo Championships in my early twenties changed me. I had always tried to avoid aggressive confrontations. In fact, my greatest fear was getting into a fight. Now, with this minor win, I developed an inflated opinion of myself. But my ego bubble was to burst some months later. The Japanese call it *karma* (what one does returns to one). I call it needing a good lesson.

I was driving late one night on the road to Durban with two friends when we stopped for refreshments at a roadhouse. As we left, a group of six rowdy locals flung a string of insults at us. I responded with an insulting hand sign. As we reached the outskirts of the town, a large, black car overtook us and forced us to the side of the road. Sure enough, it was none other than the six locals, baring fists and teeth at us. We drove around their car, but they persisted and cut us off again, forcing us to the right side of the road. This was a clear case of fight or flight, but there was nowhere to run. I jumped out and walked toward the black car. It was a dark night. As I reached their car, both the right side doors opened and I was in a brawl. While the driver taunted me, a big guy tackled me from behind. The rest of them circled us. It all happened quickly, with my friends still stuck in our car. There was a steep drop at the edge of the road, which I only felt as my opponent and I crashed over the side, rolling over bushes and jagged rocks. I was bruised and dazed as we finally fell against a barbed wire fence at the bottom. The fight had developed into a wrestling match, which suited me. As the other five rowdies came rushing down the slope, I heard one say, "Let the two fight it out." I was relieved. This one-to-one fighting was what I was learning at judo. As I applied a reverse neck lock across his windpipe, I felt him giving in.

The mob pounced on me and plucked me off him, pinning my arms. Their hero had free rein. He shook his head, swore at me, and hit me with a right hook. I felt dazed, but did not drop. They pushed me into him again and again. He must have hit me 30 times with the same blow, but somehow he couldn't put me down. I just kept staggering forward as if in a dream, trying to get at him. But my reflexes had slowed down from the punishment my head was taking.

Then, suddenly, it all stopped. They didn't want to continue. I walked up to my opponent and extended my hand, thanking him for the experience (it was the first serious fight I had been in). But it was as if he feared my attitude. He stepped backwards, saying, "Hey! Watch it!"

Beyond Spirit of the Empty Hand

I have not feared being hit since that day. Although the left side of my face was a mess, I really felt good inside.

For the next year my judo career comprised losses and more losses. As we neared the black belt grading, rivalry between my colleagues and I reached fever pitch. Try as I might, I was always a half-point or two behind the dynamic Dennis Clarke and the calculating Jimmy Coker. They made their black belt first *dan* and I didn't.

"You need more finesse," said my coach, Jimmy White. Then, he took me in hand. He had the uncanny knack of dropping my spirits one moment and raising them the next instant. He would have me on my back, more often than not, with his tricky, changing combinations. He would turn in for a hip throw and, as I resisted with all my power, he'd change direction and have me falling backwards, using an inside leg throw. For the next stage, Jimmy kept pitting me against Claude Chanu, a big fourth *dan* (black belt degree) who had exercised his grappling skills on the beaches of Brazil, South America. He was an expert ground worker who enjoyed tying us up in the most unconventional knots imaginable. He was a formidable opponent, and he stayed that way well into his sixties.

Then I was told to face sixth *dan* World judo Champion Norman Robinson, in a line-up of 10 men at the nationals. I lasted about 10 seconds and marveled at his speed. It made me train harder. I was a provisional first *dan* at the time, which meant I needed that extra something to get a first *dan*.

A few months later, I was graded first *dan*. I was told to enter in Norman's line-up, and I lasted the longest of the 10. Norman praised me, and his father, Professor Jack, announced that his association also recognized me as a first *dan*. Shortly afterwards, I entered in the Senior South African Kodokan Championships and reached the semi-finals. But I had fractured a bone in my leg earlier on and, hobbling around the mat on one leg, I was unable to defeat the two-meter giant, Mark Glaser.

It was that cracked ankle which led me to discover a virtually unknown art—karate.

I was angry with myself. I had just missed the South African judo title and here I was, sitting in my bedroom with my leg in a plaster cast, unable for the first time in two years to do any judo training. I asked myself what I was going to do for the next six weeks, and the answer literally landed in my lap.

Meeting Myself

"Read that!" said Jimmy White, entering the room and flinging a book onto my lap. "Maybe it will teach you how not to break your leg. You're too wild in your fighting." Jimmy White, my instructor, was a fourth *dan* judo-ka (*ka* means practitioner), who had learned his skills the hard way in Singapore. I valued his advice. It was blunt and to the point, like his judo.

The book with the strange title, "Karate," immediately captured my attention. Clean-cut Oriental athletes clad in white with black belts around their waists, literally leapt out of the pages at me. Jimmy, who sensed my preoccupation with the book, said, "I'll leave you with it; you need to stew for a while."

One particular line in the book captured my imagination. "The karate man never stops training."

With a crutch under one arm and the book in the other, I made for the backyard. Thus, sitting on an old wooden chair, my new training regimen began. In this seated position I went through the various blocks, punches, and strikes in the book. I wasn't able to do the moving techniques, but I had a wealth of exercise doing repetitions of the upper body techniques. I remembered Dr. Sebastian Hawkins (principal of the judo school) once showing me how one could practice striking techniques on a young tree or pillar. You drew four lines. One represented the nose, the second the chin, the third the throat, and the fourth line the solar plexus.

A friend called out any one of the four areas and you had to strike immediately to the appropriate line with the edge of your hand. I adopted this kind of training using the techniques in the book, aiming them at a brick pillar that held up the old coal shed. There was also the stem of a peach tree, which I padded with old straw cushions, and then struck with my fist from a seated position.

By the end of the six weeks, my hands were becoming hard with traces of callus developing on the knuckles and the knife edge. My upper body had grown stronger, but when the doctor removed the plaster cast, I was upset by what I saw. My leg was pale and painfully thin. I immediately launched into a strenuous set of drills ranging from leg squats to roundhouse kicks, and from heel raises to doing back kicks against the coal shed wall. As usual, I overdid it and limped around for weeks with sore muscles and bruised heels, but the muscles began to thicken.

Beyond Spirit of the Empty Hand

From My Back Yard to a Dojo in Orange Grove

Jimmy Coker called me one day saying: "Stan, meet me at lunch time. I want to show you something."

I worked at a bank in Orange Grove, and he met me outside.

"Come with me."

We walked a few blocks up Louis Botha Avenue and he stopped outside a small shop.

"How do you like it, Stan?"

It was a vacant shop.

"What do you mean, Jimmy?"

"I mean, Stan, you're ready to have your own *dojo*. I'll go in halves with you and we can teach people judo. It's in you, man!"

"Wow!" That was all I could say at first. I had never thought of doing this.

"The rent will be 20 pounds a month. I'll pay 10 and you pay 10, okay?"

"I like the idea, Jimmy, but I'm only earning just over 30 pounds a month in the bank."

"Be positive, Stan. We'll do demos and we'll get students. I guarantee you we will be making a profit within two months. Are you in?"

"Yes, Jimmy. Thank you for thinking of me."

When I told my mother I had signed a lease and was liable for 10 pounds a month, she looked extremely worried. We struggled each month to make ends meet. But she nodded her head and wished me luck.

Within one month Jimmy and I were paying the rent from members' fees and making a little pocket money for ourselves. We called the place Zenith Judo Dojo. Within a couple of months Jimmy Coker came to me and told me, "Stan, you're on your feet now; I'll be moving on. You are secure enough to do this on your own. I saw your potential and just wanted to get you going."

That was Jimmy Coker, an amazing person with vision, and a true friend. After he left, I took in various partners who were also close friends—John Davies, Ginger Halpern, Ken Wittstock, Neville Kenmuir and his wife, Dawn—and each helped my progress in many ways. (Dawn Kenmuir later became Secretary-Girl Friday-*Boss* of our national organization, South African JKA Karate Association. As of the date of this writing, the association has more than 250 *dojos* and over 15,000 practicing members.)

Meeting Myself

My small judo club in Orange Grove was going well. With banking during the day, judo at night and now this new karate in the mornings and on weekends, I was forever tired. I participated in Doug Baggot's judo Black Belt Club three times a week where all one did was fight other black belts one after another. On the other nights, I taught, and after the class, fought my co-instructors, who would just lie on me while I struggled to get free. It made one tough, but it was exhausting. At the bank I yawned my way through most of the day. At times I felt I was getting weaker so, instead of getting more quality rest, I increased my training by doing weight training during lunch breaks.

Something had to give. I broke my other leg, in exactly the same place as I had broken the first leg. I had become over-exuberant fighting Claude Chanu. I tried to force him over my leg and got my foot caught in a gap in the mat.

"You're using too much energy. You need to flow more. Become more gentle," he chided. Little by little, Claude Chanu's philosophy began to penetrate my thick skull.

"Read this." He wrote out these words for me: "My eyes are God's eyes. I see with the eyes of the Spirit. There are no obstacles in my pathway. I see clearly the perfect way."

Karate training increasingly dominated my interest. One day, a scrawny teenager who had been watching us, said he wanted to join the club. As I began teaching him judo, he stopped me, saying: "No, I want to learn that stuff where you kick and punch."

"But I don't know much about it myself," I replied.

"Please teach me," he stubbornly insisted. And thus started our first primitive style karate class.

Twelve years later, the scrawny youth, Ken Wittstock, took third place in the All Japan Karate Championships, the first non-Japanese to place highly in a world class tournament.

By 1960, I was 23 years old and my small judo *dojo* in Orange Grove had quite a large group of students. I still trained out a few times a week at judo, but karate training now captured most of my free time. If I wasn't back-kicking the coal shed wall at my mother's home, I was doing *mae-geri* (front kick) on a sandbag, or hammering my hands against a large concrete block we had dragged into the *dojo*. The word got around and many top judo men, wrestlers and body builders visited to work out with us at our primitive book-learned karate.

Norman Robinson had also been doing a similar thing, and he and Doug Baggot, along with Ken Wittstock, Ginger Halpern,

Beyond Spirit of the Empty Hand

Jimmy White, Cecil Wolov, Neville Kenmuir, John Davies, a few others, and myself, would work out in the most unthinkable ways. Our unwritten maxim was: *You've got to be tough!* We bashed our limbs against walls, trees, bricks and against each other. We were very bruised most of the time, and in a free-fighting match we knew little of self-control. A good win was when your partner either submitted or was winded, or on occasion, knocked out cold. But I think our saving grace was that, in essence, we were good friends, believe it or not. Each one had some excellent quality that the others admired and tried to emulate. For instance, Norman Robinson and Jimmy White were expert at throwing you if you got too near to them. Claude Chanu was like the Boston Strangler with his neck-breaking techniques. Ken Wittstock, then an up-and-coming youngster, was full of unorthodox tricks. I am told that my back kick was something special at the time, thanks to the coal shed wall that I had marked with a cross and at which I aimed and kicked every day.

The initial small group of karate students at Orange Grove began to grow until it was larger than the judo group. I tried everything to keep the interest which, although it never flagged, I knew deep down was lacking something that the book-learning could not provide. I had begun teaching new students, yet I was not qualified. We had even developed our own system for grading. White belt was beginner level. After about nine months we could go for green belt and the final top level was red belt. We had only half a dozen "qualified" red belts at the club. Among them were Ken Wittstock, Jimmy White, Ginger Halpern, Tom Langley, Ervine Katzer, Neville Kenmuir, and Cecil Wolov. I used to invite other top martial artists, such as Doug Baggot, Norman Robinson, Claude Chanu, and my bodybuilding instructor, Peter Arundale, to help me test the unfortunate candidates. These were tests that made the demands on the recruits in *An Officer and a Gentleman* look timid by comparison. One of the tests I remember went something like this: "Break that brick with one blow; now block those kicks (everyone in the class had to throw kicks toward the poor student). Now get out of this hold. (Somebody of your own body weight had to hold you down). Do 60 push-ups. Now fight each one in the class." And so on.

That was the ad-lib kind of test given by a very tough and uncompromising panel, which sat in a straight line shooting orders and questions at the single examinee. Those who got through green or red belt may not have had the prettiest techniques, but they sure could handle themselves. Our grading system was primitive. Basically, only the tough in spirit got tougher while the weak fell by the wayside. Jimmy Coker, who had been watching our enthusiastic body-crunching regimen from the sidelines, one day said, "You can't go on like this. You'll end up as a has-been by the time you're 30 years old. Go to Japan; do it properly." At first his words did not quite register. I had never thought about *that* before. This Jimmy Coker was either a genius or a complete fool.

"But how can I do that? I'm in the bank," I replied uncertainly.

"Think!" he said. "And go!"

Then it all happened at once. My grandfather passed on and left me 500 Rand for further education, and the bank granted me a three-month paid leave of absence. I married Judy, with whom I had been going out for the past year, and we pooled our meager resources. We left for a three-month honeymoon-*cum*-karate expedition to Japan.

"You've got courage," quipped a friend as we left. *Chutzpah*, I think, would have been a more accurate word.

Beyond Spirit of the Empty Hand

3

ORANGE GROVE TO TOKYO

Meeting Myself

Thanks to the urging of my judo colleague, Jimmy Coker, my wife and I were about to step onto Japanese soil. The year was 1963. I was 26 years old at the time, and my mission was to learn this new, strange martial art, karate.

I had previously done some soul-searching regarding the school of karate I should join, but after much correspondence with Japan, I finally chose the Japan Karate Association which was recognized by the Japan Ministry of Education.

Shunsuke Seto had maintained a regular correspondence with me over the previous year and we were fascinated by his writing style. Every letter began with a poetic paragraph revealing the nature of things and weather conditions in Tokyo.

The misty sun struggles to show its face
yet the fallen leaves smile,
laughing—warming my heart.

As Judy and I stepped into the narrow, bamboo-lined lane in Yotsuya, a suburb of Tokyo, we instantly became aware of dynamic sounds emanating from a small wooden building at the end of the pathway. As we reached the flimsy wood and glass door, it slid open, revealing a smiling Japanese face. The young man took our shoes, and invited us into the vibrating building.

This very polite and happy individual was none other than my pen-friend, Shunsuke Seto. I was pleased to meet him but the astounding actions and sounds that were dramatically unfolding on the shiny wooden floor behind him distracted me to such a degree that my wife apologized to Seto for my lack of good manners.

"Ah, he like karate, I see," said the ever-smiling Seto, as 20 hardened heels crashed to the floor in unison. This was followed by a blurred set of arm movements. Their whip-cracking action resounded across the small *dojo*. Then the compelling sounds of what seemed like a regiment of lungs expelling air as their lightning arms changed to a slower pace. The 20 black belts were now rooted deeply into a *kiba dachi* (horse riding) stance, knees braced, their eyes alert, yet seemingly unaware of the rivulets of perspiration flowing down their cheeks. Their hands described a perfect arc, which seemed to blossom, fade away, and then consolidate.

It flowed from the soles of their feet. Then the final gladiatorial shout, or *kiai,* reverberated deep into my innards.

"Phew!" I exclaimed, shaking my head and looking at Seto as the group ended their *Tekki Shodan kata*. (Kata are formalized routines of techniques) "I can't believe it. I've never seen anything like this in my life. They're fantastic!" He laughed, enjoying my undisguised enthusiasm.

"You very lucky," he said. The 20 were lined up in the straightest line I had ever seen. The group knelt and faced an older man, who had been taking them through their paces.

"You have just seen the instructors' class in action."

"Who is he?" I asked, pointing toward the man in front.

"Nakayama Sensei, Chief Instructor of the Japan Karate Association," said Seto in a tone of reverence.

As Seto led us to a man seated at a desk, I noticed that while the group training had ended, the instructors were now doing training of their own particular choice. Some were lightly sparring, others were pounding the *makiwara* (sprung, padded punching and striking board) at the back of the *dojo*, stretching into the splits, or checking each others *kata*.

I was introduced to the director, Takagi *Sensei*.

"Why do you want to do karate?" he asked.

"Because I love karate," I answered without thinking.

"You must look at other schools," said Takagi, sternly.

"I have," I shot back bluntly, "and I want to join this one," I added with conviction.

"Welcome to Japan, Stan-*san* and Judy-*san*!" he said unexpectedly, his stern countenance changing into a sunny one.

Confusing Days

My first days of training in Japan were totally confusing. I was neither a beginner, nor was I advanced because I had done four years of book-training-style karate in South Africa. When Enoeda Sensei asked me what belt I was, I said, "Red Belt." This was an arbitrary grade we had given to ourselves in South Africa.

"What belt is that?" he asked.

"Like beginner," I said, trying to correct my *faux pas*.

In Japanese terms this kind of statement is usually taken to mean, "I've been training for some time but I won't blow my own trumpet." That was that. I was categorized and without further ado was told to join the General Class. This meant, unbeknown to me, that I had bypassed the Beginners' Class without yet having stepped on the floor.

Meeting Myself

My next loss of face was when suddenly the buzzer sounded and an assortment of white, green, purple, brown, and black belts scurried on to the floor leaving me standing at the side, dressed in a shirt and a pair of denims. There was a strained silence until the instructor sent over a senior class member.

"Where is your *gi* (karate suit)?" queried the sub-instructor.

"I haven't got one," I answered, realizing I was holding up the class. An instant later there was a suit in my hands.

"You change quickly!" he urged.

My real problems started when I stepped onto the floor. All the commands were in Japanese, and I didn't understand a word. On short, sharp, clipped commands, the class would move sideways, exchange blows in complete unison, and I was the one and only confused body, forever turning in the wrong direction and bumping up against this synchronized squad of shaven-headed Japanese, peppered here and there with a few *gaijin* (foreigners).

First Grading Attempt

"You must take grading examination," I was told by a class senior only three weeks after my arrival in Japan.

I sat on the polished floor, among a large group of *kyu* (student level) examinees. As I sat waiting, I noticed that the students at my table did their *kata* facing Table B. Then my name was called out from the other table, Table A. Somebody nudged me and I dashed across to Table A which was facing in a completely different direction to what I expected. Confusion again.

"*Hajime!* ("Begin!")" commanded the chief examiner.

I moved in a mindless state. Halfway through I bumped into another examinee going through the same *kata*, *Heian Nidan*. It threw me. I apologized, stopped for what seemed an eternity, tried to gather myself, and then completed the last four moves of the *kata*. I walked off, certain that I had failed.

"Congratulations, you are now a 7th *kyu* (second rung of the student levels)" Enoeda informed me.

Now, with a month's intensive training in Japan, I was a very tired 7th *kyu* who had been subjected to thousands of repetitions of blocks, punches, stances and kicks, up and down the wooden floor of the *dojo*. Although the training drills in this class made immense demands on my body and mind, we did very little free-fighting. My wife told me that the instructors' class did plenty of free-

Beyond Spirit of the Empty Hand

fighting. This I wanted to do, so I waited after my class and approached the first Black Belt who entered the training area and asked him in broken Japanese: "*Jiyu-kumite* (free fighting)?" He bowed and we were into my first sparring experience in Japan. I hadn't noticed, but this informal match had drawn the attention of a number of instructors who, so my wife said, watched from the corners of their eyes. My opponent moved in a low, fighting stance and within seconds had scored with a well-controlled *mawashi-geri* (round kick) to my neck. Without thinking, I attacked his shin with an ankle sweep. He dropped to one knee. It happened a second time. Then he suddenly moved like a windstorm attacking me with a flurry of blows. Instinctively, I spun around and delivered the unorthodox back kick I had done so often against the coal shed wall in my backyard. It wasn't a very hard kick, but it caught him directly in his solar plexus because he dropped and clutched his knees. He was winded. I felt embarrassed. I was fully aware that he could have taken my head off with his first kick, yet as I helped him from the floor, he congratulated me, saying, "Good—your technique brown belt level, but your fighting maybe *sandan* (third degree black belt)."

I was astounded by what he said, and his attitude revived the enthusiasm of which I had been drained since I had begun training in Japan. I learned later that this black belt was a fourth *dan* and an All Japan Champion.

This incident turned out to be a worthwhile one for me because it spread around the *dojo,* and from that day on, whenever I was introduced to Japanese karate-ka, they would invariably greet me with, "Ah! Mistah Back Kick."

Three months had passed, and the Japan Karate Association was preparing for the 6th All Japan Championship. The training was intensive. It had become traditional for the two top Westerners in Japan to put on a demonstration of attack and defense from a chair-sitting position at the Championship. A week before the tournament, Enoeda Sensei, who had been giving me extra coaching, called me onto the floor.

"You please fight him," he said, pointing toward a tall, powerful, 4th *kyu*, who I will call Morton. He was my senior. A number of people had gathered to watch. They included the instructors, the director (Takagi Sensei), the secretary (Maya-san), and Judy. The fight lasted about 20 minutes. My wife told me later that my actions had the audience of instructors and staff in hysterics. I had still not been entirely weaned from my book-learned, unorthodox

Meeting Myself

karate. I attempted all sorts of unusual tactics, such as pointing to the side of Morton and then attacking him as he looked at where I pointed. Evidently, the way I executed my moves was hilarious, to say the least. I would do six or seven fresh-air hand moves from a *kata* and then suddenly shoot out a side-kick. Morton got confused and fell down a lot, much to the amusement of the Japanese Instructors. Evidently, he had bullied a few beginners in the past and because of Japanese politeness, the instructors had said nothing to him about it.

After the fight, both our karate suits were torn and we were drenched through with perspiration. Enoeda Sensei slapped me on the back and with a hearty laugh told me I had been chosen for the foreigners demonstration.

"Also, tomorrow, you take special grading test," he stated, becoming serious again.

I arrived at the *dojo*. Except for the instructors' class, regular classes had been canceled because of the forthcoming championship. I watched from the side, and halfway through I was called on to train with them. The pace was unbelievable. I felt totally worthless, like a cart horse against race horses, and yet, I had in three months come down in weight from 200 pounds of muscle and fat to 180 pounds of sinew, muscle, and bone.

After the class a table was set out, and the examination began, with me being the sole examinee.

"You go back to South Africa soon, so we will give you a special examination," said Nakayama Sensei, the Chief Instructor.

I assumed I was being tested for 6th *kyu* the next level, as there is normally a three-month waiting period between *kyu* levels. The test was extensive. After completing many variations of *kihon* (basic techniques) and *kihon ippon kumite* (basic, one-step sparring), I was told to do *Heian Sandan* (kata number three), then the 4th and 5th katas, and finally, *Tekki Shodan*, which is a brown belt *kata*. After this they asked me to do *Bassai Dai*, a Black Belt kata. I told them I was still unsure of it.

"Okay," said Nakayama Sensei, after leaning across the table and talking to the 4th *dan* instructor whom I had winded with the back kick, "You are now 3rd *kyu*, brown belt. Next year, when Kase Sensei goes to South Africa, you can try *shodan* (first degree black belt)."

I couldn't believe it. Brown belt in three months! It was unheard of. But then I had done all of that training from books. It must have helped a little.

Beyond Spirit of the Empty Hand

Enoeda beat Shirai in the final of the Sixth All Japan Championships and my chair demonstration with Tom Ryan was well received by the audience as well as by ABC-TV.

Quiet Bank Clerk Can Kill ...

Judy and I returned to South Africa in July 1963. A large crowd, consisting of judo and karate enthusiasts and family members, met us at Johannesburg's Jan Smuts Airport, flinging laurel wreaths around our necks and pressing us for details of our Japanese adventure.

It wasn't long before I was giving my first press conference. I remember I felt both confident and insecure at the same time, a paradoxical mix of pride and uncertainty. I was proud of my new found karate status, yet uncertain of who I was in relation to the South African community.

When questioned on karate, I was a sage on the subject. I knew it all. In fact, I felt I literally owned it. Dogmatism was my middle name, yet on the other hand, I felt out of place in social circles, unable to converse intelligently on anything but karate. When someone spoke of sport, I would say, "Other sports are nothing compared to karate." I must have been a real pain in the backside. "We train much harder. We're doing something useful. You PT men just exercise for vanity; we karate men (there were no women doing it at that time) are not only getting exercise when we punch and kick, we're also learning self-defense". I found people seldom argued the point with me. But, in retrospect, I guess one doesn't argue with a 200-pound, six-foot-two karate zealot. There was just nothing better than karate, and I was more than willing to get onto the line to prove it.

During my first press interview with the *Star* newspaper, I was asked by a reporter, "Can a karate man kill a person with a blow of the hand?"

"Oh yes. Quite possible." I never pondered a question or thought twice in those days. My answers had to be direct and quick like my techniques.

The next day the following headline heralded my first write-up:
"Quiet Bank Clerk Stan Can Kill a Man with One Finger"

I was astonished when I arrived at my *dojo*, then situated above the Central News Agency in Orange Grove, to find that the membership had grown from 30 to about 100 members in one day, and

Meeting Myself

all because of one write-up. I was happy but worried. I had to do something. I didn't want to be seen as a phony. I resolved that I had better live up to my newspaper image, or else. So from the next morning, and each following morning at six o'clock, I began building even larger, uglier calluses on my fists and on the edge of my hand. I never succeeded in building up much muscle on my finger. So be it, the morning regimen had begun with me alone, at first, in the backyard of my mother's house.

Judy and I had spent all our savings in Japan. In those days a few Rand went a long way. We had spent our life savings on the three-month Japanese trip. Totaled up, it came to R1,500, a fortune in those days, when R1 bought more than 500 Japanese Yen. Nowadays, R1 buys 25 times less. So it was back to the bank for me and back to typing for Judy.

Early mornings I trained, and evenings I taught my Grove members karate, the Japanese way. Aiming to verify the image the press had bestowed upon me, I created a daily regimen that did not allow enough time for a moment of weakness to creep in. I rose at 5:30 a.m., trained until 7:00 a.m., washed, breakfasted, and clocked in at the bank by 8:30 a.m.

I worked with stock brokers, getting reports on shares from them on behalf of bank clients. I started my own imaginary portfolio and within a year had made myself far in excess of a million Rand. That was only a hypothetical profit, of course, because I didn't have an extra cent to my name. At times I acted as teller. This I liked, as there was a nice pillar in my box against which I hardened the side of my hand when no one was looking. A female ledger supervisor called it my teething ring.

At lunch time I would run to Reg Park's Gym and pump weights with Peter Arundale. My body was going lean from the karate training, and I was scared I would get weak, so my reassurance was heavy bench presses, curls, and squats. Thus began the inevitable inflating and deflating process. Karate, which hones and strips you down, making you fast, lean, and cable-hard as compared to weights, which pump you up and build strength and size. I realize today that weights done systematically in the right doses can enhance one's karate skills, but in those days it was just a case of the more the better of both karate and weights.

As a consequence, I would walk out of the gym red-faced, exhausted, and pouring with sweat, seeking out the nearest milk bar. Four double-thick chocolate malts later I would arrive back at the bank and would collapse behind my desk, yawning the afternoon

Beyond Spirit of the Empty Hand

away, willing 4:00 p.m. to arrive. By the time I arrived at my *dojo* an hour later, I was raring to go.

If ever the expression "kicked ass" suited anyone, it suited me. Every day I paid the price in my training, and now it was the turn of my students to suffer. I have been told by many of my students that I was a tyrant then. If there was any lapse in concentration or a small mistake, such as missing a count by a student, he would pay dearly, usually by being severely scolded: *"More spirit! Hop around the dojo ten times!"* And they hopped. I switched on when I was on the floor and never has a student refused to do or try to do "the impossible." I believe I have grown too soft today. My old way proved one thing to me: The most unlikely students were often capable of the most unexpected feats.

One evening while I was endeavoring to get an idea through to my senior class, two young men, who were seated on a nearby bench, were talking animatedly about something. Piqued by their lack of demeanor, I confronted them, commanding, "Hop around twice!" They hopped.

My wife came running from behind the reception desk calling, "Stan, Stan! What are you doing? Those people just came to look, they're not even members!" I let them finish one circuit and stopped them.

"Nice spirit," I told them, trying unsuccessfully to hide the grin on my face.

"Thank you," they responded.

The next night they were on the floor, this time in karate-*gi*. They had signed up.

It is all very well to be dedicated to hard training, and our athletes today do just this, but they also know when it's time to lay off. In those days I had a point to prove. I had read that, "The karate man never stops training," and I took this literally. For five solid years, I trained seven days a week. I honestly felt that if I missed one day, I would grow weak—like Samson after he had his hair shorn.

When, for the first time, my wife demanded that we take a week's holiday in December, I rebelled against the idea.

"What about my training?"

"You need a rest. You've earned it," she would answer.

"Rubbish!" I would answer, and come up with some inane reply like, "When you are on the back of a tiger, you can't get off."

"I don't see any tiger," she would reply, quite calmly.

Meeting Myself

"You just don't understand," I'd say, sulking for the rest of the day.

In the end, she won. She kept at me. We went on our holiday to Umhlanga, a resort town on the East coast of South Africa. One week. I had to creep out of the room at dawn.

"Where are you going?"

"To swim," I'd lie.

Then it would be sprints up and down the beach, interspersed with press-ups and splits in the shallow water. Then to the tarred car park at the rear of the hotel, where I would go over every *kata* I knew. This incessant training produced certain results. It made me tough and uncompromising with karate. In my mind I was like superman. My reasoning was, "I train the hardest; therefore, I must be the best."

The Japanese had told me, "You're the chief instructor; now set the example for your students!" I took this seriously and grew very tired and weary, drained of energy. And as a result of the overtraining, I caught colds and flu easily and would snap at times like a threatened, wounded animal. For example, if a student of mine happened to get a stray blow through on me when we were sparring, I would descend on him like a ton of bricks, sweeping him to the floor and tying him up in a lock until he submitted.

One evening, just as we had finished the last class, an onlooker approached me in front of my students, saying, "This new karate thing is all very well, but you stand no chance against a knife."

"Are you a knife fighter?" was my immediate reaction. I was already on edge from the day's training, work, and teaching.

"Yes, from Kenya. I have seen a lot of action."

"Try me!" I snapped. I was riled that he had the audacity to confront me in front of my students, who all waited for me to respond. Considering what I now know about people and fighting, I must have been insane to say that.

"Okay!" he said. "You serious?"

"Of course," I shot back. "Where's your knife?"

"I haven't got it here," he answered, "but have you got a ruler or something?"

"Some knife fighter," I retorted. "A knife fighter without a knife!" I was really rubbing it in.

Someone fetched him a ruler. He came at me. He did a few slashing movements. I blocked them.

"I've just cut your arms up, you see," he teased.

"Didn't you see me whip my jacket off and wrap it around my forearm?" I taunted back. Of course, I hadn't, I was just bantering with him. Then he lunged, a straight stab to my solar plexus. My back kick hit his solar plexus before the knife was half way. He dropped, winded. We revived him.

"Where did that come from?" he asked weakly.

"I don't know!" I responded, now worried that I had hurt him. And I honestly didn't know because those kind of responses just happen. It's like your instincts take over.

"Are you crazy?" scolded my wife on the way home in the car.

"You don't understand," I replied.

"He could have had a real knife, Stan."

"True. That was a bit stupid of me," I agreed. "But all the students were watching."

4

KASE SENSEI THROUGH THE BACK DOOR

Meeting Myself

1964 heralded the arrival of two people: my first daughter, Caryn, and a top Japanese karate instructor, Taiji Kase *Sensei*. Because of South Africa's immigration regulations and restrictions on Japanese citizens at the time, Kase was brought through the back door of Johannesburg's Jan Smuts Airport, so to speak. Clad in a dark blue and white kimono, he literally leapt over the barrier separating the arriving passengers from the waiting crowd.

"*Jyslaaik* (an Afrikaans expression of surprise)" exclaimed one customs official. "Who the hell is he?"

"A sixth *dan* karate man from Japan," I stressed.

"He looks bloody dangerous to me," said the official. "I won't *sukkel* (interfere) with him!"

Kase *Sensei* beamed at the man. "Sank you bery much," he exclaimed, bowing deeply.

"You may move through, sir," said the official, who moved away without so much as laying a finger on Kase's baggage.

Sitting on the grass outside the airport building, Kase *Sensei* talked to us.

"All instructor must try *oi-zuki* (stepping punch) all day until fall down." He talked like a machine gun spitting bullets. Whatever he said was reinforced by dynamic fist or feet movements, which had our little group of instructors enthralled. Each technique was a whip-like crack, and his flowing kimono became alive with each movement he made with his arms and legs. He was a short, thickset man with a big face and bright, shining eyes.

Kase's first teaching stint was at George Higginson's Kodokan *dojo* in Durban. The training area overlooked the Indian Ocean, a perfect setting for hard, healthy training.

One night at about 9 o'clock, as I was wearily preparing my bed on a couch in the small lounge area of the *dojo*, Kase called me.

"Stan san, you now take *shodan* test! Okay?!"

"*Osu!* Sensei!" I replied. His word was law, and my "Osu" (pronounced Oss) meant that I would do my best and keep a strong spirit of fortitude. We'd done three hard sessions that day comprising two hours of *kihon*, two hours of *kumite* and two hours of kata. I was aching and tired, and bed was all I could think of until then.

"Tonight good meaning for you, this test." All of the other students were summoned and they watched me go through my paces. I must admit I cannot remember much about that test, except for one thing. Halfway through *Bassai-dai* kata, I went into another kata called *Kanku-dai*. Kase stopped me.

Beyond Spirit of the Empty Hand

"Once more," Kase commanded.

My heart raced. "I had better do it right this time," which I did.

"We all go out now. Must make party." We weren't about to argue with Kase that we were tired and that we were not relishing the idea of tomorrow's early morning training at 6 a.m.

"Stan now *shodan*," he informed the group as we walked to a nearby restaurant. "Must celebrate—all night, okay? First black belt very important. Big celebration, all night. Okay?" he repeated. "Not think of tomorrow. Today is today. Tomorrow is tomorrow."

My tiredness disappeared in an instant. We celebrated, captivated by Kase *Sensei*'s stimulating anecdotes on karate and life.

"Ah, today some Japanese *kenchusei* (student Instructors) very weak," he told us.

"No, no, *Sensei*. *Kenchusei* very strong," I argued, slurring my words. The mix of Lieberstein wine and Castle beer was taking effect.

Kase ignored my protest and went on. "My University time we have no judges or referees. Now too much control. Too much hand guards, groin guards, gum guards. Before, when University teams fight, it is real team fight. One big *dojo*, two doors. One University walk in one door, other university walk in other door." Kase's words were blunt and to the point. No *ands, ifs, buts*. Just straight info. "Instructor shout '*Hajime!*' and everybody fight."

"Each other?" I queried. I was picking up his short clipped way.

"No, no, Stan. Everybody fight anybody. Very dangerous. Team with most member standing is winner."

We laughed and laughed at this.

"Did you ever get hurt, *Sensei*?" someone asked.

"Ah," he pondered, looking up at the light fixture. "Nearly."

"What happened?"

"Ah. Many member of other University attack me. I block all. But one pull me onto floor. Hold me. Other members begin attack," he paused.

"And then, *Sensei*. What did you do?"

"I get out," he paused again.

"How?"

"I catch his banana. Nearly make 'banana split.'"

We found this very funny.

I was mindlessly drunk by the time we returned to the *dojo*, where we sat on the floor, the *Sensei* talking to us. It was a never-ending evening, or was it morning? By three o'clock in the morning I sobered up somewhat and realized that he was talking on three tracks all at once—a kind of *Zen* talking. On the one hand he talked about karate training in general. In the middle of that he brought in some comments. For example:

"Tournament karate not complete. Only half of karate. Stan, you pick your toe with small finger. Not hear." I realized I was trying to pick some hard skin off my little toe and stopped. "Because, if we do only tournament, (he was back on the first track again) we lose *Budo* (martial way) spirit. Tournament only game—not real. Stan, you not go other side." (This was the third track he was on).

"Other side, *Sensei*?" I queried.

"Other side very dangerous," he said. "Other world not for you. I see other world. Now I cannot sleep. Not happy. Stan, you stay in this world. Never play with other world. Karate is better. More real."

"Thank you, *Sensei*." I began to realize what he meant—that I should not ever dabble in the occult.

"It," he said, "is like death." Then he switched back to the first track. "Real karate is hard training, hard kata, hard sparring, every day. Stan! You pick your toe!" My hand shot away. I realized how unaware I had been of my actions. This lesson I have never forgotten. Kase's message was a simple one: Be aware of what you are doing and be in the present time. Don't try to exist in the past or the future. Now, is where it is all at.

Kase *Sensei* on that night had tasted the full range of South African wines and beers. He fell on his side, snoring. It was around 4:00 a.m. We flopped down near him. Someone said: "He's far gone. We're off the hook for 6:00 a.m."

"Yes," I agreed and slipped into a deep sleep. But it was short-lived.

The Initiation

"*Ohayo gozai masu!* ("Good morning!")" the ringing voice of Kase *Sensei* echoed across the room. There he was, freshly showered and clad in white. His hands were tying his black belt around his waist.

"Come, come, come! You all very late."

"Oh, no!" groaned someone.

My head felt like it was twice its size, like an over-taut bass-drum being hammered on by an unruly child.

Beyond Spirit of the Empty Hand

"Oh, no!" we moaned, dragging ourselves up.

"Oh, yes!" he beamed. "Very special training today. Mr. Stan *initiation!*" He looked my way, waiting for a reaction. I gathered myself, stood as upright as was humanly possible in my aching state and said, *"Osu!"* which signified fortitude that I really didn't have. This was my outward bearing. Meanwhile, my insides were wailing, "Oh, Shit! Not an initiation now. What's an initiation? How am I going to get through this?"

When all 30 of us were lined up on the floor in our positions, Kase *Sensei* said, "Okay." He always said okay. Okay with Kase *Sensei* always meant okay like, "Okay, let's go," or like in, "Okay, be reasonable, do it my way."

"Osu!" we all echoed. That resounding *osu* from 30 trained brown belts had every blood vessel in my brain holding on for dear life. My head felt as if it was about to explode.

If Kase meant to break me down with his initiation, he had already succeeded—*before* the initiation. I was plain scared and, to top it all, I had forgotten to go to the lavatory. My bladder was not only full, it was also very uneasy about whether it would get through all of this without bursting. What I heard next nearly caused me to faint. In fact, I was praying to God that I would faint. "Please, God, let me faint. Let me be released from this impending madness."

"Kanku Dai," he announced sternly.

"Kanku Dai," we echoed. At least I knew it well. The relief was short-lived. "Sixty five times."

"Sixty five times!" my incredulous insides yelled back at him silently. "I don't believe all of this. This is not happening to me. Oh, yes, it is." It had begun. Kase did every move with us.

Kanku Dai is a kata with 65 moves in it. You go backwards, forward, sideways. You jump upward and drop to the floor. It's like life. It has its ups and its downs. It has its mountains and it has its valleys. Plainly speaking, *Kanku Dai* is the meanest, hardest, most testing kata in the book. Do one *Kanku Dai* properly and your pulse is way up, and you feel like bending over real low to get precious oxygen into your lungs. Well, the first 25 repetitions were the most agonizing. After that I moved as if in a dream.

When Kase finally called *"Yame!"* ("Stop!") I was way off somewhere else. The headache had gone. My worries were gone. I was in another world, but certainly not in the dark world Kase had warned me about. I felt light as he announced: "Zat was Mr. Stan's initiation. *Naote!"* ("Relax!")

Meeting Myself

I sprinted to the lavatory. As I achieved total relief, I chuckled at Kase *Sensei's* approach. I thought about it. If that was 'Mr. Stan's initiation', why did those other 29 guys have to suffer along with me? Thank God they were there, though. Their presence had given me strength.

New House, New Dan

By the end of 1964, Judy and I had saved enough money to put a deposit on a small house of our own in Gardens, a middle-class suburb in the North of Johannesburg. The first thing I did when we moved in, was to install a number of outdoor *makiwaras,* sandbags, and a chinning bar in the backyard. By this time Kase *Sensei* had returned to Japan, but now a bigger visit was being planned with the *Japan* Karate *Association* for 1965. Four instructors were coming to South Africa for a six-month stay, and they were the cream of the Japanese crop. Great they were then, and great they are today. Pandemonium broke out in the South African martial arts circles with their arrival. Seeing these living dynamos in action made all who witnessed their prowess take up karate immediately. The four Japanese Juggernauts were none other than Taiji Kase (returned for the second time), Hirokazu Kanazawa, Keinosuke Enoeda, and Hiroshi Shirai.

Kase is today resident in France and is renowned worldwide as a master of karate-*do*, as are Kanazawa (who heads his own international association), Enoeda (chief instructor of Europe), and Shirai (top instructor in Italy).

Each would teach in one of the main centers of South Africa. Enoeda in Johannesburg, Kanazawa in Pretoria, Kase in Durban, and Shirai in Cape Town. On the first day of their arrival, after taking them around the Johannesburg Zoo, I was suddenly informed by Kase, "Now time to train! Enough sightseeing. Where is nearest *dojo*?"

"Central Gym in town," I answered.

As we changed into our karate-*gi* I thought, "No wonder they are good. Training comes first."

As we lined up on the *dojo* floor and bowed (only the four of us, Kanazawa hadn't arrived yet), something quite unexpected happened.

"Okay, Stan. You now take *nidan* (second degree black belt) grading."

Beyond Spirit of the Empty Hand

My heart jumped. Had I heard right? I must have looked nonplussed because Kase *Sensei* stated, more than asked, "You train hard this last 12 months, *neh*?"

"*Osu,* Sensei!" I affirmed.

"Of course. Therefore, you now try *nidan*."

I couldn't believe this. I was awarded first *dan* only a year ago and now they wanted me to try second *dan*. Normally a two year period would have to pass before the Association would allow one to try for second *dan*, but I figured that I had been training three times as hard as the average student, so I was probably eligible.

I started with basics in combination form. Then the kata I chose was the one I had been doing for the last year. In actual fact, it is a small man's kata, called *Empi*, which means "flying swallow." Then the surprise.

"Okay, *kumite*."

I stood in the middle of the floor surrounded by these three formidable *senseis*. I was hoping that they may have arranged a couple of South Africans for me to fight, but none were forthcoming. Who am I going to fight, I wondered? Would it be Kase, the danger man who splits bananas and other things; or Shirai, the 1962 All Japan Champion; or Enoeda, the 1963 All Japan Champion? One was as dangerous as the next. Or would it be all three?

"Shirai!" Kase called out. The fight was on. Shirai fought very relaxedly, placing his kicks and his punches expertly and with control on various parts of my anatomy. But I was wild, like a semi-tamed horse. After all, I was the one going for *nidan*, so I figured that I had to be more than impressive. At one point, after Shirai had neatly snapped his roundhouse kick next to my temple, I reflexed too quickly snapping in a *kizami-zuki* (jab punch) to his face. My control was not as good as his. He got it on his nose— cracked, he later told me. But there was not any sign of aggression from him. He fought on as if nothing had happened. A true karate man. I was awarded second *dan* right after the fight. No parties like with the first *dan*, only a bow and a word of serious advice from each of the *senseis*:

"You have responsibility now. Keep hard training."

5

ENTER ENOEDA

Meeting Myself

The Warrior Gentleman

"What's he doing now, Judy?" I kept calling Judy from the bank whenever I had a moment. It was eating at me that I could only train with Enoeda *Sensei* in the early mornings and evenings. I wanted to be with him all day, but I could not afford to leave the bank just yet.

"He's outside."

"Doing what?" I asked impatiently.

"Hitting a tree."

"What? Tell me exactly what he is doing. What's he dressed in? How's he standing? Everything, Judy!"

"Okay, okay. Relax, Stan. Just give me a chance. He's got a straw thing on the tree."

"A *makiwara*," I interrupted.

"Oh, is that what it's called."

"Which tree?" I asked.

"Right out in the front of the house. The one near the garage, next to the trash can."

I wanted to know everything. Every detail. How hard he was hitting, what he had on his feet. Then I would get back to work and call again when I had a chance. Enoeda *Sensei* was always hammering away on a *makiwara* when I phoned, for hours at a time, non-stop. The pillars in the bank building were now getting much more of a thumping from me since Enoeda's arrival.

Enoeda's first evening lesson at Grove *dojo* was an event that no one will ever forget. There were no introductions. No time for them. Enoeda just emerged from the change room, strode onto the floor as only Enoeda can stride, and commanded, *"Yoi!"* ("Ready!") He stood up front, the indomitable warrior, upright and powerful. His awe-inspiring gaze took in the entire scene.

"Kiba-dachi!" he ordered.

We sprang into the deep horse-riding, or straddle-leg, stance which, evidently, was not deep enough, because Enoeda shouted, "More down!" Enoeda had the loudest *kiai* (spirited shout) and the loudest voice of any Japanese instructor I have ever met. You get a fright when he speaks, let alone when he shouts. Well, he was not satisfied, and Enoeda is very forthright when he is not satisfied. He is a simple and direct man, and he took the most simple and direct course. He wanted us *down* in our stance and if we didn't go down, he would assist us a little. He proceeded to kick us all down—a "soft" *mae-geri* (front kick) to each and every one of us, in the gut. He had made his point. Before his instructive kicks, we looked like double-decker buses; now we looked more like low-slung racing cars.

How our thighs felt was another story. Mine felt as if they were bleeding inside, but I was not about to do anything to attract that sledgehammer foot onto my stomach for a second visit.

Although Enoeda only had two moods, a good mood and a bad mood, he had many sides to him. While karate training was his daily bread, he studiously applied himself to two other things: Learning English and playing golf.

Cecil Wolov, a middle-aged first *dan*, gave him daily lessons in English. It was also Cecil's idea that Enoeda listen to the latest pop tunes, learn the words, and sing along for English practice. One day as I alighted from the bus in Grant Avenue, a whole block away from my house, I heard a loud voice ringing across the rooftops.

"Lo-o-ove, is a many splendid thing...." it sang.

As I reached the front gate, I realized that the singing was coming from my lounge. There was Enoeda, together with Cecil, and he was singing with a gusto that would have had Pavarotti pale into insignificance. As the record ended, Enoeda looked my way.

"Nice way to learn English," he laughed.

A couple of weeks later when I phoned Judy from the bank and asked where he was, the reply was the same as before: "He's outside."

"Oh, hitting the *makiwara*?" I ventured.

"No, pushing the pram (baby carriage)."

"What?" I couldn't believe it. I hardly ever pushed Caryn in the pram. It was infradig for a karate man to push a pram. Debbie, our second daughter, was born during Enoeda's stay. So while Judy was attending to her, Enoeda sometimes offered to take care of Caryn.

"This Enoeda is full of surprises," I thought. My pram-pushing frequency increased after seeing just how gentle he could be with our baby. In those days I always tried to read meaning into everything anybody did, especially Enoeda. Was he doing this pram-pushing because he liked it, or was he doing it to teach me a lesson or two about fatherhood? Today it doesn't matter which it was, except that I had learned something of value from him.

It was also because of Kase and Enoeda *Sensei* that I eventually resigned from the bank three months after their arrival. It was all getting to be too much to handle: training, teaching, entertaining the Japanese, and giving the family a little attention. The number of students at my *dojo* was increasing. Finally, after Kase had urged, "You must be chief instructor of JKA; cannot do part time," I left the bank, but I was very financially insecure at the time. So I joined forces with Bob Zager, the owner of Central Gym, as I felt I needed the security of someone who knew the gym game. The two of us became partners in Grove and Central Gym, which had weights, PT, and karate, while I ran Grove, which was only a karate studio at that time. We pooled our resources.

Now I had time on my hands to train. Enoeda *Sensei* and I would rise at 6:00 o'clock every morning and either train in the garden or drive to a park. All the training was outdoors. Our outdoor training included hand hardening on different kinds of *makiwara*, ranging from an upright pole planted in the ground with a pad on it, to several trees varying from small to large. We did front kicks, side kicks, and back kicks delivered with running shoes on, against the trunk of an old oak. Roundhouse kicks we did against leaves. We did fast snapping work while keeping the knee elevated, for repetition upon repetition. We always ended our training with kata.

Happy Hacking Golf Then Some Serious Confrontation

Having resigned from the bank, I now had my mornings free. Our afternoons and evenings were devoted to teaching beginners and advanced students. After Enoeda and I had finished our early morning training, the rest of our mornings became occupied with two main things: swimming at a nearby pleasure resort and learning to play golf. Sam Belnick, a lawyer black belt who had a farm in Rustenburg, an hour-and-a-half drive from Johannesburg, invited us to play golf at the Rustenburg course with a top businessman. Up to now, Enoeda and I used an old number three wood and a seven iron when we visited a nearby driving range. Now we were into our first official golf invite. Up until this time we had played actual golf about three times. We were real rookies at the game.

"We had better buy some clubs," I suggested.

"Of course," he beamed.

So we visited the Pro Golf Shop. I didn't have much money in those days, nor did Enoeda, so I scratched around and came up with about 25 or 30 Rand. With this we naively set out to buy two

Beyond Spirit of the Empty Hand

sets of clubs. After spending an entire morning at the golf shop trying and testing the most superb clubs, we walked out of there with three second-hand clubs, six balls, and a packet of tees. Under Enoeda's arm was a box containing a pair of neat, spiked golf shoes, and on his head he wore a new golf cap. We were ready for Rustenburg. We hopped into my old Volvo and were on our way.

We kept promising each other how we were going to annihilate the two Rustenburg golfers. Sam Belnick, Enoeda, and I spent a relaxed and enjoyable evening sitting outside Sam's big farmhouse, which was on an orange farm on the Golden Mile near Rustenburg. We were watching a magnificent sunset, sipping beer, and grilling different kinds of meat on the log fire. The main talk was how we were going to whip Sam and his partner the following day at golf.

At 6:00 o'clock I awoke. The first thing I saw through my window was what looked like Ben Hogan himself. A second glance told me that it was Enoeda, complete with golf cap and golf shoes, warming up, hitting at an imaginary ball. He really looked the part.

"*Ohayo, gozai masu, Sensei*," I shouted through the open window.

"*Osu!* Stan. Today I feel very good," he shouted

"You look good, *Sensei*. I hope we both break 100 today."

"Of course!" he shouted, sending an imaginary ball into the distant blue mountains.

As we arrived at the members entrance in Sam's Mercedes Benz, our golf opponent stood waiting. He was perfectly attired in spiked shoes, smart slacks, golf cap, and leather gloves, and a huge state-of-the-art golf bag and kit stood regally between him and his caddie.

"This man is very serious about his golf," offered Sam.

"Is that so?" I replied. Meanwhile, inside, I was saying "Oh, no!" I glanced at Enoeda. He merely winked one of his cat's eyes at me, as if saying, "Not worry, Stan".

As we stepped out of Sam's car a horde of motley-clad, adolescent caddies descended upon us. We chose three and dismissed the rest, who stood watching. Sam opened the boot of his car and handed his bag to the first caddie. The other two caddies were waiting to shoulder our two bags which, of course, were nonexistent. Instead, I handed two clubs to one caddie and three clubs to the other. Then I handed each of them a sock with three golf balls in it and a few tees. The two caddies had never seen this sort of thing before, and they couldn't hide their surprise. Their mouths were agape as we handed them our pitiful equipment. This was not lost on Enoeda. The look on his face had me clutching my sides trying to suppress my mirth, but now was not the time. I told the caddies to move their asses to the first tee quickly. I didn't want to shake up our Mr. Vermeulen too much. Sam introduced us as two champions from Japan. Through habit, Enoeda and I bowed to Mr. Vermeulen. Both of us just said, *"Osu!"* Not much more was said as Sam and Mr. Vermeulen became engaged in some discussion as we approached the first tee.

After we had duffed our first drives, I overheard Mr. Vermeulen talking to Sam in Afrikaans, "But I thought you said they were Japanese champions?"

It hadn't taken long for Vermeulen to discover that Enoeda and I were not golf pros from Japan.

"No, Vermeulen," laughed Sam, "don't be stupid. They're karate champions, man."

I noticed that Vermeulen maintained a respectable distance from us for the rest of the game.

Enoeda and I chatted with each other in a mixture of broken English and Japanese that only the two of us could understand. Like, for instance, when I hit a fresh-air shot, Enoeda remarked, "More *kime* (focus), Stan," and I responded with, *"Osu, Sensei!"*

Sam drifted between Vermeulen and the pair of us, always the considerate gentleman conveying messages of praise at even the lamest of shots. One time Enoeda uttered a loud *kiai* as he teed off. A golfer in another foursome nearby, who was attempting a close putt at the time, missed the hole.

Vermeulen, who knew the group, just gave a sheepish smile and averted his gaze toward the distant mountain range.

One time, near the end of our very hot and laborious game, it took me about four attempts to get the confounded ball out of a bunker. I overheard Vermeulen whisper in the Afrikaans language to Sam, "That tall Jap with the sunglasses isn't as good as the other one."

Sam dropped his putter and doubled up.

"Vermeulen, you nit-wit. The tall guy might walk like a Japanese and talk like a Japanese, but he's no Japanese."

"What!" Vermeulen moved closer to Sam. "Now I've really balls'd things up," he whispered. "Who the hell is he, then?"

"That's Stan Schmidt. He's a South African who has just trained in Japan. He's not Japanese!"

Beyond Spirit of the Empty Hand

Later, in the pub, Sam explained to Enoeda *Sensei* what had happened. Enoeda was so tickled by this episode that he exploded with laughter, slapping the table. The drinks and peanuts flew in all directions.

"Very funny!" he shouted and kept repeating, "Mistaah Stan, like man from Japan! Ha, ha, ha!"

Enoeda's laughter was infectious. Soon every person in the pub was laughing along with him.

---oOo---

We had hardly gotten back to Johannesburg when Enoeda called me into his room after our morning training was over.

"Sit down, Stan. Very important we talk now!"

He looked serious. Why, I don't know, but I felt a little uneasy.

"Stan, I just finish speak with Kase *Sensei* in Durban on telephone. We decide we must have First South African JKA Karate Championship in Durban. Mr. Higginson organize. Very nice. We have four Japanese judges. Every karate-ka must participate."

"When, *Sensei*?" I ventured.

"Soon. Maybe five weeks. You must win."

"I'll try, *Sensei*."

"Both kata and *kumite*," he added.

My stomach gave a lurch, like a heavy truck does when the driver shifts down to challenge a long, steep hill. My mind had shifted instantly into a high revving gear.

"What kata must I do, *Sensei*?"

"*Kanku Dai!*" he said without any hesitation.

My thoughts went back to my initiation with Kase *Sensei*. Sixty-five *Kanku Dais*. *Kanku Dai* and I were old friends. But that was endurance training—okay for an initiation but not good enough to win a championship where one needs a high degree of precision, coordination and *kime,* a perfect balance of muscular contraction, and relaxation, the correct application of fast and slow movements, and the right control of hard and soft movements.

Finally, to win kata one had to exhibit charisma, that special individual charm and dynamism that every champion must project. The Japanese call it spirit.

"*Kanku Dai* is number one Shotokan kata," stressed Enoeda. "It has many variations of technique in it. Very difficult challenge. But you try, okay?"

Meeting Myself

"Okay, *Sensei*," I replied. I then tried to get him outside to start coaching me on *Kanku Dai* immediately.

"More relax, Stan. You too tense. We first drink tea. We talk."

Reluctantly, I sat down again. He went to the kitchen and came back with a tea tray. He poured tea for both of us. After we had taken one sip he announced, "Friday is *jiyu-kumite* day for you and me. You must win First South African Championships. So you fight me."

I felt a nervous twinge in my stomach. It wasn't so much what he said, but rather the way he had said it. And today was Thursday. To make things worse, he proceeded to tell me all about his *kumite* fighting experiences in the Japanese instructors' class.

"Maybe some instructors happy I leave Japan." He seemed to ponder his words, his expression growing more serious. He had answered my question before I could put it to him.

"My spirit maybe sometime too strong. Maybe too much like old *samurai* spirit. Some instructors not like this."

Enoeda *Sensei* has a long *samurai* heritage, his roots stemming from the Southern island of Japan, Kyushu.

"I like hard *kumite*. Must be real. Sometimes injury happen." He shook his head seriously. "I try study *ashi-barai*. Many times I practice on my student's ankle. He tie big padding around ankle, and I keep sweeping.

"When fighting, I not like to sweep one leg. I like to sweep both legs. One time my opponent stand, not move. I sweep, he fall down. But I very sorry because his leg broken. This is *kumite*."

Enoeda sat opposite me. The weather was hot, and he wore shorts. The muscles of his legs rippled as he demonstrated the sweep, still sitting. His legs were strong and symmetrical like the legs of a weight-lifter. No wonder he had broken the opponent's leg. All this candid communication made me feel very uneasy. I ventured a glance toward my lean, long ankles and shuddered at the thought of what might happen to them if this tiger sitting opposite me attacked them with his formidable leg sweep, but I had no time to think further on this matter as he was now telling me about a neat tooth extraction job he had performed on another fighter who just moved in slightly too close, just as Enoeda released his piston-like punch.

"Ah, perfect timing," laughed Enoeda. "He move in to attack me. I see perfect distance. I release *gyaku-zuki* (reverse punch). Perfect power. Perfect control from me, but he make little mistake. He jerk head maybe two centimeter forward as I punch. We separate. I think maybe little touch and everything okay. Then hear sound like not-cooked rice falling on wooden floor. Very strange. I quickly look in his mouth. All his top teeth still in mouth but not so long any more. Very clean break. Bottom half of top teeth now lying on floor. *Why* this happen?" He prolonged the "why," tilting his head to the side. "Me not understand. This very funny."

I laughed nervously along with him but I did not think this very funny at all. I have always prized my teeth. As a boy, my mother had told me that my teeth were more precious than jewels, and I didn't savor the idea of having them shattered and scattered over a *dojo* floor. No way. No thank you. The thought made me clench my jaw tightly as if to protect them. That night I didn't sleep.

When I knocked on Enoeda's door at 5.30 a.m. the next morning, I expected the usual "Hello, Stan". Instead, I heard a stiff, gruff, "Mmm." Normally, as we drove to the park in my gray Volvo, Enoeda would comment on the freshness of the morning. "Ahh, flowers very beautiful. That big bird sing sweetly." But today was Friday, and his bearing was serious, to say the least. I found the silence unbearable, so I ventured, "Ah, lovely day, *Sensei*." All I got back was a gruff "Mmm," so I said nothing further. When we got to the *dojo*, Enoeda chose the part of the change room farthest away from me to change. "Oh, boy," I groaned to myself. Things really looked bad. What's going to happen? Images of a gigantic leg sweep and teeth falling like a hailstorm of corn pips flashed across my mind. Then we were on the *dojo* floor. We bowed and started almost one hour of free-fighting. It turned out different than what I expected. Enoeda's control was superb. There were times when we stalked each other for minutes on end without exchanging blows and then there would be a combination of moves at each other. I learned an immense amount from this. Every Friday was the same pattern. A serious, formal start to the day, with great warmth and jollity expressed by Enoeda *Sensei* as we finished and had breakfast together.

As the time of the Championships grew closer, so my special morning training sessions with Enoeda increased in intensity. We did repetition after repetition of *kihon* combinations against fresh air and against leaves of trees, stopping just short of the leaf, "to develop aim, focus, and control," said Enoeda. We used the bag and *makiwara* for penetration. But always on Fridays, I had to face Enoeda himself.

Meeting Myself

We practiced many kata done in different directions—the five *Heians* and *Tekki Shodan,* which were the prescribed kata for the tournament and, of course, *Kanku Dai,* my *tokui* (favorite) kata.

I felt dead-beat by the time the last Friday of sparring with my *Sensei* came up. I had lost about 10 pounds of body weight. By contrast, Enoeda looked tanned, fit, and energetic. He had done an equal amount of training with me.

"More relax," he would always say to me. "Your head too busy. Too tense."

I never felt I was good enough.

Our final Friday of sparring arrived, and it was the same serious routine. My back kick and *kizami-zuki* were working well, but now I was trying to score with *mae-geri* on Enoeda. He just kept blocking me.

"Harder, Stan!" he would say.

I'd go harder, but his *gedan-uke* (downward block) felt like an iron bar blocking every kick with great force. When I managed to get one in, I got carried away and tried with all my spirit to do another one. This second *mae-geri* was short-circuited in its forward and upward arc by a crushing *kakato-geri* (downward heel kick) by Enoeda's right heel, which descended and crashed down onto the nerve plexus situated at the center of my kicking thigh, before I could release the kick. I dropped, feeling like I had been shot with a .44 magnum. Up to the present day, this is the only time I have ever been put down by a blow.

I dragged myself to a nearby wash basin and nearly threw up. Enoeda thought my antics very amusing.

"That my special technique," he quipped, as I limped out of the *dojo* with him afterwards. He had to drive the car; my leg was too painful. I couldn't straighten it completely for days.

When we got home he told me, "Stan, first time I drive car." I couldn't believe it. But on second thought, the drive did seem a bit jerky, and he had kept on asking me all sorts of questions, like, "How start car? Where to loose hand break?" Now I was really impressed with him, in more ways than one.

"What about the championships?" I asked him at breakfast.

"By end of week your leg better. Easy win, Stan."

"But what about training?" I moaned.

"Your training finished. Just a little light training every day. But now time we rest. We eat, drink, play golf. Must make new energy. No worry."

Beyond Spirit of the Empty Hand

By the next Saturday we were all in Durban. My leg was better, and I won both kata and *kumite*, thanks to Enoeda Sensei's unique training methods.

Returning To The Source

Soon after *Sensei*s Kase, Enoeda, Kanazawa, and Shirai had left South Africa to teach in other parts of the world, a small group of karate seniors joined me in my early morning training sessions.

I was training for my second visit to Japan, which was scheduled for the spring of 1966. On my first visit I had met many interesting and inspiring people, and I could not wait to see them again.

Of the Caucasians I had met, two stood out in my mind. One was Gary Friederich, a tough and plucky little guy who could do a hundred or more push-ups at the drop of a hat. The other non-Japanese, who is now a Japanese in almost every sense of the word, was a Canadian by the name of C.W. Nicol, better known as Nick, a blue belt, 4th *kyu*, who loved and lived the Japanese culture even then. He was destined to become the most famous of Caucasian authors living in Japan. His first work, *Moving Zen,* published in 1975, took the karate world by storm. This, I believe, was due to its true and inspiring message of a *gaijin* experiencing the deep end of what Japanese karate-do is really all about.

Even back in 1963, Nick was a natural storyteller. It was always a pleasure to sit with him and a small group of Westerners over a Sapporo beer, hearing of his experiences. We usually sat outside, near the *dojo,* on make-shift furniture—a set of used *sake* (rice wine) containers made of straw. A bottle of Sapporo beer plus *soba* (noodles) was our late lunch.

Soon I would be back in Japan again after three years, and I could not wait to see Nick, Gary, and Seto. Shunsuke Seto was Nick's best friend who I first met at the *dojo* door in 1963. And then there were the instructors who had inspired me and whom I wanted to emulate more than anything else in the world.

The ones with whom I had made personal contact in 1963 were *Sensei*s Nakayama, Takagi, Itoh, Sugiura, Kase, Shoji, Enoeda, Kanazawa, Asai, Ueki, Yoshimasa Takahashi, Nakaya, Isaka, Kisaka, Ochi, Okuda, Seto, Sugiyama, and Maya-san, the JKA secretary.

I badly wanted to impress these people, so I did an average of three hours training a day in preparation for my trip: One hour of *kihon,* one hour of *kumite,* one hour of kata, plus bag and *makiwara* work, weights, and running.

When I arrived in Japan in the Spring of 1966, I stayed at a house Kase *Sensei* had arranged for me together with three other South Africans—Clive Himsworth, Roy Braun, and Alan Gooderson.

Later I booked into the Asia Center, the little hotel in which Judy and I had stayed in 1963. The staff was virtually unchanged—always helpful, friendly, and courteous, as they still are today. But the JKA *honbu dojo* had moved from Yotsuya to the old Kodokan building in Suidobashi, a suburb of Tokyo. This building had been the previous premises of the world judo fraternity.

6

THE GOLDEN ERA OF JKA

Meeting Myself

[**Author's Note:** Much, but not all, of the next three chapters are extracted from my previous book, *Spirit of the Empty Hand,* in which I compressed time in order to communicate the character of the training at the Suidobashi *dojo*. I will call the Suidobashi training "The Golden Era." This chapter depicts the training of that era—from December 1964 to April, 1974, when the JKA headquarters moved to the Ebisu suburb of Tokyo. The events in this following chapter, while not necessarily being in exact chronological order are, nevertheless, true and factual. I have made more than 20 visits to train in the Japanese instructors' class. Each of these visits has lasted from four to 12 weeks at a time. It would be impossible to record every training session in this book. Therefore, what I have done is to compress The Golden Era into these three chapters. For the sake of flow, I have dealt with the most typical type of training I experienced in that 10-year period under *Senseis* Nakayama, Shoji, and Sugiura (who always taught kata on a Friday) as well as with other *Sensei* both in and outside the *Honbu dojo*. The *dojo* described in *Spirit of the Empty Hand, p. 115,* was the very spacious Ebisu *dojo* which the JKA moved into in April, 1974. The *dojo* I describe now is the Suidobashi *dojo* which the JKA occupied from 1964 to 1974.]

Welcomed by Mr. Takagi

Even though I had been in Japan three years ago, everything seemed completely new to me as I took the subway from Aoyama Ichome to Yotsuya and from there changed to the Japan National Railway and headed for Suidobashi. From the windows of the train I noticed that many taller, new buildings had arisen from the old and that an American influence was beginning to make its mark with American-style restaurants surfacing here and there.

The familiar JKA insignia, that of the red rising sun superimposed against a larger white moon, indicated to me the entrance of the *dojo*.

As I ascended the wide concrete stairs my senses were alerted by a set of sounds that grew louder as I approached the first floor landing. I felt like a moth being drawn to a flame. These were familiar sounds. Sounds of feet swishing across a wooden floor, *kiais,* the sharp commands and count of a *sensei*.

But these familiar sounds, nevertheless, sent a cold shiver up my spine. At the top of the stairs was the JKA office and reception area. As I approached I was greeted by none other than Takagi *Sensei*, Director of JKA.

"Welcome to Japan, Mistah Stan!" He wore a big smile. "Sit down. I telephone your friend, Mr. Seto. He soon come to meet you."

As I settled onto the flimsy fold up chair in front of his desk, he asked: "How is your beautiful wife, Judy *san*?"

"Very well, *Sensei*. She is looking after our two children back home in South Africa."

"Boy or girl?" he inquired.

"Two girls," I replied, "Caryn and Debbie."

Mr. Takagi sat back and nodded a few times. He had a serious expression on his face which broke into a smile. He chuckled. "You bery strong, Stan *san*."

"Why, *Sensei*?"

"Because you make two girls. Bery strong!" He paused, then added: "Me too. I have only girls. Also bery strong."

He proceeded to pour tea. As I raised my cup and sipped the steaming, light green liquid, I could not prevent my hand from trembling. The training seemed to be reaching its peak, judging by the crescendo of sounds that penetrated the thin office wall. He asked what was an unlikely question, especially considering the tension that had built up inside of me.

"What you think of Japanese tea?" I hadn't really thought about how it tasted.

"Uh, very good," I ventured, at which he proceeded to top up my cup. It occurred to me that this tea tasted more bitter than anything I had ever consumed in my life.

Judging by the sudden quietness, I concluded that the training had ended. It was one o'clock in the afternoon.

"You wish to take practice?" he questioned.

"Yes, please, Mr. Takagi," I nervously replied. Out of the corner of one eye I noticed that a karate man had entered the room. He searched through some files, found what he wanted, bowed and made his exit. Judging by his wet forehead and damp karate-gi, he had no doubt been part of that class. I was not only fascinated by his serene attitude, but also by the fact that he was the tallest Japanese I had yet seen. Sensing my interest, Mr. Takagi offered, "He berry big Japanese. Mistah Tabata, berry strong instructor, but he such good manner." Mr. Takagi's pronunciation of the word *very* intrigued me.

"Mr. Takagi, which training class should I attend?" I asked.

Meeting Myself

"Of course, instructor training," he said as if it went without saying. "You now *nidan, neh!*"

"Can I start tomorrow?" I requested nervously.

"Good idea!" he exclaimed, rising to meet a group of men who had entered the office. Seto arrived a few minutes later and treated me to a delicious *sukiyaki* (steak and vegetables) meal, informing me that I was to report for training at 10:30 the following morning.

---oOo---

I arrived at the *dojo* entrance early the following morning and climbed the well-worn concrete stairs. As I reached the landing, I noticed long wooden shelves upon which an assortment of shoes and *geta* (sandals) were neatly placed. Beyond the shoe racks, the foreigners class was in action. I recognized Y. Takahashi Sensei. He was conducting the main class, while four or five white belt beginners were being taken by a black belt instructor I didn't recognize.

There was a mixture of Japanese and Westerners in both groups, and the belts the students wore revealed that their levels ranged from white to black belts.

The tall karate man I had seen the day before in Mr. Takagi's office now joined in with the general class, which was doing front kicks, moving up and down the breadth of the *dojo* in military precision. Tabata's kicks were high and snappy, and the rest of the class looked well drilled.

The *dojo* was a rectangular shape, about 10 steps wide by 25 steps long, with two pillars about eight paces apart propping up the roof at the back end of the floor. Each pillar had been bound with a kind of sponge rubber, which looked badly battered. The floor was covered with long strips of plastic tape. There seemed to be more tape than wood visible. It occurred to me that this was a place where a lot of hard work had happened. The floor had taken a hammering, no doubt from the numerous foot stamps, jumps, and karate-ka being thrown on to it.

I waited at the entrance, watching. It fascinated me how smoothly the Japanese moved. But there were a couple of Westerners who were also moving with well articulated actions, their centers of gravity down. I didn't recognize any of the foreigners in the class. No Nick, no Gary.

Takahashi Sensei called, *"Yame!"* and the class stopped for the traditional halfway mark rest. Takahashi came striding across.

Beyond Spirit of the Empty Hand

"Stan san, welcome. It's a long time no see you. Your wife, Judy, come?"

"No, Sensei. It's good to see you again."

"You take instructor training." His voice had taken on a serious tone.

"*Osu*, Sensei."

"OK, you change into *gi*." He pointed to a door. He turned and ordered the class to recommence. With the warm-up and *kihon* parts completed, they now began doing *gohon kumite* (five-step sparring).

I placed my shoes on the nearby shoe rack and entered the change room, which consisted of a small open changing area, two make-shift showers, and a Japanese toilet. I made use of the toilet—squatting style—and almost fell into it as I stood up, trying to find the tiny flush chain. After changing into my *gi*, I folded my clothes into a neat ball and jammed them into a small, open locker. No locks, no doors. Nobody stole anything from you in Japan in those days. As I picked up my tog bag and made for the door, I remembered what Seto had told me the night before: "Nobody steal in Japan," he had said. "If police catch someone stealing, it is big dishonor for him and his family. He lose face. To kill someone is bad, but to steal is worse. Japanese not like these kind of people."

The *gohon kumite* had revved up to a fast pace. Big Tabata *Sensei* had joined in. I felt sorry for some of the karate-*ka* who had to face Tabata. They looked terrified, yet he was gentle with them. He flowed forward and backward smoothly for such a big man. He looked completely at ease. Yet all of his blocks and punches were crisp and accurate. A short Japanese brown belt led most of the counting. He was like a dynamo. He had a tenacious spirit, and he clearly stood out as the leader.

After about 15 minutes of five-step sparring, Takahashi Sensei allowed the class to do light free sparring, which became not so light as each fighter endeavored to get the edge on his or her opponent. The last 10 minutes of the class was devoted to doing the five *Heian* katas, twice each; once to the count and once freely, without any count. I watched the kata training, carefully noting the subtleties of technique that I was personally lacking. The class ended with a short warm-down, and then they lined up on a sharp command from the short Japanese who turned out to be the *sempai* (senior) of the class.

The students sat upright, forming two straight lines facing the *shomen* (front) wall of the *dojo*. This wall was wood-paneled with a small shelf attached to it. On the shelf, vases with flowers and some twisted paper formed a little shrine. On one side was a picture of Gichin Funakoshi *Shihan* (master), and on the other side of the shelf was a sheet of cardboard tacked to the wall bearing the five maxims in English:

> Seek perfection of character
> Be faithful
> Endeavor
> Respect others
> Refrain from violent behavior

"*Mokuso!* (Meditate!)" ordered the *sempai*. Everybody's eyes closed in unison. Takahashi *Sensei* sat a few yards in front of the line on the left side. Slightly behind him sat Tabata *Sensei* and two other *kenchusei* who had instructed the new white belts.

After about two minutes, the *sempai* ordered: "*Yame!*" Then the class repeated after him the five maxims in Japanese:

> "*Jin kaku kansei ni tsutomuru koto.*
> *Makoto no michi o mamoru koto.*
> *Doryoku no seshin o yashinau koto.*
> *Reigi o omonzuru koto.*
> *Kekki no yu o imahsimuru koto.*"

These words were repeated with a spirit of fortitude that left the atmosphere in the *dojo* charged and electrified. A pause, then, "*Shomen ni rei!*" ("Bow to the front!") Still kneeling, Takahashi turned around gracefully, returning the bow that the class offered him. He said a few words to the class in Japanese and ended, for the benefit of the foreigners, with, "Keep training hard every day."

The *sempai* then called the class together at the back of the *dojo* floor and ticked off an attendance register. Finally, he gave a sharp command, and the class members rushed off to fetch a bucket of water and some rags. They soaked their rags, rinsed them out, lined up the entire length of the *dojo* floor, and proceeded to push the damp rags across the floor on all fours, butts in the air. When the *sempai* was satisfied that the already clean floor was clean enough, he ordered, "*Yame!*' and the bucket and rags were again packed away out of view.

As Takahashi Sensei left the floor, I approached him, "What must I do now, Sensei?" He didn't look like he wanted to converse.

Beyond Spirit of the Empty Hand

He was already making ready for the forthcoming training. "You warm up and wait. Class begin twelve o'clock."

It was now about 11:40 a.m. according to the wall clock. I bowed and stepped on to the floor and went to the back part of the *dojo,* which led onto an outside porch. This was the *makiwara* and conditioning area. There were four or five well used *makiwaras* in a line; a pile of broken ones lay scattered behind them. Bound onto one *makiwara* was a sheaved straw pad, while the others bore canvas-covered sponge rubber pads. The pads were a dark brown color and had been flattened out by the many punches they had absorbed. Much blood had been spilled on these *makiwaras,* judging by their color.

I set myself into a short *zenkutsu dachi* (forward stance) and began lightly punching the sheaved straw *makiwara,* which afforded me a view of the *dojo* floor. It had an unusual feel to it, just enough give. I preferred this sheaved straw to the rubber pads to which I was accustomed.

A number of young, clean-cut looking black belts filed onto the back corner of the floor near to me. Some sat, conversing quietly, each going smoothly and easily through his own stretching routine. Some of them were doing light free sparring. Not sure of what I should be doing, I kept my gaze toward the *makiwara,* but I was able to observe their actions out of the corner of my eye. What I saw amazed me. This was the most flexible group I had ever seen. Total splits in all directions seemed to be a natural habit to them.

Then a short stocky Westerner with a crew cut arrived and came right up to me.

"Hi, Stan. I heard you'd arrived." It was Gary Friederich, my friend from Yotsuya *dojo* in 1963.

"Hello, Gary. I'm happy to see you. Where's Nick?"

"Probably hunting whales in the Arctic or writing some book."

Meeting "The Animal"

I asked Gary to guide me with regard to the proper protocol for this instructors' class.

"Sure," he said, "come and stretch with me." His voice had a marked American drawl. Gary was more my match, both of us being far less flexible than the student instructors, or *kenchusei,* as Gary described them.

Meeting Myself

"The *kenchusei* usually stretch for about 30 minutes before the class," he said, gradually coaxing my legs out as wide as they would go, using his own feet as levers and holding onto my belt with his hands.

"Why so long?" I asked. "They don't seem to need it."

"Because their seniors have told them to do so," he explained, pushing my legs to their painful limit. "Breathe more deeply and try to relax your face and neck," he encouraged. "In just a moment, the 'big guns' will arrive, so be ready and do just what I do."

We changed positions, and I stretched his legs.

"Oh, man," whispered Gary suddenly, looking across at the *kenchusei* group. "Guess who has arrived."

"Who?" I asked.

"The animal," he said slowly, only loud enough for me to hear. I stole a quick look, and what I saw caused a violent reaction within my innards. A square, blunt-faced powerhouse stepped onto the floor. His narrow eyes were set deeply into a clean-shaven head. He ignored the group, moved past them, and headed for the sandbag with deliberate mechanical strides. He was different from the other athletes. What now had entered the *dojo* looked less like a human being and more like a huge pit bull. It is strange how one can move placidly through life and then unexpectedly come across a total stranger who instantly spells danger. My entire being had just told me that this man was "trouble."

With my heart beating harder and faster against my ribcage, I swallowed the invisible lump in my throat and asked Gary: "Is he an instructor?"

"No, he is also a *kenchusei*. Been second *dan* for about two years now. A real loner. The other day he put his only friend in the hospital.

"But I thought we were supposed to use control."

"Control in this class is a relative thing. What may appear to be a very hard blow to the average person from the general class, is a controlled blow to this group. But yes, Mr. Yano often goes too far." (Author's Note: Yano is his real name. I gave him the pseudonym, Sado, in *Spirit of the Empty Hand*.)

"Don't the seniors stop him?"

"Yes, but then it is often too late. He goes through the ritual of kneeling and bowing his head in penance. Their theory is to forgive, if he shows enough repentance. This is in the hope that he will mend his ways, but so far this leopard hasn't changed his spots. I guess he needs a good lesson from someone. But who's to do it?"

"Search me," I said, feeling as timid as a lamb.

The "big guns" stepped onto the floor. The *kenchusei*, then Gary and I sprang upright and bowed to the impressive group of instructors (fourth *dans* and above) who filed onto the floor and formed two straight lines. We, the *kenchusei*, lined up beside them, with me as the junior on the far end of the back line. A distant clock struck twelve. Nakayama *Sensei* kneeled in front of us. We bowed, and the training began.

A command had us all forming a large circle and doing calisthenics conducted by one of the *kenchusei*, who led us by example with a short-clipped utterance every time there was a change of exercise. This brisk limbering lasted only about five minutes. It was expected that we warm up before the class.

Next, still in a circle, we did repetition punching rooted in a front stance. Each member of the class counted to 10, starting with the most senior and working around the circle to me. The actions were dynamic, and we had completed 100 kicks on each side before the master ordered, *"Yame!"*

I felt more exhausted from this opening 15 minutes than I had ever felt in my own country. After the first 50 kicks, my legs had become like lead weights. One or two of the trainees had missed the odd repetition, but Yano, I noticed, had applied himself totally to every move.

During a 30-second rest period, it dawned on me that my abnormal exhaustion stemmed from a sense of insecurity and overtension. This alien environment, the demanding standard of excellence, the strange language, fast pace, and to cap it all, "the animal," all contributed to my present discomfort.

For the next 30 minutes we practiced a series of interactions with a partner. Before each action, the master carefully demonstrated and described the technicalities. His demonstrations were intricately clear, but my sparse understanding of Japanese didn't allow me to comprehend any deeper meaning that, no doubt, he was communicating verbally.

We were half way through this special *kumite* when both my forearms began to ache badly. The only thing that relieved me was that Yano was in the same row as me. Thus, in changing from partner to partner, I had not yet had to face him. However, this was but a small compensation, for I had been on the receiving end of the most potent kicks I had ever faced. The attacking side was re-

Meeting Myself

quired to do front kicks against us with the expressed purpose of making contact with our stomachs using direct force, strategy or both. Over the 15 minutes of repetitive blocking, we practiced three different approaches.

In the first, *go no sen* (taking the initiative later), we had to try to move directly backwards, blocking the kick, and then return forward doing a counter. My main problem was that I could never seem to propel myself far away enough from my opponent's foot, and thus I was unable to ride the force. I took most of it on the forearm and sometimes on the stomach. These short men had the uncanny knack of suddenly developing the longest of legs.

In the second approach, *tai sabaki* (swiveling), we were required to pivot to the side, blocking the kick and almost simultaneously delivering a counter measure. This was comparable to the sidestep of a bullfighter. Here I found I was not dropping and rotating my hips quickly enough, and two or three times I took too much impact and struggled quickly to get air back into my lungs trying not to reveal the fact to my attacker.

With the third approach, *sen no sen* (taking the initiative earlier), we had to move directly forward into the attack just as the kick started, countering at the same time. This approach is also sometimes known as *kamikaze,* or suicide, approach. I found that when I luckily moved in early enough it worked, and I did not hurt myself. Mostly, I sensed the attack too late. My late forward propulsion caused my blocking arm to clash with my attacker's fast-moving shin bone. The very bones of my forearms felt bruised as we made the last change, and the big instructor, Tabata, stood facing me. I expected the worst, but it turned out to be one of the best confrontations. He was very kind, slowing his attack down and giving me helpful advice, not via the spoken word, but rather through a very comprehensible sign language.

For the next fifteen minutes we were the attackers, and my shin bones became the painful victims of repetitive blocking. For the last fifteen minutes of the class, we practiced kata, and the prolonged intensity of the training brought a red flush to my face and a burning to the soles of my feet

I literally dragged myself out of the *dojo* like a wet rag. I was too tired to eat. Back at my room I swallowed volumes of liquid, anything on which I could lay my hands. I then stretched out on my bed and slept.

On waking the next day, I felt stiff and sore all over, and to make things worse, I found myself limping toward the communal bathroom. I had two huge blisters on the soles of my feet. My arms, from wrist to elbow, were swollen and were all colors of the rainbow. Desperately, I telephoned Seto, telling him what I felt and looked like.

"Ah!" he said, "jet lag. Your body not yet ready. But you start training, so you never stop. Go to drugstore and tape yourself. Be like *samurai.* Never give up."

I did what he said and attended the second, third, and fourth days of training. By the fifth day, I felt nauseous. The training had been similar to the other days except for one difference. We did different attacks on each consecutive day. By this time, I was so covered in tape, I must have looked like a mummy. In addition to my discolored arms and legs and raw feet, I now had a number of extra swollen features: my small finger from blocking with an open hand; my right big toe from accidentally kicking someone's bent elbow instead of his stomach; and a swollen nose from stupidly going forward into my attacker's punch with my eyes closed. All of this, and I had not yet faced Yano.

As we finished on Friday, Seto told me that there was no more instructor's training until Monday. "You take good rest, see sights of Tokyo." The first step in my recuperation program, set up by Seto, was a visit to an immaculate bathhouse where the healing elements of hot and cold water, massage, tranquillity, and friendship were administered.

I awoke on Monday morning to the sound of rain droplets against my bedroom window. My mind felt light and refreshed, as if a thick bank of cloud had been removed. My body had not yet healed completely, but it was well on its way, and I hummed a little tune as I showered, making ready to leave for the *dojo.*

7
CONFRONTING THE TOP GUNS

Meeting Myself

"Your Whole Body Is An Eye"

Where we had concentrated upon techniques and tactics during the past week, this week consisted mainly of confrontations that put our reflexes, timing, and ability to respond, on the firing line.

The master had cleverly conceived an approach of gradually stepping up the degree of difficulty of the confrontations. On the first day, the defenders had to stand in a fixed position. The attacker could stand as close as he liked and deliver single blows that had to be deflected without blinking an eye. The attacker announced what blow he would be delivering, but he could do it from any distance he chose and use any timing. In other words, wait and suddenly strike, not necessarily at a regular tempo.

On the second day, we had to do the same thing, but this time the attacker could do either of two announced attacks. For example, he would announce *jodan* or *chudan* and proceed to do either of the two.

On the third day we weren't restricted to a fixed position, and were thus allowed movement, except that the attacker could move in with any one attack without warning. I found that I had to resort mainly to *go no sen*, that is, moving away as the attack came. I wasn't confident enough to move in with *sen no sen*.

Oishi *Sensei*, who in later years won the All Japan *kumite* title many times, amazed me. His timing and responding were uncanny. No matter what attack I launched, be it punch, kick, or strike, he moved forward scoring on me before I could finish it. It was almost as if he were reading my mind. His control was superb, and I was never hurt by him. Interacting with masters like him and Tabata had restored some of my confidence.

But the fourth day proved to be "black Thursday" for me. Before the class, I was stretching and watching some of the *kenchusei* doing light sparring. I felt a tap on my shoulder.

"*Sukoshi kumite,*" ("A little free fighting") uttered the gruff voice of Yano. Facing him was as bad as I had imagined it might be. He stood, hands at his sides. I assumed the regular fighting stance and tried to look at his face. He looked not at me but through me, as if I didn't exist. Then, hands still at his sides, he proceeded to walk at me. It was if some invisible force emanated from him, causing me to move backwards. For the next minute or two he walked while I back-pedaled, traversing the length and breadth of the *dojo*. Not one blow had been struck when the buzzer

Beyond Spirit of the Empty Hand

rang for the start of the class, but this animal of a man had controlled me in a manner that I did not like at all.

As we meditated, I remembered the words of *Sensei* Nishiyama: "A true fighter will seek *kyo* in you and attack *kyo*. And the attack will be directed at where your greatest weakness lies. It may exist in either your body or your soul." The soul, I believe, comprises one's mind, will, and emotions.

Yano, I now realized, had managed to capture a part of my soul.

During the warm-up I spoke to myself, rationalizing that he was only flesh and blood like me and that I had only two alternatives: to stand up to him or to be completely trodden under foot. Through all of the conditioning training, my mind was not totally present in my body. I did the movements easily and automatically. My mind had leapt ahead to the *kumite* training that I knew was inevitable. I also knew that I would face Yano again, before the day ended.

Yano became my invisible opposition, the theoretical victim of every technique that I launched into that circle of energy and fire.

The master broke the circle and told us to form a line, a queue facing the most senior members of the class. This was it, I thought. Today's interaction had progressed to a stage where the defender faced a line of attackers. Taking his turn, each member of the line could deliver any one technique at the defender, without telling him what it was to be. After every one of us had delivered one attack, the next in seniority would become the defender. I would be on last and did not savor the idea.

It was well past one o'clock when Yano faced the line as defender. From the back, I watched him facing up to the various seniors. For the first time, I noticed that Mr. Takagi was watching the training from a doorway situated behind Yano. What I had observed was that Yano was very aggressive, tended to be wild, often tried too hard, and sometimes lost his balance. From his posture, I decided that he was open to a left front kick. I planned to approach him timidly, suddenly create spirit by *kiaiing* loudly, pause, and a split second later deliver my front kick.

It worked. The kick sailed through, and he almost fell over his feet rushing to counter me. But before he could get at me, the master told the next defender to take Yano's place. Almost everybody had been on, and it would soon be my turn to face the line. It came, and all I saw was Yano at the back end of the fast-shortening queue. Then he was on me. He gave a bloodcurdling yell and

Meeting Myself

stormed forwards, unleashing a running combination of kicks and punches. This sent me reeling backwards, careening into the fragile windows that framed the doorway. We both landed near the *makiwaras* amid a shower of shattered glass and wood.

I felt embarrassed as we were hoisted out of the mess and led back to the floor. Two of the seniors were admonishing my adversary for breaking the "one-blow-attack" rule.

This was not the end of my relationship with Yano, I realized. This was but the beginning. I had found myself a rival, or had he found me?

The following Wednesday proved to be another one of those black days. The training had been going well. I felt energetic, and my body was in fine condition. Although the blocking was still intense, I was no longer bruising. I had also learned to deflect the kicks more successfully, but we were onto line work again. This time the degree of difficulty for the defender was greater. He started with his back to the wall, and the attackers could do any one attack on him. This put tremendous stress upon the defender, as he was unable to escape backwards. There were two alternatives: *Tai sabaki,* pivoting sideways; or *sen no sen*, moving into the attack.

I noticed that the pressure seemed to be too great, even for the highest *dans*. One All Japan champion had been successfully moving in on each attack, when at last he faced Tabata, who used the tactic of waiting. The trainee made a number of false starts, which no doubt took the edge off his timing. When Tabata's front kick came, he moved in just a fraction too late, taking half of the impact on his forearm and the other half on his abdomen. He doubled up, the wind knocked out of him. In an instant, a senior instructor, Mabuchi, attended to him, applying a resuscitation technique that revived the trainee within seconds.

My turn came. I felt ready and full of spirit as I faced the first attacker. This feeling was short-lived. Ochi artfully hooked my front foot away with his front foot, and I went sailing to the floor. I was shaken. The next attacker spun around, and I pivoted to the side, but not quickly enough. His back fist strike made contact with my hand, causing me to slap my own cheek. It was smarting as I faced number three, Oishi. Before I could think, he closed the distance like a gale. All I felt was a light tap on the chin. If there was ever any time in my life when my head could have been taken off my shoulders, it was then. Yet Oishi had acted with benevolence, a true sportsman. But what of Yano and some of the other unknowns? Could I rely on them? No, I couldn't afford to take that chance. A fear gripped me, and at that moment I resorted to prayer. Inwardly I asked, "God, help me. Please help me face up to these men. What must I do? Give me what I need." Strangely, at that point, the master called a halt and spoke to me.

"You, too much thinking. You look only with two eyes. Don't forget your whole body is an eye."

I did not quite understand, but his few words had given me spirit. As I was about to start with the next opponent, he added, "Hips more tight. Make body one unit."

A Head Butt and a Bite

I managed to block the next few attackers but could not get my counter technique in. Then Yano faced me, his arms hanging loosely at his sides. He walked towards me as he had done on Thursday. With the wall behind me, I could not back away, so I rooted myself firmly, setting my gaze on the triangle formed by his shoulders and nose. I tried to see him generally, rather than looking specifically at any one part of him. When Yano was very close to me, he stopped and tried to outstare me. I didn't allow myself to be taken in by the stare. I concentrated on seeing all of him. My legs began vibrating from the tension in my bent knees, but my poise didn't waver. He tried to distract me by bringing his hands together with a loud clapping noise and followed up immediately with an unorthodox bola punch to my head. I blocked, but a second, unexpected punch glanced off the side of my head. As a third was on its way, I blocked it and caught his wrists with my hands. He reacted by bringing the crown of his head down in the direction of my nose. I avoided the direct impact and took the head butt against my chest. Without realizing it, my right elbow homed in against his cheekbone. For a brief moment, he looked dumbstruck, almost as if saying: "Who are you to be hitting me?" Then, like a hungry hyena, he screamed and sank his teeth into my forearm, biting hard to free himself. We broke apart and, like two incensed fighting cocks, flew at each other again, but the instructors intervened, pulling us apart. One of them took him aside and reprimanded him in no uncertain terms. He hung his head, saying only, *"Osu! Osu! Osu!"* For the next few weeks Yano and I didn't confront each other again. The instructors were, without doubt, seeing to it that we remained apart.

Meeting Myself

Human Beings Emerge

As I passed the office on my way home, Tabata Sensei called me, saying, "Tomorrow you please come to instructor party. All instructors come." I bowed deeply a number of times, thanking Tabata for the honor of being invited. He left, saying, "You good fighting spirit."

He had made my day. With a spring in my step, I walked to the subway station singing a Japanese ditty about a telephone conversation, sung to the tune of "London Bridge is Falling Down".

"Moshi, moshi, ano-ne,
Ano-ne, ano-ne
Moshi moshi ano-ne,
Ah-so, desu ka"

The passing people smiled.

---oOo---

The restaurant was a simple construction of wood and *tatami*, with separate areas for various groups of people divided by a lattice of cleanly washed wood. At the head of each area was an alcove with a simple, yet exquisite, flower arrangement. A long, low, shiny wooden table graced the center of each area. The instructors seated themselves on the floor and Isaka, the toastmaster for the evening, showed Gary and me where to sit.

We waited quietly until a tray of Kirin beer arrived. Three of the *kenchusei* sprang up and poured drinks for the seniors, who held their glasses. When all the glasses were filled, Isaka made a short speech honoring Senseis Nakayama and Shoji, who were seated in front of the alcove. Then to a rousing *kampai* (cheers) we downed the beer in one gulp. I was pleased that it was very light beer and that the glasses were small. Then other *kenchusei* moved around the table, bowing to each recipient and refilling his glass.

"This pouring of drinks is an important social custom," Gary pointed out. "It is etiquette to do so graciously, at the right time. Come on, grab a bottle and do your round."

I moved around on my knees, unable to disguise my clumsiness. The instructors were dignified, yet warm. Most thanked me in Japanese, while only one or two spoke in English.

Beyond Spirit of the Empty Hand

The atmosphere gradually loosened as the first course of food arrived.

The instructors began to move away from their initial, formalized positions to sit and converse with the various sub-groups, which changed all the time. The beer pouring tradition was a clever method of causing ongoing interaction. I noticed that although beer was used at the start, certain instructors moved on to a variety of drinks, some to *sake,* others to Coke or juice, and others to whiskey. There was a marked change in these people as their formal masks began to drop, revealing humorous and friendly human beings.

I could not believe it when even Yano came across and poured me a drink. I reciprocated later and thought I caught the faint trace of a smile on his lips. But I wasn't sure.

The spirit of the party grew with each new sweetmeat that was placed upon the table. At one point the whole group sang a *samurai* song, and then each member of the party did a solo, while the rest clapped out a steady rhythm. When it was my turn, I sang the national anthem of my country, which was very well received. It seemed to break the ice, for I had hardly sat down again when Oishi, Seto, Shunsuke Takahashi and a group of *kenchusei* called us to join them. Takahashi pulled out a sheet of paper, announcing that one of the *kenchusei* had drawn a picture, which he presented to me.

I joined their rollicking laughter when I saw what it was—a cartoon drawing of two gawky individuals in karate *gi* with one biting the other's finger. It was all in such good spirit, I wondered if they had shown it to Yano.

Suddenly, Isaka stood up, said something in Japanese, and everybody took their original places and sat in a formal kneeling position. A short speech was made followed by bows and exclamations from various instructors. Then Isaka closed the event in typical, clean-cut *samurai* fashion.

As I was putting on my shoes in the foyer, Oishi and Seto called me aside. Oishi said, "You must soon take *sandan* examination." I look disbelievingly at him. They glanced at each other, and Seto added, "Nakayama Shihan, he speak to us, okay you take third *dan* next month."

I really didn't know what to say. *"Osu!"* I replied, looking at them for a lead.

"But now you take very hard training, okay?" Oishi looked me straight in the eyes.

"Osu, Sensei!" I answered. *"Domo arigato gozai masu"* ("Thank you very much").

Gary and I shared a taxi. It didn't take us long to realize that we had both been invited to enter the third *dan* gradings.

"How many times have you tried for third *dan*?" Gary asked me.

"First time," I replied.

"You don't stand much chance," he said. "I've tried three times. This is my fourth attempt."

"What!" I said, aghast. "Why is that?"

"Because this is a very severe test. They take this *dan* level very seriously. It is what they term the 'fighting *dan*.' It is a big break-through, like passing from amateur to professional level."

"What does one have to do?" I questioned.

"Very simple. Do your favorite kata and then fight five men in a row." He boxed me lightly on my shoulder and grinned. "It's tough, my friend, really tough. I know."

"Whom do you have to fight?" I asked.

"Two new second *dans*, two from your own group of examinees, and an instructor ranked fourth *dan* or above. And you fight him last, when the others have already thrown everything at you."

"Wow!" I responded. "It must take a lot of stamina to get through that."

"Not only that. There is something else."

"What?" I demanded.

"Control often seems to go out of the window. The guys get over-excited, and it can become dangerous. You have to be careful that you don't become so excited that you fail to see what is going on. I made that mistake and ended up with a broken nose." Gary paused. His face was deadly serious. "All I can say is, remain calm in the face of the storm. My advice to you is to fight strongly and fairly, but if someone happens to lose his self-control and makes contact unfairly, then hit him back immediately; an eye for an eye. This I have found to be the soundest method of restoring order."

As I walked down the long, narrow, bamboo-lined driveway toward the Asia Center, I knew I was savoring the bitter-sweet of life. The coveted prize was within my grasp, but at what price?

Beyond Spirit of the Empty Hand

Creativity Becomes A Desperate Need

The training became geared toward the *dan* gradings. Our workload and volume was gradually increased until we were doing double the amount of training, double the amount of repetitions, double the amount of techniques. As we were reaching the peak of this marathon type training, I felt a deep tiredness creeping into my bones.

One day in the circle, we had repeated 1,000 punches and were starting the second thousand when the master approached a *kenchusei* training next to me. I heard him shouting at the man, who happened to be in a very low stance.

"More down, more lower!" The *kenchusei* replied with *"Osu!"* and looked as if he would disappear through the floor if he went any lower. The master kept doing this, and then it dawned on me that he was using English, speaking to a Japanese! He had never done this before. But he persisted: "Why don't you hear? Down, I say!"

The penny dropped. I was in a high stance. It could only be me with whom he was communicating, so I dropped into a low stance. Immediately, the master left the tired *kenchusei* and moved away to another part of the class. The Japanese sometimes have a strange way of communicating. The master's indirect approach had a profound effect on me later. I thought to myself, that without embarrassing me, he had communicated something of value, for I had eventually responded to his message, and communication was satisfactorily completed. We had spoken to each other, in a sense, a profound sense. I had much to learn from these people. What if I had not sensed his communication? If I nearly missed his point, then how many previous communications had I missed due to my insensitivity? For the first time, I realized that being sensitive and open to the communication of others was a very important asset, especially when considering the process of survival. For the first time, I knew that every utterance, every move, and every non-move was a form of communication. In order to cope with them I must learn to read and interpret their actions. They spoke with their bodies, not a language of empty words, but a language of doing, filled with thrust, and target-directed energy. When pitting myself against these martial artists, their wisdom would rub off on me, a touchstone to clarity. Interacting with them demanded clarity. I thought about my religious heritage and what I had read: "A wise man is mightier than a strong man."

It was impossible for foolishness to last long on the *honbu dojo* floor. It had to be replaced by wisdom, for only a wise man could survive the human chess game taking place in that arena.

A strange thought crossed my mind. Here I was in the middle of an alien culture and now, for the first time, I was experiencing the value and truth of my own religious background. A verse from Proverbs gave purpose to my quest: "Iron sharpens iron, and one man sharpens another."

With the *dan* grading near at hand, I noticed that the volume of work was gradually decreasing, while the intensity was increasing. In other words, we were changing from long, repetitive workouts to shorter, explosive sessions. Where before the accent had been on endurance and on a great volume of formalized training, now we were allowed to express our own creativity.

Where previously we had been restricted, now there was freedom to test and express our own tactics, speed, rhythm, distancing, and timing. The pace had more than trebled. We were now "sprinting" in short bursts, so to speak, rather than "jogging." The confrontations were short, and the actions like lightning.

Every day I was invited by various top instructors to do free fighting. While every instructor had been trained at the same *honbu dojo,* by the same instructors doing the same basics, I found that each instructor had a different and unique way of fighting. The main problem I had in confronting all of these different experts was the unpredictability of their actions.

Takahashi was small, yet artful, and moved like water. Hard to catch, yet he'd wait and always get his counter technique in.

Tabata was tall, supple, and could punch like a mule kicks. I once managed to catch him with a changing *mae geri/mawashi geri* to his face, at which he just smiled, saying, "Good!" and then proceeded to nail me on the sternum with a bola punch similar to the overhead punch in *Bassai Dai*. It was the hardest blow I had ever received. My chest was sore for weeks.

Ochi *Sensei* I could never really figure out. He later became grand champion a number of times defeating the giant Tabata in one final. Ochi was like a rubber ball: short, agile, tricky, and supple. (He used to do splits in the large communal bath after a class). He could move under, over, and around me almost at will. One time I got hold of him by the belt and had him going with a hip throw. In mid air he twisted out, landed on his feet and scissored my legs, dropping me to the ground.

Then there were the steady fighters, Takashina and Miyazaki; the artful Ueki, perfect in every technique; the sneaky Abe, with kicks that wrapped themselves around your neck, coming from nowhere; Shunsuke Takahashi, always solid and strong.

I had met Tanaka once but not yet fought him. I had been told that he always attended the *dan* gradings and fought a good many of the candidates. I dreaded the thought of coming across him in my forthcoming *dan* grading. But somehow, judging by the very nervous feeling in my gut, I was more worried that I might have to fight Yano. I felt sure that we would meet on the big day.

The daily free fights with all of these expert karate men took their toll on me. I experienced every emotion possible, both on and off the *dojo* floor, during that build-up time to the gradings. I felt fear a lot of the time, anger some of the time, depression a little of the time, and I was tired and aching all of the time.

And then the worst happened. I was surprised when Tanaka *Sensei* turned up one day and invited me to spar with him. Where "the animal" had disturbed me with his rough, aggressive tactics, Tanaka's approach caused me to become at first relaxed, then bewildered, and finally frightened. He would edge forward, moving softly like a panther. His face was calm, communicating not the slightest hint of any aggression except for two smoldering coals of fire, his eyes. They had a hypnotic effect and were all the more penetrating, since they were framed within a clean-cut thatch of short, spiky, black hair. Within the first minute of *kumite* with him, I knew I was facing an expert of experts—not a predatory powerhouse like Yano, but a deadly specialist who did not waste an ounce of energy on unnecessary moves.

The fight opened with me relaxed, moving to and fro. Tanaka had created a rhythm. He would move toward me and then a little away. He kept doing this. I watched him intently. The third time, he came close and dropped his guard. I threw a reverse punch toward his open chest. He deftly swiveled to the side. I missed him. Catching my arm with one of his hands, he leapt into the air, entwining his legs around my unsteady hips and with sudden explosive force, he wrenched me downward, flattening my back against the floor. He had used a flying scissors technique. Still trapped like a fly in a spider's web, I felt the sharp slap of a well controlled heel to my chest. Like magic, he unwound himself and was gliding

Meeting Myself

again, telling me to rise. My previous relaxed feeling had now turned into bewilderment and fear.

As we sparred on, I felt more and more powerless. Everything I tried, he turned to his advantage. My best attack, the front kick, had no effect on him. As I raised my knee to kick, his hands easily caught my leg, and every time this happened, he threw me in different ways using a variety of unique and surprising counters. His counter always found my most vulnerable area, and his controlled blow was like a firm, stinging slap. Once, thinking he had lost concentration, I tried to do a left roundhouse kick to his head. My leg was only halfway on course when his front leg lashed the skin of my stomach.

It was as if his techniques were over before they started. One saw nothing coming, and he was suddenly calm again, but not those eyes.

I went home in pain. It was not a deep-seated muscular soreness, and there was no bone pain, but there was a soreness that was much more apparent—my skin was red and on fire.

Every time he worked with me it was the same. I did not seem to be improving, and I began to dread our daily confrontations. At last, I began having sleepless nights, and if I did get to sleep at all, I kept having a recurring nightmare. There was a dark, black cloud that appeared and always began to envelop me. I would strike out wildly, but felt it smothering me. Always I became weaker and weaker, my limbs moving as if in slow motion.

Three days before the gradings I was working against Oishi. We had been chasing each other across the length of the *dojo* floor, doing our favorite combinations on each other—moving target work.

I tried my combinations on him, but he back-pedaled like a mongoose moving away from a cobra. It was very hard to reach him. I only managed it once or twice. But he was phenomenal. He covered such a great distance in a short time. He would face me and always say first, "You ready?" Then, try as I may, his explosive hips and giant strides tore at me like a Sidewinder missile finding its target. Then we would rest for a few seconds, and it would start all over again, my turn to chase him.

The humid summer days and the intense effort caused me to run rivers of perspiration. Once, Oishi and I both slipped and fell in the sweat. I thought he would kill me, but he lay on the floor laughing, finally saying, "You very clever fighter... make deep river... me nearly drown."

Beyond Spirit of the Empty Hand

I found that very funny.

Asking the Right Questions

As the class ended one day, Tanaka approached me.

"Oh, my goodness," I thought, "not again!"

As if reading my mind, he said: "No *kumite* today. I ask question. You have free time now?"

"*Osu, Sensei,*" I replied, bowing and nodding in the affirmative.

"Okay, you change, we take lunch together."

As I showered and changed, the weirdest of notions passed through my mind. On the one hand, I was excited and pleased about lunch but, on the other hand, these words repeated themselves in my head, "So the big cat is hungry. What is he going to eat? Hope it's not me."

We lunched at a Western-style, McDonald's-type of restaurant. Contrary to my expectations, I found him amiable and easy to talk to.

"You like karate?" he asked.

"Very much, *Sensei*," I replied, "but I don't feel I am very good at the moment."

"Why?" he questioned, raising his eyebrows. I still could not reconcile myself to the fact that this was the same man who had been the major cause of my nightmares.

"Well, Sensei..." I chose my words carefully. "I feel so unconfident when I fight you. I feel as if I am a new beginner."

"How long you study karate?" he asked.

"About five years," I replied.

"Oh, I study karate nearly nine years," he said. "Karate road very long. Sometimes up, sometimes down. I also have same feeling before but, please, don't give up." His expression grew serious. "I think soon big change happen in you."

"*Sensei,*" I asked, "please, will you tell me what my biggest problem is?"

"You!" he said, grinning broadly. He had taken me by surprise again. I laughed nervously, and he added, "Of course, everybody have same problem. Your technique and spirit very good, but you need more understanding of distancing."

"What do you mean, *Sensei*?"

"I not speak. You must study, then soon discover for yourself."

Meeting Myself

His change of position told me that this subject was now closed. We ate and talked about my family, his family, Japanese customs, and about my country.

As I clung to the leather hang strap, maintaining my balance in the speeding subway coach, Tanaka's spirit was still with me. His way of thinking fascinated me. Keeping time to the staccato rapping of the revolving train wheels, a voice inside me kept repeating, "What is distancing?"

From the moment the Thursday class began, the atmosphere was intense. Without allowing us to warm up, the master announced, "*Jiyu kumite. Hajime!*" Every five minutes, we changed partners, and this went on for the full hour.

I fought everybody in the class except Yano. The other instructors were "switched on," and I felt that all their fury was unleashed upon me. I gained the impression that they were working lightly with each other, but when they faced me, it was as if they were bulls and I was a red flag.

I tried to use my greater size to hold them off or to intimidate them, but gradually they wore me down, until I began moving in a mindless sea of action, sweat and tiredness. I was no longer capable of thinking or anticipating. I released blows, took blows, fell down, stood up, and kept going. I no longer worried about being injured. Some inner spirit drove me on. Winning or losing became non-existent. All that mattered was to keep going. It was as if someone else was doing the fighting. When the master ordered, "*Yame!*" I felt like I was awakened from a dream. Then we meditated. I existed in a timeless zone, merged with the surroundings, emptied of all worldly thoughts. Nothing mattered.

The class ended, and I realized that we had been sitting for many minutes, yet it had felt like seconds.

The master summoned me and told me to take Friday off and relax because I was grading on Saturday. As I bowed to him and started making my way out of the *dojo*, he called me back and said, "A truly big man must first learn to become a small man." With that, he closed the communication by calling another karate-*ka* to him.

I walked slowly along the street, a new line added to my self-made *koan* (a riddle set by a Zen master): "What is distancing; what is small man?"

It was only after I reached the Asia Center that I realized I had covered the seven-mile distance on foot instead of taking the usual subway ride. Soaking in a hot bath, it occurred to me that I had today closed the seven-mile distance between *honbu dojo* and Asia Center unconsciously. "What is distancing?" I sang out aloud. Then, surveying my big frame filling the tiny tub, I wondered how on earth I could become a small man. What did the master mean? As I dried my body off with a towel, I thought, "Maybe he means I must become more agile and move more quickly, and be compact like a small man. But this goes without saying. No, he said 'become' a small man. This is a very teasing riddle. Why can't he be straightforward with me? Why always this subtle innuendo?"

Sitting alone in the center of the communal dining hall, picking at the rice and shredded vegetable meal, my mind became busy and I began to realize that my entire body was aching—no doubt, from the hour-long free fighting. A couple of friends called me to join them at their table, but I rejected the invitation, saying that I needed to go to bed.

Try as I might, sleep wouldn't come. Although my body was tired, my mind was like an electric kaleidoscope that I could not turn off. Growing more and more restless, I finally gave up the idea of sleep, dressed, and walked out into the Tokyo night.

A sense of loneliness pervaded my entire being. "Here I am in the middle of a busy, colorful metropolis, but I feel so alone. What am I doing here?" I thought. "With Saturday drawing closer, I feel further away from myself than I have ever felt." A large amusement center decked in alluring neon signs drew me in. In the corner of the game-filled area was a group of boisterous individuals crowded around an electronic game called "Racing Car." These were the biggest Japanese men I had ever seen. I gravitated to the opposite corner of the establishment, trying to appear inconspicuous.

Hardly had I slipped the *yen* coin into the game of "Space Invaders" when I heard a booming voice, "Ah, karate man, you come here!"

I looked up, and sure enough, a beefy man was waving goodbye to me. I had recently learned that this gesture meant "come here." I considered running out and escaping but, on second thought, I walked across to them, wondering how they knew about my karate. I didn't have to wait long for an answer.

"What *dojo* you attend?" asked the same man, pointing to the Japanese characters inscribed on my T-shirt. I told him, and they did not seem over-interested. Then a Japanese girl among them said to me, "You very tall man."

"Yes," butted in the bull of a man, "but he very skinny."

Meeting Myself

They roared in delight. I forced a smile, bowed to them, and headed for the door. A Westerner who had been watching turned to me saying: "Don't feel bad. Those are *sumo* wrestlers. It's just their way of being friendly."

"It served me right," I thought to myself. "I wanted to know what is small man. Now I know. Or, do I?"

I walked on and began thinking of my wife, my daughters, my friends and students back home. If there was any one time I needed them, it was now. The distance from them felt so far. Distance is that gap separating two entities, but what is distancing?

8

THE THIRD DAN GRADING

Meeting Myself

Closing The Distance Between Self And Reality

Hundreds of shoes and straw sandals covered the floor and stairs of the *dojo*. The floor was a hive of activity. There were three groups, each with a huge crowd of karate-*ka* gathered around, watching and grading. Other karate-*ka* warmed up and practiced in any small free space they could find. I found Gary and Seto. Gary looked pale. "When do Gary and I go on?" I asked Seto.

"Much later," said Seto. "Still about a hundred and fifty people going for *shodan* and then about eighty for *nidan*."

It was now about 10.30 in the morning. Watching two brown belts doing *kumite* made me feel uneasy. They were good.

"If the brown belts are this good, imagine what the third *dan* grading will be like," I remarked.

Seto pulled us away, inviting us for a snack downstairs.

"Still plenty of time," he pointed out.

In the afternoon, we watched those going for *nidan*. Tanaka, who was also dressed in karate *gi* was testing the *nidan* candidates, not by marking them on paper, but fighting them. He must have participated in about twenty or thirty fights that afternoon, all of which he took in his stride. His opponents seemed desperate as he easily dispatched them with leg sweeps, throws, or stinging blows to their bodies. A few times, he literally slapped his opponent's cheeks with his roundhouse kicks, which came from nowhere.

Among the *nidan*s was one very aggressive and spirited individual who I will call Kaneko. In both of his fights, he knocked out his opponents with a right-footed roundhouse to the jaw. I didn't like the look of him. He was dangerous and only went forward. I made a mental note to be careful of that right foot.

The next few hours we walked up and down the stairs from *dojo* to restaurant. I couldn't stomach anything more than *miso-shiru* (soup). It was five o'clock when the three groups formed into one area. At a long line of tables were seated the most senior karate men in the world. My nerves were raw by the time my name was called out.

There were five of us facing the *Shihankai*—Gary, myself, and three Japanese. Each of us was required to do our favorite kata.

Gary went on first. He did *Nijushiho*. Midway through, he lost balance slightly. Not a murmur came from the thousand eyes focused upon his every move. It was rather like the mobs that gather around famous golf players to watch a $100,000 putt. There was

Beyond Spirit of the Empty Hand

one difference today—this crowd was almost within touching distance of Gary. The grading area was very small.

My turn came. I stood in the middle of the small area waiting for the command to begin. My legs felt like rubber; they trembled, and there was nothing I could do about it. I felt the perspiration running down my cheeks. The master told me to begin. I bowed and announced my kata: *"Gankaku!"* The sound of my sweat droplets pounding the floor was magnified by the silence. There are times in *Gankaku* when one assumes a position like a crane standing on a rock. This is where the kata derived its name. After a series of fast moves, there is a sudden change into a smooth, flowing sequence of graceful moves, whereby one leg is drawn up behind the knee of the other leg, and balancing on one leg for a time, one then slowly swivels around and delivers a high side snap kick.

I finished the kata, and to this day cannot recall the details. How good it was I will never know.

It was similar with the *kumite*. There was no time for thinking. One of the Japanese candidates in my group faced Kaneko, the aggressive *nidan*, who immediately felled him with a potent roundhouse to the jaw. Again, that right foot. The grading of my colleague had started and ended within seconds, as he was in no condition to continue. So this is what Gary had meant. Kaneko, of course, had nothing to lose. His grading was already over. I reasoned that if my colleague could not cope with a second *dan*, he was then not yet ready to become a third *dan*. One thing had become clear. I now understood the rules of this game, and that was all I needed to know. My attitude instantly changed. I went cold, but deadly cold.

My name was called, and what I had been fearing happened. Kaneko stepped out to face me. As we were told to start, he stepped in, and I instinctively moved backwards. I felt the roundhouse as it glanced off my right cheek. He had used his left foot. I didn't see it, but fortunately I had managed to ride the blow by sliding backwards. I had retreated and fallen into the ring of people watching. Walking back to the center line, I told myself that I must now only go forward; otherwise I had no chance.

On *hajime,* we both shot forward simultaneously, but my leading punch must have been a fraction of a second quicker than his kick. He dropped to the ground like a dead bird and there he lay. A voice from the judges panel shouted, "More control!" I bowed and waited, not believing what had happened, for I had definitely not followed through with the technique. My fist must have touched a nerve center on his jaw. Kaneko stood up looking slightly dazed. I then faced a Japanese from my group. We had a couple of clashes in which we both attacked and blocked each other. Finally, I surprised myself by back-kicking him into the crowd. It was a well-controlled kick delivered just as he was losing balance. How I did it I still don't know. I happened to be in the right place at the right time. Is this what Tanaka meant by distancing? But still my inner voice persisted, "What is distancing?"

My other fights went reasonably well as I began to feel more emotionally stable. "Maybe this too has something to do with distancing," I thought, "like getting closer to one's true self." I almost felt ready to meet Yano, but fate works in its own strange way. All that training, those explosive confrontations, the worrying, the build-up, and now, instead, I faced Tabata *Sensei* for my last fight. For his opening gambit, he feinted by circling his open hands in front of my face. Suddenly he switched to a powerful leg sweep that sent me tripping sideways over my own feet. But I recovered balance before I fell, only to be caught again by the same tactic.

"I must wake up," I said to myself, as we were directed back to the center of the area, for in the very moment I had thought I understood what distancing was, I was in that instant too distanced away from myself to perceive what was happening. I opened with a front kick, which Tabata blocked powerfully. He tried to sweep again with his massive right foot. I avoided it by sliding backward and suddenly out of nowhere came the favorite technique I had been practicing so hard. My left leg started off as a front kick, and he started blocking downward as before, but suddenly my foot changed from a forward direction to a round action. My roundhouse kick neatly tapped him on the side of his jaw. I showed no emotion, but felt ecstatic inside.

"Another mistake," I reminded myself. His eyebrow lifted, and his eyes went wide with surprise. He chuckled heartily and slapped me on the back saying, "Oh, very good technique" I had a feeling of *dejavu*.

The examiner cut in, *"Hajime!"* Tabata switched on instantly, swept me into a horizontal position, and before I landed, he scored with a powerful, controlled blow to the chest. Again the chest.

"Yame!" ordered the chief examiner.

I bowed to the gentle giant who stood smiling in front of me. I respected him deeply for his skill, but more so for his sincere warmth and benevolent way. "He is truly a big man." I felt this emotion strongly. "He has a soft side; he is humble. Is this not

Beyond Spirit of the Empty Hand

what Nakayama Sensei meant when he urged me to become the small man? I have been too filled with myself. This is my hardness. That is why I often miss the actions of others. I have got to learn to see clearly. And isn't this type of seeing intimately related to distancing?"

Loneliness and Then ...

The gradings ended, and no results were given. This was the way of Japanese karate. Results were seen as unimportant. As I walked across the empty *dojo* floor, I thought of a Japanese proverb: "Live with cause, leave results to the great law of the universe." Although I knew there was much wisdom in these words, I was unable to shed myself of a deeply implanted habit. I was dying to know whether I had passed or failed. I had probably failed, I reasoned. But I badly needed to know on which side my coin lay.

Takagi *Sensei* told me I must meet him the next day at the NHK TV station. I would be doing a short demonstration.

On the stairs, I passed a group of instructors. Tabata reached out and pulled me to a halt. "You come for dinner tonight."

"*Sensei*, I must go and pack. I leave the day after tomorrow." A lame excuse, but I was now overcome with a state of anti-climax. I felt empty inside and didn't want to impose my blankness upon the *Senseis*. I had the TV demo to do and, what's more, it required effort to communicate with this group, and my understanding of Japanese was limited. Mostly, we talked in sign language, in very elementary English and, for my part, in very broken Japanese.

Seto and Oishi grabbed me and dragged me along while Tanaka warned: "Tonight no sleep. Soon leave Japan. Must enjoy."

Sitting next to Tabata in the taxi, I kept waiting for a suitable opening in the conversation to ask him the nagging question. But no such opening presented itself, and soon we joined the instructors at an "Eat-and-Drink-as-Much-as-You-Like-in-Two-Hours" type of restaurant. I was still not my normal carefree self.

As we began with the singing of songs, Tabata sat next to me and, raising his glass to me, said quietly, "Maybe tomorrow you *sandan*." Before I could say anything, he joined in with the singing, indicating that I should sing louder. His ambiguous comment had not relieved my inner nagging.

From that moment, I resolved to convert my introversion to an outward spirit. I sang and even did a dance for the instructors,

Meeting Myself

which apparently looked so ridiculous that some of them rolled onto the floor with laughter.

The next day, Takagi *Sensei* met me in the foyer of NHK TV station. I had brought Clive, Roy, and Alan to help with my demonstration. We were introduced to the presenter, who shuffled us into a make-up room. We changed into our karate-*gi*, and the presenter asked me to put on a long, black, dressing gown-type garment, which concealed the karate suit I was wearing. I was told that before my demonstration I would be facing a panel who would try to guess my occupation.

As I was ushered onto the stage of a sound studio, I was welcomed by a live audience of applauding Japanese people.

"Doctor?" was the panel's first guess.

"No," I answered.

"Sport?"

"Yes."

"Some martial art?"

"Yes."

"Judo?"

"No."

"You are a karate-ka!" said one of the panel.

As I answered yes, someone helped me remove the black gown and the compeer of the show was escorting Takagi Sensei onto the stage, followed by my team.

"We have a surprise for you," said the compeer.

Mr. Takagi stepped up to me, took the microphone and announced, "Mister Stan Schmidt, on behalf of the Japan Karate Association, I have pleasure in advising you that you have been promoted to the third *dan* rank of karate—the first Westerner to receive this honor."

The audience erupted, cheering as Mr. Takagi shook my hand.

"Now for your demonstration," said the compeer.

That night, we had another party.

I don't remember how I got home, but I was awakened the next morning by Seto's call. As we spoke, my eyes surveyed the room, and it gradually occurred to me that the nature of its contents had changed drastically.

"Please wash and dress. Be ready in 30 minutes."

"Where are you?" I asked in a dazed voice.

"Downstairs. I take you to the airport," said Seto.

As I replaced the receiver, I noticed that all my belongings had disappeared. That is, except for my red suitcase and black

Beyond Spirit of the Empty Hand

overnight bag, which stood side by side in the middle of the neatly tidied room.

Miyazaki *Sensei* had helped Seto pack my belongings more neatly than I could ever have done. He had even packaged my excess baggage and would take it to the Post Office and dispatch it on my behalf, Seto told me.

At the airport, I shook Seto's hand and thanked him for everything. He produced a large carrier bag filled with parcels that were wrapped in colored paper, complete with attractively tied bows.

"From all instructors," he said, and before I could answer, he handed me a large brown envelope, pushing me forward into the area restricted to passengers.

"Please, you only open envelope when plane in sky," he added.

I was caught up in a wave of passengers moving forward, clinging to the bags and parcels precariously dangling from all sides. As I was about to turn into the first passageway, I heard his voice.

"*Sayonara.*" Turning, I saw his face clearly for an instant, and then it was swallowed by the crowd.

"*Sayonara,*" I said quietly to myself as I walked down the long corridor. "*Sayonara,* my dear friend."

Thoughts of tiredness were non-existent as the droning of the takeoff jets lulled me into the deepest sleep.

"We have just reached the halfway mark." The voice seemed to come from far off, but as I awoke I realized the captain was speaking to us over the intercom.

On my lap lay the brown envelope Seto had given me. As I began opening it, I felt a touch on my shoulder.

"Do you know you have slept for over eight hours and missed two meals? Aren't you hungry?" asked the smiling air hostess.

My hands slowly unfolded the large, white, rice paper *sandan* certificate. It was inscribed with bold, black Japanese characters. It was a work of art. Beautiful. I folded it and put it carefully back into the envelope, not wanting to spoil it.

"You seem far away." She leaned forwards speaking into my ear. "You still have a long way to go. Let me bring you something to eat."

"Really?" said I without thinking. "Yes, I do still have a long way to go, but at least I'm beginning to enjoy it all.

9

BREAKING BRICKS AND BUILDING BRIDGES

Meeting Myself

Daily Bread

"Yes, I still have a long way to go..."

These words repeated themselves over and over in my mind, night after night, as I lay awake in my bed, secure again in my small house in Gardens.

A combination of jet lag plus thoughts of all of the stimulating experiences that had happened to me in Japan, ending with my third *dan* grading, didn't allow me much sleep for the first seven days after my arrival back in South Africa.

My career of banking as a profession was over. I had chosen a new way of life. I had spent every cent of our meager savings on this Japanese trip. What we now possessed were two lovely daughters with a third on the way; a house with a first and second bond over it; a *dojo* in Orange Grove with the burden of a high monthly rental; and a group of very keen karate students.

While I was proud of being described by the Japanese and local press as "the first non-Japanese to achieve the third degree black belt in karate," I also saw this as a tremendous challenge and responsibility. I continually reflected upon the meaning of third *dan* and began to study all types of books related to Japan and frequently wrote my thoughts down.

The third *dan* had earned me status, and I developed quite a large membership base at three *dojos*—Orange Grove, Central Gym, and the University of the Witwatersrand. But, I wasn't making money. What I earned was a joke compared to what my school pal, Gary Player, the famous golfer, was earning.

"All these members and Judy still has to go out and work," I once complained to my friend and student, Ray Joffe, a prominent attorney.

"It's because you are only charging 40 Rand a month," he told me. "You should be charging at least 100 Rand!"

I was reluctant to make my fees too high for fear of being labeled "commercial." I had read somewhere that the *samurai* warriors did not like handling money.

I told Ray, "If I train hard and teach well, the money will come."

He just smiled, but behind his twinkling eyes he must have been thinking how naive I was.

I remembered what Kase *Sensei* had advised me when he told me to go full-time into karate in 1964: "Karate, very difficult ca-

Beyond Spirit of the Empty Hand

reer. Up and down. Sometimes rich. Sometimes poor. But good life. You try, Mistah Stan!"

I had chosen my path: To dedicate myself to hard training and good teaching. I was back home on solid ground, and there was a lot of hard work to be done.

Judy helped with reception work at the Grove *dojo* while I was a tyrant toward my students. Fortunately, Judy tempered the atmosphere in the *dojo* and managed to prevent some of the members from leaving.

"No," she would say, "he is not angry with you. It's just the way they do it in Japan. Keep trying!"

I was uncompromising in my demands regarding how karate training should be approached.

The first morning after my return from Japan I was back training at 6:00 a.m. with the Early Birds. This instructor training took place six times a week—four times a week at Grove *dojo* and twice a week at my house. At the house we trained outdoors, *gashuku* (outdoor training) style. We trained on a half-slate, half-lawn area. The perimeter was fitted with crude *makiwaras* and bags of all sizes. Included in our equipment was a chinning bar, a dipping bar and an assortment of trees, which we kicked and struck to harden our hands and feet.

The training ranged from bag and *makiwara* striking, to resistance training with dumbbells and barbells, to moving forward and backward against the resistance of rubber bicycle tubes tied around our waists or ankles, to free fighting wearing boots, to wrestling judo-style on the grass until someone gave up, to doing repetition after repetition of a kata like *Bassai Dai*, to breaking bricks, tiles, or wood.

At first Judy complained, "What are we supposed to do with all of this rubble?" (The broken bricks and tiles.) Later, she gave up, telling me that I was totally unreasonable.

After dinner one evening in our kitchen, I teased her by reaching out and grabbing her around her shoulders.

"Come on. What are you going to do now?" I challenged.

Hardly had I spoken when she shot out a double fist punch to my relaxed solar plexus.

"This and this," she laughed.

I doubled up. She had winded me, and I could not believe it. Winded for the first time in my life and to cap it all, by my wife! And she hadn't even had one lesson in karate. I think it was from that time onward that I began listening to her a little when she spoke.

We weren't pulling in enough money from the *dojo*. We needed to build a room onto our house with our third daughter, Tia, on the way. Also, we needed to go away on our annual holiday. So Judy, while still pregnant, went out with a friend, Doreen, to sell toilet sets door-to-door.

My fanatical involvement with karate must have been hard for her—Early Birds every morning, teaching children every afternoon, teaching adult beginners every evening, and teaching the black belt club later in the evenings.

There was also the SA JKA national association, of which I was Chief Instructor, comprising *dojo*s in all the provinces of South Africa, with two national black belt gradings a year, two national *gashukus* a year, two national tournaments (juniors and seniors) each year, and an annual visit from at least one Japanese Instructor.

Then there was a championship, a *gashuku,* and four gradings a year for my own *dojo*. In addition, I would visit and teach in the various areas around South Africa.

We also put on demonstrations at schools, theaters, universities, and shopping centers, and participated in a number of documentaries and movies. Then there were the annual visits to Japan, which I always looked forward to.

I always enjoyed writing. After a hearty evening meal with my wife and daughters, I often wrote late into the night.

At that time Judy began to instruct aerobics at the *dojo* along with her other chores.

Nasty, Unwelcome Visitors

Often there were those nasty, unwelcome visitors, like an aching toe. (All too often I had at least one broken or severely bruised toe); a puffed-up elbow (breaking too many boards in demonstrations); swollen knuckles (overdid it hitting the underpadded *makiwara*); and the numerous occasions when I made contact with my opponents elbows instead of his mid-section. And last, but not least, my sore lower back. I had seen the Japanese easily bend their torsos over to touch their straightened legs while sitting. So I made Ed Dorey, the biggest karate-*ka* in South Africa at the time, sit on me as I strained to get my head to my knees. I heard something popping out of place.

My chiropractor, Dr. Phillips, would shake his head in disgust.

"You're too extreme. You over-do things. Your reputation has preceded you. Take it easy, Stan. Be fair to your body. You only have one."

I was a fool. I didn't listen. He would work on my back, click it back into place and I would be back training. I wanted to be like the Japanese—hard, serious trainers.

But then, what I hadn't figured out was that every time I had visited Japan it was during the All Japan Championships. In other words, the training was always peaking during that period—fast, very intense workouts with ultimate focus of spirit and energy. And this in the earlier years, the 60s and early 70s, was the way of karate in South Africa.

It was only a few years later that it dawned on me that the break-neck pace I expected from my students and from myself was too harsh.

Various Japanese Instructors like Nakayama Sensei, Ochi, Yamaguchi, Enoeda, Shirai, Kase, Kanazawa, Tanaka, Chinen, Higaonna, Kawawada, Kagawa, and Omura visited South Africa and stayed at my house. I trained with them, watched them, and gradually began to see that their training methods were essentially gentle most of the time. Their free-fighting was smooth-flowing, like their kata, with focus, but not forced.

Along with this gradual realization I visited Japan at other times of the year and saw that the instructors trained in different ways, focusing on different aspects of their art, according to the seasons and according to the task at hand—gradings, demonstrations, tournaments or in many cases, for health and fitness.

It took me nearly two decades to begin to understand the delicate balance between hard and soft, the balancing of quiet time and intense time, necessary to produce effective techniques.

Only in the early 1980s did I begin to appreciate the admonishment of my doctor friend and student, Dave Berson: "Your gentleness shall, more than your force shall, move them to gentleness."

Aching to Return to Japan

Always at the back of my mind, whether I was training, instructing, writing, or relaxing, was Japan. The *honbu dojo*—to train

Meeting Myself

again in the Hornets' Nest with the dynamic Japanese. And then to enter in the event to beat all events, the magnificent All Japan Championships.

I would often reflect back to my last visit to Tokyo in 1966. So much had happened. Forgotten experiences filtered through my mind, and these memories motivated me to return.

Our little South African team of Clive Himsworth, Roy Braun, and myself had done quite well at the 1966 All Japan Championships held at the colossal Nihon Budokan Martial Arts Stadium. Well over 2,000 contestants took part in the tournament. Our team had entered merely to gain experience. There were about 50 teams competing in our section. We couldn't imagine even making it through the first round, but to our surprise we won our way through four rounds and ended up in joint fourth position.

-----oOo-----

In 1968, I again entered in the All Japan Championships and won a gold medal in the team event, doing *Chinte* kata. As they presented me with the huge floating trophy, they told me, " Keep it, Mister Stan. From next year we will have three-person-teams."

Up to the present time, the team kata event required that just one participant compete on behalf of his team. I gave the beautiful trophy to my friend, Shunsuke Takahashi, chief instructor of Australia, to be used as a trophy at his University Club championships.

A few days before the Championships, I was fortunate to run into the famous novelist, Yukio Mishima. After a workout I walked out of the change rooms and almost bumped into a middle-aged Japanese man clad in karate-gi. He was poised and upright in stature, possessing a presence and charismatic strength that commanded respect. I bowed deeply. He returned my bow and commenced teaching a group of about 20 young men, each wielding a six-foot *bo,* (wooden staff). Their movements were precise and spirited and were performed in rigid military fashion.

They were rehearsing for a demonstration that they would be performing at the forthcoming championships. I discovered later that this group was part of Mishima's personal army, the Tatenokai.

I was never introduced to Mishima in person, but Nakayama Sensei, after Mishima's death by *hara-kiri* in 1970, told me that Mishima had studied karate with him.

"A very versatile and controversial man, Yukio Mishima," Nakayama had said. "He was more than a famous novelist. He was also a playwright, a sportsman (engaging seriously in body building and the martial arts), and a film actor. A man of many talents."

The theme of ritual suicide, *hara-kiri,* appeared in nearly every one of Mishima's works. He endlessly rehearsed his own death, so to speak. With Japan's surrender after World War II, Mishima felt Japan had lost her spirit, so he formed his own personal army as an example to the authorities.

"Japan needs new teeth," he told Japanese in high places. He wanted Japan to return to the old feudal way. Thus, he would give his life for his cause, which was to make Japan the most superior fighting nation on earth.

In November 1970, Mishima and a small group entered Eastern Army headquarters in Tokyo and took over in an attempted *coup d'état.* They captured and bound the general, and Mishima addressed a few hundred army personnel from a second floor parapet. The regular army soldiers were not impressed, and dismissed him as crazy. Mishima then returned to the General's office and taking a sword, committed *hara-kiri,* disemboweling himself.

Teacher Becomes Student

Back in South Africa, I sometimes found it hard not having my own teacher. I would train on my own and with the Early Birds, but I felt the need to be put through my paces like I was doing to my students.

Cecil Wolov, one of my students, emerged as the one to put me under the whip from time to time. He was a natural-born coach, older than me, wiser than me, and, coincidentally, he had a build similar to Nakayama Sensei. He was short and eagle-eyed. Sometimes we called him "Little Nakayama." I wrote to Cecil at the end of each week's training in Japan. He studied those letters thoroughly, and when I returned to South Africa, I would meet with him once a week, and he would whip me into shape. When I told him he was getting carried away, he would chuckle fiendishly, saying, "Another 10 reps." Then he would present me with a copy of a letter I had written to him.

"Read that. Carefully. Your own words. Don't tell me I am getting carried away. Now get onto one leg and kick."

I was thinking, "My number one worst form of torture."

"Front kick and roundhouse kick. *Ichi, ni, san ...*"

"It's not so bad," I would think. "I like to do roundhouse kick."

"No! Keep your knee up! Higher! Higher! Now put in a few side thrust kicks."

I thought, "This is utter torture!" Side kicks were not among my favorite techniques.

"No! Don't drop your knee!"

"*Osu!*" I would grimace in time with my attempts to do side kicks, harder and higher, with my hip flexors, back, and lungs all burning like fire, sweat running down my forehead, and the kicks feeling totally ineffectual.

"Knee up, Stan. This is Nakayama Sensei speaking. Read the letter again!" Cecil would shout.

"*Osu!*" was my only reply. I had quickly learned that any other reply definitely would result in extra repetitions.

"Remember the letter." He would stop counting and start talking. Cecil loved talking.

"*Osu!*" I would respond again, like a lame parrot hopping around on one leg. If I so much as dropped my leg an inch, he would hit me with one of his two favorite remedies: a dose of sarcasm or a dose of praise. Usually the former. But he always had such a nice way of saying things.

"You told me that Enoeda could stand for hours on one leg and easily do kicks in all directions without getting tired! Are you sick, or what? You've only been on one leg for less than five minutes."

"Cecil, I'm not Enoeda, and I didn't exactly mean *hours*. It's only an expression."

"Oh! So you're a bullshitter on top of it?"

Cecil would laugh out loud like a cackling duck, while I was nearly dying on one leg, holding my ankle up with one hand and losing all semblance of dignity. Cecil enjoyed the sound of his own voice. He suddenly would begin praising me.

"Look, Stan. I don't want you downing yourself. You're too humble, always putting those Japanese ahead of you. That's why you only came fourth. You're better than them, man!"

"Like bloody hell," I would think.

"You train harder than them; you're bigger and faster."

"And stiffer," I would add, unable to take this unwarranted mix of praise and pressure. "They're like India rubber men. I'm like a telephone pole."

"Shut up, Stan! That's a negative remark, if I ever heard one."

"*Osu!*"

"That's better. Change to the other leg."
"Thank God," I muttered to myself.
"What was that?"
"*Osu!*" A very useful expression.

Later, in the change room, Cecil would still be at me.

"You've got guts, Stan. You don't give in. Even with all the shit I give you. But get one thing straight. I can't do much for you, if you go on thinking the Japanese are your superiors. You rate them too highly."

Now I hit back. We were not on the floor any more. Cecil is my student, after all.

"Look, Cecil, I rate them as superior because they *are* superior. They invented the art. They are *great*. And that's how I want to be. They can do techniques that I will never achieve in one lifetime."

"Maybe. But, Stan, you have got certain things *they* can't do."

"I don't see them."

"Well, until you do, you'll only have yourself to blame. You keep limiting yourself. Never do that. Life is hard enough. You're good. Believe me!"

"Thanks, Cecil." I like what he says, but I only half believe him. It's always the same. Every training session with Cecil ends this way.

10

HEAVEN AND HELL

Meeting Myself

The Gates of Heaven

Although I am now a committed Christian, I went through a period in the late 60s and early 70s, where I wanted to know more about what lay behind the Japanese way of thinking. I read many books on *Zen* and I was particularly impressed with Paul Reps' *Zen Flesh, Zen Bones*. It is full of little stories and anecdotes. The one I liked most was "The Gates of Heaven."

As the story goes, a *samurai* named Nobushige came to Hakuin and asked him if heaven and hell were real.

"You couldn't possibly be a *samurai*," replied Hakuin. "A true warrior wouldn't ask such a stupid question. Only a blockhead or a jackass would waste my time with such nonsense!"

So enraged was Nobushige by this that he began chasing Hakuin around the room, shouting that he was going to beat him senseless.

"Beat me up?" cried Hakuin. "I knew it! You're probably a beggar in disguise who doesn't even know how to use a sword!"

The furious warrior instantly drew his sword, and Hakuin shouted, "*That* is Hell!"

The *samurai* hesitated and returned his sword to its scabbard.

"*That* is Heaven!" said Hakuin

In Alan Watt's *The Spirit of Zen*, (New York, Grove Press, 1958), there were passages from *The Samurai Creed* that motivated me.

"*I have no magic power; I make inward strength my magic.*" (This pointed me back to my culture: "The Kingdom of Heaven is within.")

"*I have no limbs; I make promptitude my limbs.*" (Using this principle I was able to move and strike much faster.)

"*I have no enemy; I make incautiousness my enemy.*" (Simple, common sense.)

Eugen Herrigel's *Zen in the Art of Archery* (New York, Random House, 1971) is a classic work read and absorbed by top martial artists and sportsmen world wide. The following extracts appealed to me:

> "The sportsman or artist moves above worldly sordidness and restlessness to transcend physical technique so that his art becomes 'artless art'."

"Learn to wait properly. 'Let go of yourself,' is what a great archery teacher advised his student."

"Just as one uses a burning candle to light others, so the teacher transfers the spirit of the right art from heart to heart..."

One-Day Zen

It was on a training visit to Japan in 1969 that I became taken up with the idea of going to a *Zen* teacher to learn the techniques of meditation. I felt that with the daily hard training I needed something like this to soften and balance out my daily regimen. So after training one day, I approached Nakayama Sensei and told him I wanted to study *Zen*.

"Why do you want this, Stan? No need. Karate training is already enough."

"Sensei, I'd like to try."

"Okay, if you want. Please speak to Mr. Oishi."

I spoke to Oishi *Sensei* and he told me there was a *Zen* temple nearby the Asia Center. He made a call and told me, "You go 5:30 a.m. tomorrow. Seven o'clock finished. Okay?"

"Thank you," I nodded.

This I hadn't bargained for. So early, but I had asked for it. I couldn't back out now. I had thought of doing *Zen* in the late afternoon.

The next morning I eased my tired body out of bed, dressed in an old, blue JKA track suit and made my way on foot to the temple. (It turned out to be a 30-minute walk). I admonished myself: "This is not such a bright idea. I'll just get back to the hotel to change and then I will have to rush off to the *dojo,* which is also a 30-minute walk and traveling time by subway. And then there will be two classes—one general and one instructors' class. By one o'clock I'll be a corpse. I'm dumb," I thought as I reached the double doors of the temple situated near Roppongi.

The door opened, and a man dressed in a loose fitting robe greeted me in Japanese.

"*Ohayo gozai masu,*" I said, and bowed. Then, running out of Japanese vocabulary, I pointed to the JKA emblem on my track suit. He nodded once and invited me in. Immediately he demonstrated a sitting lotus position, one bent leg folded across the other. For me this was like trying to tie my long legs up in an impossible

Meeting Myself

reef knot. I tried but couldn't connect up. He then demonstrated a half lotus. Still I couldn't connect. I kept falling over backwards.

"What position can you take?" he asked in understandable English.

Breathing a sigh of relief, I slipped into *seiza* position, the standard karate kneeling position.

"Ah, ha!" he commented. "This position very severe. Do you wish to do this?"

"*Osu!* Eh, I mean *Hai* (yes)." You don't say *osu* to normal Japanese people. It's mainly karate-ka that use this kind of slang word to convey a spirit of fortitude.

He sat next to me for a few minutes. By now I was beginning to feel some pain in my ankles. He adjusted me into a more upright position and then he said, "Okay, please stand up. Follow me."

"Phew! That was a short lesson," I thought. "Now for some tea and a talk."

But instead, he led me into a long narrow hall. An aisle ran down the middle with two long raised platforms on either side of the aisle stretching the length of the hall. The two platforms were covered in fresh green *tatami* mats. On each of the platforms were perched about 10 black, square velvet cushions set neatly on the *tatami* nearly two meters apart, like little soldiers in neat formation. The hall was beautifully crafted in rich oak, and at the entrance was a simple wooden stand with a drum resting upon it. Everything was so neat, so clean, so serene. I realized later that this was a meditation hall.

My mentor stopped at the first cushion on the left and asked me to climb up onto the *tatami* platform. I did this easily, as the platform was only about half a meter above floor level.

"Please turn around and face the wall," he ordered.

"Must I use the cushion?" I asked meekly.

"If you want. But your *seiza* no need cushion."

I nodded and took up the *seiza* position. I jammed the cushion in between my bottom and my heels. It felt slightly more comfortable than not having the support of the cushion. He must have been amused by my awkwardness and unconventional way of meditating, but all he said was, "Sit quietly one hour. No move." He walked out, leaving me on my own. I nearly fell off my cushion. Those six words caused a kind of gut reaction in me I had never thought I was capable of mustering up in one second flat. It was a cocktail of emotions, with fear being the predominant ingredient.

Beyond Spirit of the Empty Hand

Although I was sitting stock still, my inner voice was complaining, "One hour sitting like this! When I do this for 10 minutes my ankles want to fall off."

Then a second shock. I heard it first—a clacking sound and the chime of a bell. Again the clacking, louder, like two flat sticks were being banged together. Out of the corner of my eye, (I wasn't sure whether to keep my eyes open or shut, so I opted for the former option), I saw a long line of beings entering the hall behind me, filing sedately past me, each stepping up onto the rostrum effortlessly, placing himself upon his cushion, and assuming a double lotus position. They sat quietly, like living statues, exuding peace.

"*Shabat shalom,*" flashed through my mind. Ray Joffe's considerate words to me every Friday afternoon. *Shabat* meaning Sabbath. *Shalom* meaning peace. But this was not the Sabbath, nor did I feel at peace.

"They've put you in with the pros," my anxious little inner voice warned. "You had better not give in. It was you who chose to be here." I should have heeded Nakayama *Sensei*'s subtle advice: "No need. Just karate training enough."

Pure silence claimed the hall. The only sound was the soft swish of the stocking-clad feet of one monk who floated up and down the aisle, keeping watch. He carried a flat type of stick. I had read that the flat stick was used to wake up "nodding off" meditators. A sharp rap across the shoulders would wake up the snoozer or, alternatively, if the meditator felt he needed this stimulating sting to get him back on track, he could place both open hands together in front of him, indicating to the "stick man" that he was requesting "a shot."

After 10 minutes I was uncomfortable, but I didn't dare move. No one moved. I could not let JKA down. My honor was at stake. So I sat fast, grimly gritting my teeth as about 20 minutes dragged by. By this time I was perspiring profusely. At about the halfway mark, I felt I had to do something. I was dying of pain in my lower extremities. The sweat pouring out of every pore was not from heat. It was from pain, and to make things worse, the more pain I experienced, the more serene the pro meditators looked to me. I was learning fast how to look sideways without turning my head. My eyeballs were having a field day.

Then I had to do it. I picked up both hands indicating to the passing monk that I wanted to be hit with the stick. He ignored me, allowing me to slip further into my self-made hell.

Meeting Myself

Now, at about the 45-minute mark, my entire lower half was just about numb. Along with this, my stomach was busy doing internal gymnastics. It was like a nest of worms, butterflies, and serpents had awakened inside of me and were celebrating my discomfort with much gusto.

Feeling I wanted to just give in and stand up, I instead placed my hands together, begging for a pick-me-up.

"Thwack!" Like a blessed bolt of lightning, the monk's stick struck me square across the shoulders. Temporary relief. I felt like saying, "Again, please!" But he resumed his catwalk patrol, and my suffering was returning with renewed vengeance.

I began imagining: "No blood flowing in my legs. Gangrene. Amputation." I tried to keep my entire body from trembling. This silent shaking was from nausea and the effort of trying to remain still and quiet and upright. I felt like death, but I was, in fact, filled with life. Pain is a great indicator of being alive.

How I held out I do not know. I suppose it was pride. I heard the beat of the drum, or was it a gong? I'm not quite sure which. The monks arose and began moving out of the hall in a neat single file. With their exit, heaven entered. I knew it was over. I was alive again.

I tried to stand up, but couldn't. My lower half was dead numb. I checked to see that there was no one around to witness my next undignified move—a sideways roll off the platform onto the floor of the aisle. Barumph! I lay there wound up like a human question mark. It took me about five minutes to finally unwind and straighten out and allow the pins and needles of returning blood to abate.

I stood up slowly and peered out of the door into the foyer of the temple. Not a soul in sight. Suddenly I moved out of the front entrance, like Jumpin' Jack Flash. I turned, bowed once in case anybody was watching and made my way back home past Aoyama Cemetery, where I saw pink and white cherry blossoms in full bloom. Never had the Sakura blossoms smelled more fragrant or looked more beautiful.

I began singing as my strides lengthened, "It's a lovely day today..."

I never returned to that *Zen* temple, but in my heart lay only admiration and respect for those dedicated monks who face this challenging task with such tranquillity.

My one and only *Zen* lesson was a valuable lesson, in many ways.

Beyond Spirit of the Empty Hand

Reading, Wrestling, and Ruminating

I would read as much as I could lay my hands upon concerning Japan, the martial arts, the Japanese way, culture, philosophy, and arts, and I tried to integrate it all into my university studies, my karate, and even my way of life. For a period I even went as far as talking like a Japanese would, in broken English, to my students in class.

"OK (pronounced ookeh). Everybody try. More down. You..." I would point to a nervous student, "...very good, but need more *kime!*" He would nearly break his neck to do it. "Better. I like!" and so on.

I suppose they call this identifying fully with something, but I went overboard and would almost bring the discipline of the *dojo* into my home, ordering people like my wife, my children, and my friends around, as if they were my karate students. It was becoming a habit and often I did it without thinking: "Get this, do that!" But I always said "please," thinking that good etiquette would get me everywhere. I was rudely awakened one day by Dr. Dave Berson, who had quietly watched my dominating ways.

A few months after my one-day *Zen* experience in Japan, my third daughter, Tia, was born.

"*Mazeltov*, Stan," Dave congratulated me, hearing the good news. "Your family's growing big. Are you going to deserve them? Be careful, or one of these days you'll be pulling rank at the dining room table."

"What do you mean?" Dave's reprimands were usually subtle, but not this time.

"Picture this, Stan. You are so into your karate, the next thing is you'll be bringing it into the family dinner." He demonstrated.

"*Yoi!* Get ready, grab your knife and fork. *Hajime!* Begin eating."

"Don't talk rubbish, man, Dave." I shook my head.

"And then when you're finished gobbling your food down at the alarming rate that you do, with such well-practiced mayhem, it'll be '*Yame!* it's over' and your family will be about halfway through their meal, and off you go with your poor gut cursing you for overloading it in such record time."

By this time Dave was shaking with mirth. I just shook my head again.

Meeting Myself

"Dave, you're too much." But, of course, he was right. I was far too fast an eater. Not a very good example to follow.

Miyamoto Musashi, the "Sword Saint" of Japan, particularly influenced my way of thinking.

Musashi was the greatest of masters when it came to defeating others with his sword, but he also sought out other masters in other arts and skills. He befriended them and would study with them until he had learned their craft.

He was as skilled with an artist's brush as he was with a sword on the battle field.

Both his brush and sword mastery flowed from his soul, an aware mind, a committed will, and balanced emotions, with the spirit of strategy as his mentor and guide. He possessed an insatiable desire to know the truth, and once said, "There is no way *to* the truth. Truth *is* the way."

I was fascinated by Musashi's courage, his methods, and his unpredictable fighting approaches. He was continually balancing out the scales of life and death in his life, harmonizing the inevitable ravages of war with the art of creativity, the godly music of poetry with the bloody battles of human wills—balancing out the harsh and gentle realities of life on that small but distinguished island, Japan.

I felt I needed to temper my blazing karate training regimen with the cool waters of poetry, music, and studying. And I was realizing that I needed others to help me in my various pursuits. My first priority was the desire to be a true karate man. Then, as I grew up a little, I also wanted that illusive thing called enlightenment.

Later, the idea of wisdom claimed my aspirations, so I began studying, and it led me into realizing just how limited I was. It came to me from Plato, who, more than 2,000 years ago, uttered the wise words, "I would rather die in truth than live my life in error." I liked what he said.

I managed to live in truth some of the time. But the rest of the time, I fear I lived in self-justification. Put another way, self-justification is that little suburb of the city called Error, which borders on the city called Truth. These places appear similar from the perspective of an inflated ego or a deluded mind.

Looking back, I can see now that while most of my intent was pure, much of my content was questionable.

Beyond Spirit of the Empty Hand

Claude Chanu, Ground Worker

Claude Chanu, the Frenchman who worked as a diamond cutter in Johannesburg and had trained in judo in South America, had a great influence on my thinking. He would level me out from time to time. Of course, in the karate world I was something of a king. As I have said before, I sometimes felt I owned karate, but every time Claude arrived at my house or *dojo*, I would experience the stark reality of being defeated time and time again by this past-master of *ju-jutsu*-type wrestling, and this occurred at quite regular intervals over a 20-year period. Claude was a loner, who would often go away on his own mission. He would disappear for a month or two, always to return, more powerful than ever.

We often did ground work on my front lawn. As we knelt facing one another, I would ask him where he had been. His square, powerful face would light up, a young twinkle coming out of wise, old eyes.

"I've been swimming with the sharks up at Balito Bay," he would say, his voice bearing a distinct French accent. "Last Friday I hitched a ride on the back of a manta ray."

He was about 10 years older than me, but I never found out what his actual age was. He died tragically a few years ago.

He was an adventurer with no fear of man or nature, but he had a great respect for both. At one time he became a mercenary, fighting a bush war against the Mau Mau in Kenya in the 1960s.

He never taught his unique type of ground wresting professionally, and he never once charged me a cent.

"I don't like to teach, but I like you. You're enthusiastic; you want to learn my art, so I will teach you many things," he said when I first started with him.

For 20 years I wrestled with him, and not once could I get him to give in, for this was the rule: "Until your opponent taps you twice, submitting, you have not beaten him." To just hold him down on his back was not enough.

He told me that when he had fought in tournaments in South America, this same rule applied to the final match. The preliminary matches, however, were decided on the normal judo points method—throws and immobilizations. But in the final match, there were no points or time limit. The first contestant to give in, to submit, was the loser.

Meeting Myself

Claude told me he once reached the final. When I wrestled with him he was always around 100 kilograms of solid, mature muscle. However, in his South American wrestling days, he was a lean, cable-hard, 75 kilograms. The man he met in the final was nearly twice his weight. One day, as we were getting prepared to wrestle, Claude told me about that final match.

"Within the first few seconds he had me on my back, and he kept attempting to beat me down with slaps, attempted strangulation, arm locks, and a few punches here and there. I could hardly breathe at times, he was so heavy on me. The match lasted nearly one hour, with me underneath all of the time. I had to be patient. All I could do was protect myself by staying close to him and blocking, keeping my arms and neck to myself—to not let him get at them to apply a firm head lock or arm lock or strangulation. He worked hard to get me. I tried to relax wherever I could, in small ways. For instance, he would get his arm around my neck and begin squeezing. I would have been 'lights out' but for the fact that I would tuck my chin in, like a little bit of armor covering my throat. Then I would wait, edging myself into the most comfortable position possible in the tight situation. I would keep breathing evenly, even when my air passage was sometimes close to being shut off. Even a slight adjustment, like a little twist to the side, would bring some relief. As the match progressed, my opponent was working harder, and I was learning to use a minimum amount of my precious energy. Finally, he became frustrated and reckless. He tried a risky tactic. I was waiting for this. He switched arms and began to bar lock my throat with his less tired forearm and began stretching his weight across me, using his body as a lever. As he reached slightly past his point of balance, I bunched up my body in a ball and kept him rolling in the direction he had taken. His upper arm became trapped against my neck. So, as I rolled him onto his back using his own momentum, I wrapped my arms around his neck, with his entire arm trapped between my neck and his own. This was about the only focused move I did in the entire match and he tapped out, submitting immediately.

"Claude," I said, "that's amazing. Can you show me how you got him?"

"Like this," said Claude, rolling me onto my back and applying what he called "the scarf hold." I tapped out immediately. His power and his perfect positioning were awesome.

"Now do it on me," he would always say after catching me with one of his specialties. He had about 10 basic techniques as

Beyond Spirit of the Empty Hand

well as a basketful of little tricks and variations he would incorporate if he felt I was getting to him. We mostly started our matches with him lying on his back saying, "Go ahead, Stan. Remember last time. Try it out. See what you can do."

One time, feeling I was getting nowhere with a variety of neck locks (he just lay there and laughed), I simply tried to strangle him with both hands, similar to the technique a murderer uses on his victim. I wrapped my fingers around his neck and squeezed as hard as I could, plunging my thumbs into and below his Adam's apple. Claude didn't even try to remove my hands. He just gazed into my eyes with a gentle expression on his face. He laughed, patted me on the shoulder, and merely said, "You're improving nicely, Stan. And you will improve even more when you begin to realize where true power and guidance come from. When you find this, you will be able to do anything." Then he added, "But it must be for a good and just purpose."

A spiritual message always embraced Claude's physical actions.

One day just prior to his death, he came to me. It was uncanny. He did not say much, just, "I feel I am not really part of this world." He wore his usual smile, but there was an underlying sadness in his countenance.

"I will, of course, be here until God calls me. But when that happens, I'll be very happy."

Then, as he was leaving, he put his hand on my shoulder and said, "Stan, you have come a long way in your groundwork, but I want you to take it further, into your standing karate. You will begin to apply the moves through your karate in an upright fashion, not necessarily lying down. Just allow it to happen. You will see. I believe in you. May God bless you, my son." And with that he was gone.

I never saw him again. He died on his own, an alone man. But he was loved and respected by all. Hundreds of people from all walks of life attended his funeral. I was among the men who cried.

"Like a Guardian Angel, he has come and he has gone
To share—and to depart
His gentle spirit living on
In many a heart."

With my father and mother, Theo and Anne

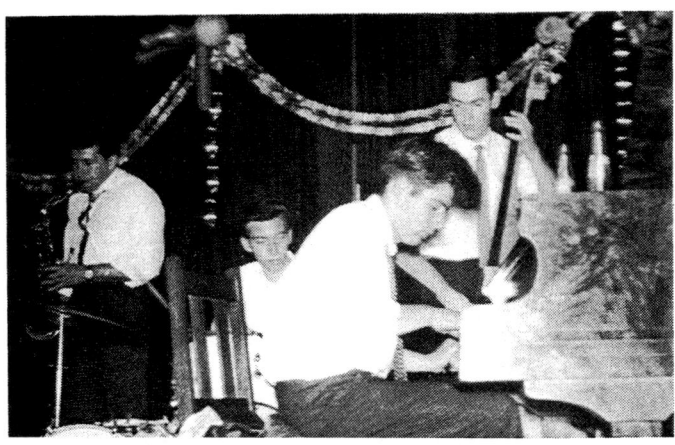

I was playing bass with Mannie Lubowitz, who later would become Manfred Mann of Manfred Mann's Earth Band.

At the entrance to the original JKA dojo at Yotsuya

Years later with Masatoshi Nakayama at the entrance to his personal dojo, the Hoitsugan

My first attempt at the *makiwara* in Japan. Judy observes.

A 1963 class at the Yotsuya dojo. Second from left in the front row is my friend, Gary Frederich. C.W. Nicol is in the second row between the fourth and fifth men in the front row. I am behind the sixth and seventh.

My school mate and friend, the great golfer Gary Player, tests my muscles.

Enoeda Sensei tests me in another way.

Taiji Kase Sensei on his first visit to South Africa.

The 1965 Japanese examining board in South Africa. Next to me (L to R) are Hiroshi Shirai, Keinosuke Enoeda, Hirokazu Kanazawa, Taiji Kase, and assistants George Higginson and Dave Maas.

Masatoshi Nakayama Sensei hunts big game with his camera.

On my personal *gashuku*.

My winning trophy for the team kata event at the 1968 All Japan Campionship.

Ken Wittstock scoring on Osaka. Ken placed third in kumite at the JKA 50th Anniversary World Championships in Tokyo.

Kenske (L) and Shunsuke Seto.

Practicing with Takeshi Oishi.

Practicing my infamous back kick.

The back kick in action at the All Japan Championships.
Wild but workable.

At the Philadelphia dojo of Teruyuki Okazaki in 1980.

Tanaka teaches me to fly. Thank God it was only a demonstration.

"Tanaka Made an Impression"

During filming of *Kill and Kill Again*, Tanaka and I attack the star, James Ryan.

University graduation day with my family. Standing are (L to R) Debbie, Caryn, Judy. Lisa (L) and Tia (R) flank me.

The Melrose dojo.

Karate with top members of the P.A.C.T. Ballet Company. Sensei Johan Roets in the foreground.
"Grace and Power"

Dolph Lundgren, star of *Rocky IV*, an Early Birds visitor.
He is flanked by Keith Geyer and me.

5th World Shoto Cup Champions
Left is Jason Khumalo, Junior World Kumite Champion, with Pavlo Protopapa, Individual Men's World Kumite Champion.

"Jason, you are a role model."
Jason Khumalo and I are joined by Minister of Sport Steve Tshwete and Jason's mother, Numsa.

1995 reunion in Japan.
L to R: Our host, Ikeda, me, C.W. Nicol, and Seto.

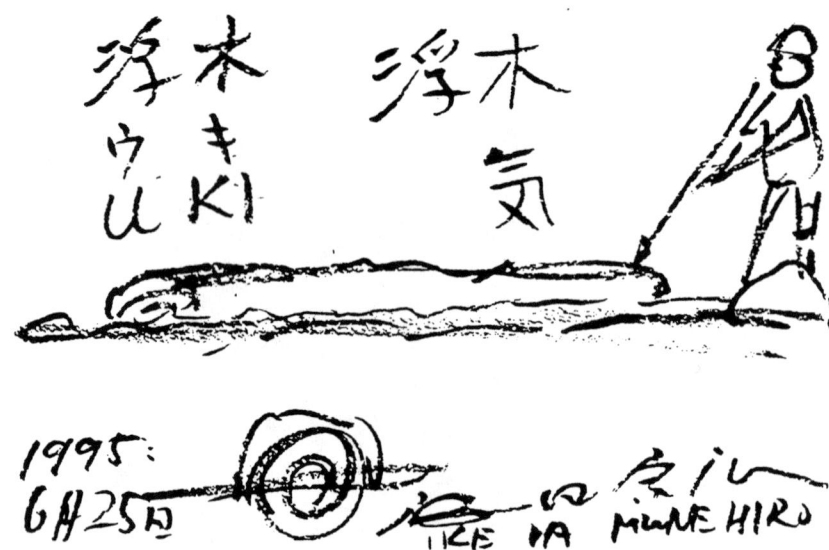

The card Ikeda created for me on the occasion of naming my personal kata.

11

A RE-LOOK AT THE JAPANESE AND THEIR UNIQUE WORLD

Meeting Myself

Although we were forever short of money, and I increasingly wanted to visit Japan, people would say to me, "What do you want to keep going there for? It's expensive. You've learned all there is to know from the Japanese. Save your money; you can do fine on your own now."

No matter how low our finances were, when the time came for me to re-visit Japan, they money was there, somehow.

Well, if I knew one thing in my life I knew this: Those no-go advisers were wrong. The desire to train with the Japanese, learn about their country, their customs, and their way of life, was like a burning fire within me. Furthermore, from the first day I saw Japan, I liked the Japanese as a nation. And I still do. I have also learned, that no nation or person is perfect, either. Japanese people also have their shortcomings, as we all do, but there is a wealth of wisdom and knowledge to be learned from them. Every time I interact with the Japanese, or go to Japan, I learn something of value.

My different experiences went through the full range of emotions—from the sublime to the ridiculous, and often embarrassing. The Japanese believe in *karma*—whatever you do returns to you, sometimes immediately, or sometimes at a later stage of your life. From a Western perspective, *karma* may be thought of as, "As you sow, so shall you reap."

One day in 1970, I experienced *karma* of the immediate type. After training, I was relaxing in my small fourth floor room at the Asia Center, Tokyo, writing and sipping coffee. I finished, stood up, picked up the coffee mug and, without thinking, flung the cold remains of my coffee out of the window. I undressed and was about to squeeze myself into the small square bath tub, when my telephone rang.

"Is this Mistah Smieedt?" came the woeful voice over the phone.

"Yes," I answered brusquely. I was tired. I was sore. I was nude, and I wanted to bath.

"Mistah Smieedt. Did you throw water out of window three minutes ago?"

Suddenly my voice was shaky and I answered, "Yes."

"Please come down to front desk. A Mistah Sugimoto is complaining his suit very wet. Please, you come soon. He very angry."

"Oh, shit, I'm stupid," I kept saying to myself as I hurriedly threw on some clothing. "What do I do now?"

Beyond Spirit of the Empty Hand

As I exited the lift into the lobby, there was a typically well-dressed Japanese gentleman standing at the registration desk, obviously complaining. His face was bright, beetroot red.

I went straight up to him and said: "*Gomen Nasai.* I am very sorry."

He turned toward me and started waving his hands in the air and shouting something I fortunately did not understand. But he kept pointing to the dark droplet marks on the shoulders of his light gray suit. Some other residents of the hotel stood near the desk, not looking in our direction, but obviously very curious about what was going on.

Suddenly, automatic pilot took over in me, and I began bowing, 60 bows to the minute, in his direction saying in English-cum-Japanese, "Me very stupid man. I very, very sorry. *Gomen nasai. Gomen nasai.*" I turned to Mister Arai at the front desk and said, "Please tell him I want to pay for his suit to be cleaned."

Mr. Arai conveyed my message to him. He bowed toward Mr. Arai, grunted, and walked away, grumbling under his breath. When he had gone, Mr. Arai turned to me.

"Mistah Smieedt. Okay now. But please you not throw water out of window again."

I heaved a huge sigh of relief and bowed to him.

"Mr. Arai, *that* I will never do again!"

A little smile crossed his face. He was no doubt amused by the episode.

And I never told him that it was not water, but coffee.

Musashi Says—Nakayama Does

Miyamoto Musashi had written in his "Book of Five Rings" that he would always stop and learn the skills of other experts. This attitude was confirmed to me by my fellow instructors at JKA *Honbu dojo* in Tokyo in their approach to karate. While karate remained their central focus, many of the instructors would study other arts on the side.

In addition to his karate activities, Nakayama *Sensei* was also an accomplished calligrapher, writer, and producer of technical books and videotapes. The five maxims, which you see on many a *dojo* wall throughout the world, were penned by him. Many years ago, he presented me with a sheet of paper, upon which he had inscribed one single character.

Meeting Myself

"For you, Stan," he had said at the time.

Like the artist, the character had appeared simple at the time. "Very old *Kanji*" (character) or, "Very difficult," or "Very deep," were some of the responses from Japanese people who saw this work. I can now see that Nakayama *Sensei*, like the character of his calligraphy, was a very deep person. Basic and wise, all at once.

Mori Sensei, the big JKA all-styles champion with the devastating leg sweeps, loves to sing and play the flute.

Senseis Iida (the first All Japan All Styles Champion) and Mabuchi (now an accomplished acupuncturist), studied *aikido* ("way of spirit harmony") techniques, and I could detect this in the way they moved in their *kumite*—smooth, rounded, circular, and very deadly if they got hold of your wrist. I am now beginning to realize that numerous aikido moves are inherent in our very own traditional karate kata. It is just for us to look deeper and discover them.

Oishi Sensei (four times All Japan Champion), who I call "Mister Lightning," had a thorough *kendo* (competition swordsmanship) background. His ability to intercept the strongest attack, bravely moving *in,* when most karate-ka would move *out,* has made him a legendary figure in the annals of karate-*do*. "Kendo timing," somebody once remarked, as we watched him applying the winning blow by dropping forward and under an onslaught of face punches and scoring on his opponent's exposed abdomen.

"Oishi's got courage," I once said to Nakayama Sensei. "I wish I could do that."

"This is Oishi's *tokui-waza*" (favorite, or special, technique). Other people cannot do this. Very dangerous," he added.

And that is exactly how Oishi beat me once in the All Japan Championships. It took him all of two seconds. On, "*Hajime!*" I shot out my so-called "fast" *kizami zuki*. He merely dropped under it and scored half a point on me. Like a fool, I repeated the same tactic, and Oishi repeated his. Another punch, a half point, and the match was over. For a whole year I kicked myself in the butt for being so dumb.

In the 1973 JKA 50th Anniversary World Championship, I again met Oishi, this time in the quarter finals. I had, in the interim, been studying a little aikido at Sensei Uyeshiba's *dojo* in Japan. A top-graded Frenchman, Tissier, took me under his wing.

What I learned from him was the art of slipping around an opponent doing *tai sabaki* as the attack was launched. I was basically a *hard,* linear-type fighter. Tissier showed me how to move in a *soft* and circular manner, still remaining close to my opponent.

This time the match with Oishi went nearly the full distance, without either of us scoring a point. I had nobody to coach me, so I thought of a plan as we mounted the rostrum.

"I will move in circles, not only straight forward like I normally do."

My plan worked well for about 115 seconds. We had numerous sharp exchanges of blows. It was a dynamic match.

Then I heard someone advising me, "Watch him, Stan. Only five seconds to go."

I must have turned my head ever so slightly to heed the advice. In that instant, Oishi detected my *kyo* (open to attack) state and executed a perfect example of *kake waza,* that is, charging in and scoring before I could initiate a move.

"Very good match," Nakayama said later to me. "It should have been the final."

This remark made me feel good. But I was going to have to work on my awareness factor—on how to stay in the zone and not get distracted.

Many years later, after I had come to know the instructors better, this little story came out. It was on a train after a *gashuku,* that one of the older instructors said to me, "Remember, you fight Oishi. Now I tell you this. When you come to Japan to train at *honbu dojo,* Oishi, he telephone Shirai in Italy and ask Shirai how he must fight Stan because Stan big man."

I'm not sure of the exact words, but Shirai, who I have fought a number of times, and who I class as one of the best all-round karate men I know, advised him something along these lines: "Stan is a big man with a big spirit. He is a strong fighter, but he always fights in the same way. That is forward, in a straight line and he likes to start with *kizami zuki.* He has a habit of ..."

So Shirai must have told him to watch for my regular habit, which to this day I have not discovered but hope I am rid of.

My student, Ken Wittstock, took third place in the individual *kumite,* and we placed third in the team kata and *kumite* events.

Sumo, Kendo, Nunchaku

Whenever I visit Japan, Seto and I meet, and he takes me to dinner. I am still trying to work out how I can pay for at least one meal. But he always has it worked out. "I already have paid, Stan," and, "When in Japan, you don't pay." I always invite him to come to South Africa.

"I will pay for your ticket," I would say.

"Thank you, Stan. Maybe soon I come." And that is where it always ends.

We talk for hours on many subjects ranging from rifle shooting (he was on the Japanese National Squad), to business in Japan, to life and its deeper meanings. We speak about karate and the people involved—their lives, aspirations, their successes, their hardships—and I often ask him for advice.

"Stan," he once said, "sometimes I feel that what Sensei Gichin Funakoshi said is so true: 'Life is a hard serious struggle'. Sometimes I am down, but I keep spirit. I keep focus on my purpose, then, next day, next week, or next year ... all okay again and much stronger. Man without purpose, is like log floating in sea—soon destroyed."

Seto does business with China, where he spent a number of his childhood years during the second world war. Despite his being Japanese, he survived at a Chinese school in Manchuria.

"That is where my 'karate' started. Every day I was in a fight on the playground. I would be ridiculed because I was Japanese."

Seto is not a big man. He is a very small man, in fact, but with a very big spirit. So I guess he became extremely resilient and able to "get up eight times when knocked down seven," (one of his favorite sayings).

The paradoxical thing, though, was that when Seto and his family left China to return to Japan, the entire school congregated to bid him farewell, and many of the boys were crying. Today, more than 50 years later, some of those rival classmates are now his very loyal friends and business associates.

We always talk about our mutual friend, C.W. Nicol, author of *Moving Zen* and many other books. Seto keeps me up to date:

"Now he is very famous in Japan. He speaks Japanese fluently. He has his own forest station in Kurohime. Many rangers and conservationists train there for ecological education. He is a famous TV personality and is involved in numerous shows—children's programs and documentaries. Also he goes on expeditions to the Arctic, Africa, and South America."

"I would like to meet with him again, Seto. It's a long time since I last saw him."

Beyond Spirit of the Empty Hand

"Okay, next time you come to Japan, I will arrange it. Now he is away from Japan."

Seto always gives me good advice.

"I know that you are 'karate crazy' like Mr. Ueki, Mr. Oishi, and Mr. Tanaka, but you need to take a break sometimes. You should also try to understand the ways of other martial arts."

A few days after telling me that, Seto took me to visit a Sumo wrestling stable. Believe me, this was a stable in the true sense, complete with mud floor and a herd of human rhinos.

I was greeted with deep bows and placed on the rostrum of honor, overlooking a small training arena. I was told that Sumo was originally known as *sumai*, meaning struggle. What I saw amazed me.

Beefy bodies constantly crashed against one another. Others were throwing each other. One small group did almost 1,000 squats, then slipped easily into the splits.

Another group kept the building vibrating by heavily slapping a thick wooden pillar. For 90 minutes the action continued, non-stop.

"The class has ended," whispered Seto, but the activity had not ceased.

The entire stable focused its attention on one very tired individual. They harassed him, taking turns to push him, throw, trip, and pour cold water over him, all of this while a *sempai* kept slapping his body with a flat plank.

This went on for at least 20 minutes. Never did the novitiate lose his temper. Here they were breeding a species that would just keep coming—no matter what.

"Gee, that was heavy stuff," I exclaimed as we left.

"Young *sumotori* take initiation every day for one year," said Seto. "Next year, he'll do the same to new member."

-----oOo-----

On another trip I enrolled at the Nihon Budokan for Kendo classes, which were conducted three times a week in the evenings. I did kendo for nearly three months, and it certainly gave me some valuable insight into the origins of my karate-*do*.

Repetition work with a bamboo *shinai* (fencing stick) was the keynote—particularly the overhead strike. And the moving up and down, forward and backward across the polished wooden floor brought out a crop of fresh blisters on the soles of my feet and toes. Furthermore, stiffness in my shoulders, back, forearms, legs, and hands indicated to me the holistic, total body commitment needed in this excellent art of timing and sharp-honed reflexes.

---oOo-----

Nunchaku (flail) is my favorite weapon, as martial arts weapons go. Its simplicity appeals to me, and I find it a perfect extension of karate arm techniques. It is an unobtrusive, deadly weapon in the hands of an expert.

But, in essence, I am a purist—an empty-hand practitioner. Nakayama once said to me, "A man who relies on a weapon is lost when he loses his weapon. The spirit of the empty hand is more pure, powerful, and just."

When I studied under Nishiyama Sensei (head of the International Traditional Karate Federation) in Los Angeles, he told me something similar. "Aim of karate expert is to develop empty-hand techniques and methods to take the weapon away from the assailant and, if necessary, use it on him," he said.

Okazaki Sensei (head of the International Shotokan Karate Federation) in Philadelphia, said, "Carrying a weapon in our society is a big responsibility. If people see your weapon, this can be the cause of big trouble—both for the victim as well as the user."

I learned nunchaku privately with Johnny, an Indonesian instructor who visited the Asia Center every afternoon and taught me every trick in the nunchaku box.

After learning from Johnny, I began to integrate the moves into the five *Heian* Shotokan katas and *Tekki Shodan*. When away on holiday in the countryside or at the seaside, I often arise early and do these kata—first empty-handed and then with the nunchaku. It keeps me aware, for I have found that if my attention strays, I receive a rap on the knuckles or head, which can be a painful lesson.

In November 1996, a man came up to me at the WKF All Styles World Championships held at Sun City in South Africa, and greeted me.

"Hello, Stan. Remember me?"

It was Johnny, my *nunchaku* teacher from 26 years before.

I Felt Insecure

After being promoted to fourth *dan* at the age of 34 in 1970, I decided that I was not shaping up to the Japanese instructors in a number of ways. While the lack of suppleness was one of my shortcomings, what nagged at me most was that I'd not had any formal education outside of my schooling, except for working at Barclays Bank for 10 years, whereas the Japanese instructors at JKA had some kind of degree, either from a university or technical college. I forever heard them talking about their university—Takudai, or Komazawa, or Nichidai, or whatever—about their training, their teachers, and *gashukus*. I felt out of it.

"What University you attend in South Africa?" was often asked of me. My answers were self-protective justifications like, "I work in Bank..." They seemed satisfied with that answer, but I was not.

Another answer I tried once or twice on the Japanese when asked which university I had attended was, "The University of Hard Knocks." This, I soon realized, was a quip that just didn't work on them. It left them stone cold. They would merely react as if I had said nothing and change the subject to something more suitable to my simple mind like, "Which hotel you stay in Tokyo?" or "You storng man. How many kilo you?"

Not having had any tertiary form of education, I felt insecure in that class of instructors. My insecurity was heightened when one of my students, Dr. David Berson, called me aside one day after training and simply declared, "*Sensei* Stan Schmidt, I want to be candid with you, and you may or may not like what I am going to say." He paused. "That is, if you will allow me to." David always had impeccable etiquette.

"Go ahead, shoot," I replied, shrugging and wondering what this was all about.

"*Sensei* Stan, you know that you are an impressive kind of animal. Tough on the floor, a competent teacher, right at the top of your art, but..." He paused.

"But what?"

"Humpty Dumpty was also on the top of his wall, and what happened to him when he fell?"

I laughed, but David remained serious.

"So?" I queried.

"So?" David mimicked me. "So what have you got as a back-up? What have you got up there?" He placed the tip of his forefinger against the middle of my forehead.

"Not enough." I agreed with what he was intimating.

"Look, Stan, I'm not saying you're dumb." A fiendish little smile crept across his face. "I'm saying you could make far more use of your potential."

I was intrigued.

"Look, my friend, you reckon you can take a little kick in the scrotum?"

"Try me." My voice didn't sound too confident anymore. He began prodding me in the solar plexus with his finger. David Berson is not a tall man. The top of his head reached the top of my chest.

"Look, Stan," he challenged, "you may be able to wrap me up in a physical knot. You are an impressive giant of an athlete. But intellectually, my friend, you're a dwarf." Then he added, "A nice dwarf."

He had a way of saying things that broke me up. He was like an intellectual Charlie Chaplin. Despite my nervous laughter, I would take him very seriously. Here was a true friend who wanted to help me progress in an important way.

"What must I do?"

"Study."

"Okay, but what? I already read all sorts of philosophy and novels and I write poems."

"University!"

"What? Varsity! Me? I'm 35 already!"

"My heart bleeds for you, *Sensei* Stan. So old."

Dave's stomach was shaking with laughter. He was around 50 and still studying. The axiom, "the greatest masters are the greatest students," flashed through my mind.

"Okay, show me how, Dr. Berson."

"All right, but first come and see something. Tomorrow. Breakfast."

"Thanks. Where?"

At the Medical Research Institute in Hillbrow, where I work. Staff canteen. Eight a.m."

Healthy Company?

We ate a hearty breakfast in the company of some esteemed medical men. It took less than 15 minutes for me to see them in an entirely different light. I had always perceived doctors, surgeons, pathologists, physicians, and their kind, to be serious, staunch, and somewhat somber beings, not of this planet. But here I was being entertained by an ensemble of comedians with Dr. Dave wielding the conductor's baton. For example, David, a pathologist, asked the

Beyond Spirit of the Empty Hand

two surgeons sitting with us, "How does a surgeon commit suicide?"

"How?" one asked.

"He jumps from his ego to his IQ!"

After breakfast, David stood up and told me to follow him. Dressed in his white coat, he marched off, with me close on his heels. Feeling like a dutiful *samurai*, I strode along, my bearing upright, feeling strong. The route took us through a maze of corridors. "This little king's castle," I mused to myself.

Then I saw it. "What now," I wondered. My upright posture sagged and I immediately knew what it was. It was a head bobbing up and down, a human head. That was all I saw at first, but I knew.

"Oh, no!" I groaned. A sick sensation claimed my innards. As we entered the room, I saw that it was a man, a dead man, a human cadaver, lying face up on an operating table.

His torso was split apart from neck to groin, and a man dressed in green was removing some organ, which he then carefully placed in a nearby container. Aghast, I stared at the dead man's face—head thrown back over the edge of the table, a lifeless doll being shaken up and down by the cutting motion of a scalpel-*cum*-saw.

"Dave," I whispered hoarsely, "I don't know if I can take this for much longer."

"All right, Stan. Sorry. I realize this may be a shock for you, but this is reality, my friend. We can go when you wish."

I took one last look, bowed toward the body and attendant, and exited with Dave.

"He passed away yesterday. Miner's pneumoconiosis (black lung disease). Affects the lungs. It's the fine mine dust particles over the years. He was only 50. Sad, isn't it? What you saw was a post-mortem. His family will receive compensation."

That was the first dead person I had ever seen. And as Dave had predicted, it changed me.

"You'll maybe appreciate life more now, Stan. Make use of all of your faculties while they're still in good working order. A good body you already have. But when you grow a little older, you may well regret it if you haven't exercised your mind, just a little."

"Do you really think I can do it, a university degree? I've never been a scholar as such. Always passed by the skin of my teeth. I don't know if I have the brain or the time for it."

"What one fool can do, another can do. I tell you, Stan, and you had better believe this: The brain you have; the time you will have to make."

123

Meeting Myself

I must have looked forlorn, for he added, "Just cut out lounging around after your early-morning training. Put in two or three hours a day, regularly, say 8:00 to 10:30. Even then you will still have the whole day ahead of you."

"That I can do. But what about lectures, the various times...."

Dave told me that South Africa had one of the largest and most excellent correspondence universities in the world, UNISA, University of South Africa. "People across the globe study, write exams and attain degrees from this university," he explained.

This unique institution had developed out of *apartheid* South Africa to fulfill a desperate need—the education of people young and old who were not permitted to attend "white" universities, or for people who needed to *work* in order to put themselves through university, or for those living in rural or distant areas.

This was great. I became enthusiastic. I could study from home, and should I not understand something, I could attend the odd crucial lecture provided for that purpose from time to time.

"Takes discipline," said David. "I've just done my History of Art B.A. Degree and I'm going further, to do honors."

"What? All of this in addition to that string of medical degrees?" I was amazed.

"So what kind of a degree should I do?"

"What are you interested in, Stan?"

"I like reading, writing, and anything to do with philosophy, psychology, and knowing about people. Also I am interested in studying about why I am on this planet and where I am going to."

"Well, that's a whole universe of study. Why don't you start with a B.A. majoring in something like English and psychology, and in the beginning do only two or three subjects a year. A regular B.A. one can do in three years, but I recommend that you get into it slowly at first. Take a little longer about it."

After much discussion with David, I enrolled at UNISA for a B.A. Degree as he had suggested. With regular and unswerving encouragement from him, I learned that the mind is just like a muscle. Train it properly, and it will work for you. As with any muscle, it grows when you put it under extra stress. It may rebel at first, growing tired and sore. Finally, though, if one persists, heavier loads become easy to manage.

Thus went my studies, with the first and second years being the hardest. It took me a full six years to achieve B.A., finally majoring in psychology and communications.

Beyond Spirit of the Empty Hand

The Japanese in My Own Back Yard

Although sporting bans during the *apartheid* era prevented South African teams from competing internationally, we were fortunate to receive many top masters in our disturbed country.

While Kase *Sensei* was the first to visit in 1964, he was followed by many others from JKA Shotokan as well as from Goju-ryu and Shito-ryu (Shukokai). I was extremely fortunate in that I literally was able to have the world's most famous masters living with me for periods of time, in my own backyard, so to speak.

Having the top Japanese exponents living with me at my house was certainly very different from interacting with them in Japan. In Japan I saw mostly the serious, focused, hard working side of them. The open, communicative, warm, and humorous sides of their character emerged when in my country.

Enoeda's second visit occurred in 1972, seven years after his first visit. He brought with him his wife, Reiko, and his baby son, Daisuke. Gone was the spiky, short-cropped head and that cavalier bachelor swagger. What entered our home was a well groomed English gentleman and family man. This was off the *dojo* floor, of course. On the floor he was still as potent as ever.

During his stay, an incident occurred that I will never forget.

"Get The Hospital Truck Ready"

It was a warm, lazy Friday afternoon, about 4 o'clock. We'd had a tough week of teaching and touring the country, and we were enjoying a well-earned rest, when I received a call from my receptionist at Orange Grove *dojo*.

"Stan, there are two men here to see you."

"Tell them to come on Monday. I'm resting."

"Stan, the one is very aggressive—says he's come to challenge you to a fight."

I turned to Enoeda Sensei, who had just showered and was reading a book, and I quickly told him what was happening.

"Stan, go kick him!" he shouted without any hesitation. "You want me to come?"

"No, Sensei. There's only one guy."

"Okay. You go. Come back soon."

Meeting Myself

That was all the motivation I needed. I told my receptionist I would be at the *dojo* in five minutes. I must admit that butterflies were playing the field in my stomach.

As I entered the *dojo*, I clearly heard some "uplifting" words uttered by a thick-set man, who aptly fitted the description, "well-dressed thug." Gold chains, rings, and chunky bracelets hung from his every appendage.

"You'd better get the hospital truck ready," he loudly told my receptionist. Next to him was a nondescript individual in a plain gray suit. My butterflies instantly multiplied when I saw the big, black, convertible Buick standing right outside. Big, black, convertible autos have, ever since I can remember, conjured up unpretty images in my head—they go well with mobsters, sawed-off shotguns, revenge, and a nestful of other nasty things. This was probably very immature thinking for a 36-year-old fourth *dan*.

"Is this the big brass?" crooned the thug, pointing his ham-sized hand toward me.

I didn't like him. His ugly attitude jarred my spirit, especially in front of my students. There were two or three of them doing free training on the floor, and they most certainly were hearing every word.

"That's me!" I answered, walking right up to him and looking into his eyes. He was slouching across the counter and he couldn't match my now hostile gaze. Something had snapped inside of me. This was a classic choice of fight or flight. Amazingly, my butterflies had instantly flown away and I had become tuned in to what I had to do. I didn't have to think. The words just came out.

"What can I do for you?" I challenged.

The man in the gray suit became the spokesman.

"I'm from the *Transvaler* (an Afrikaans newspaper). At lunch my friend and I had a bet. We've both read all about you in the newspapers—'Fourth *dan* martial artist, top karate man, best in the west!' He said he could take you out. I bet him he couldn't"

The thug butted in, addressing the gray suit, "I'm a street fighter. He's a gentleman, probably never been in a real fight." He turned to me and sneered, "You've got a pretty face. A pity to damage it, but a bet's a bet. I'm going to flatten that nose of yours."

I cut in, my anger rising above my reason and this is what came out of my mouth.

"Look, mister, I've been waiting 10 years for an opportunity to test out my punching power on a real human." I rolled up my hand

Beyond Spirit of the Empty Hand

into a fist and held my ugly, callused knuckles out in front of his eyes. He said nothing. I carried on. "I do hundreds of punches every day on that boring *makiwara* board over there, and now the bonus arrives—you! Let's go. I'll get you a karate suit."

I started to move off but a further torrent of "wisdom" emanated from my mouth. I don't know where it came from. Survival, I suppose. I turned to my receptionist and then to the gray suit and said, "Just write this on a sheet of paper and have this 'street fighter' sign it."

I noticed the first signs of doubt, as it flitted across the thug's brow. It was a fleeting expression of confusion mixed with a little doubt. Interpreting body language was a hobby of mine, and my words had caused a chink to appear in his armor.

"Write this," I commanded. The receptionist started writing furiously. "*I, Mr. Street Fighter, or whatever his real name is, hereby absolve Mr. Stan Schmidt from any responsibility should I become crippled or severely maimed as a result of my challenging him to a serious fight.*"

The thug gave a little squirm as his hand smoothed back his oily hair.

"Now wait, Stan," offered the gray suit.

"In the *dojo* call me Sensei!" I instructed him.

"Oh, sorry, Sensei, but you are getting too serious. This was just a little bet."

The receptionist handed me a karate *gi,* which I passed on to the street fighter.

"Put this on," I ordered, "there's the change room."

They went to the change room.

I was ordering, and they were obeying. When they returned, I was already changed into my *gi*.

"He just wants to wrestle against you," said the gray suit. The street fighter started doing a mock fight preamble—press-ups, then a swing or two at the sand bag, which he nearly took off its hooks.

"We will wrestle. I don't want to damage your handsome face," he shouted at me.

"Look," I said walking up to him, "punching and kicking is my game." I paused, thinking of Claude Chanu, "but if you want to wrestle, okay, I'll wrestle you, and I'll even make it easier for you."

I sat down on the floor and said to my challenger, "Be my guest. Take me in any hold you like."

Meeting Myself

He couldn't believe his luck. He immediately went behind me and wrapped his thick arms around my neck in a type of head lock, trying to make me submit. I had armored my throat with my chin, but he was getting me at one stage. He was like a bulldog attached to my neck. Eventually we were rolling around all over the hard floor. Then I heard his heavy breathing.

"Do you give in?" he wheezed.

"Never!" I shouted in his ear.

I felt him relax slightly. In a flash I rolled him over and clamped a tight scarf hold against his neck. He went limp. But I was turned on and would not let go. I was so angry, I would have done something extremely irresponsible had not the gray suit, my secretary, and my karate students pulled me off. The gray suit couldn't stop apologizing to me.

"Sensei, you are a real champ. I'll print this. You'll be all over the papers."

We went to the change rooms. He ridiculed his friend, saying, "You don't play with these karate men, man."

The street fighter was sulking. I was half clothed in my underpants and shirt when he suddenly clapped his hands together in front of my face shouting, "This is how we fight," and he dived for my legs. This move of his was totally unexpected. To this day I don't know how I did what I did. All I know is that I somehow had his testicles clutched in my fist, and he was screaming.

"Let go! You win! You win!"

"That wasn't very sporting," I remarked to the gray suit as we left the change room. "Your friend is a dangerous man. I'd hate to meet him in a dark alley."

The street fighter never smiled once. The gray suit left my receptionist with a check for his first month's installment for karate lessons. He would be back to learn karate, he said. They never returned again, nor was there any big write-up in the *Transvaler*.

Going back to the car, I felt exhilarated. "A good experience but next time if you are silly enough to take up a challenge, do it for a lot of money," I admonished myself.

Back at home, Enoeda asked me what had happened.

"I kicked his butt."

"Good, Stan," he laughed, and poured me a beer. "This also happened to me before."

"What happened, Sensei?"

"When I was first in London, some crazy guy came to my new *dojo* at Marshall Street, Picadilly. He wanted to fight me. He said

Beyond Spirit of the Empty Hand

he studied karate in China and Korea. I told him, 'okay, but you must first take training. After class I will fight you.'"

"Very good idea, Sensei." I laughed

Enoeda was grinning from ear to ear.

"Yes, Stan, because I gave a very sweat-up class. Many *geri, zuki,* and squat and kick training. Then we did five-step sparring. I watched him. Very strong, but he telegraph before stepping. So, I joined the line."

This I was liking. "How cunning and wise the Sensei is," I thought.

"Then what, *Sensei?*"

"He was at end of line, I was on the other side. Maybe 20 black belts in class. I say 'change' many times, and soon he was standing and facing me. Now I shout, *'Ippon kumite!'* (one-step sparring).

"I count, *Itchi!* (One!) He attack *jodan* (face level). I block and say, 'Again, you no good balance. You try again!' Now all class is watching. I see his face puff up like a blow fish. I count, *'Ni!'* (Two!). He made a swinging attack to my face. I jumped back. He missed, but he became very angry when I asked him, 'Why you so slow?' He lost his temper and attacked me before I could make a count. But I made a good timing *mae-geri* to his stomach. My kick was not so hard, but he fell down to the floor.

"I helped him up. His face was very gray. He looked sick, and I helped him to lie down on a bench. Then I told him, 'Okay, I am ready to fight you'. Very funny, Stan. This big man, he cried out like baby, 'No! No! Please, no!'"

"And?" I prompted.

"He never came back to my *dojo* again."

"I wonder why, Sensei."

Beyond Spirit of the Empty Hand

12

THE DAN RANKS. STEPPING STONES TO...?

Meeting Myself

New and Higher Mountains

Every black belt *dan* rank has its very own characteristic challenges, criteria, and demands.

In my case, each level achieved meant that I had to make some kind of radical change. Often, quite different and unexpected circumstances and directions led me to my goal. But always the demolition and growth process was prevalent.

No change, no *dan*. And mostly it was only after achieving a *dan* degree that I might have given a thought to what changes *had* taken place.

While the criteria for each JKA Shotokan black belt degree are basically the same (minimum number of years, set syllabus, and so on) each karate-*ka* has his or her own unique struggles and challenges over which to gain mastery. For me, training for each *dan* was like climbing an uncharted mountain. The day I reached the peak of my first *dan* mountain, another bigger and more challenging mountain suddenly loomed out in the distant mists of my mind, inviting, "Climb me!"

As Master Hidetaka Nishiyama put it, "In engaging in karate, one is like an explorer going on an exciting, challenging adventure. A voyage of discovery. Always something new to learn about and understand."

After I achieved first *dan*, Kase *Sensei* had said, "Ah, Stan, now you put foot on first rung of karate ladder. Still long climb to understand true karate-*do*. Now for first time you are a karate-ka."

"Only now, Sensei? But..."

"Before, your training through the *kyu*-grades like screening process. People with no strong spirit fall down. Stop before get *shodan*. Karate way very hard, but very good for your body, your spirit, and your self-control. All student know this. It good. So why so many give up?" He dropped his head to one side. "Human being like easy way. Do things that are bad for him. Good way, more hard way. I like hard way, I never stop karate."

"Me too!" I added enthusiastically.

"Stan san. Please keep your spirit."

"*Osu, Sensei*! I will."

"Because you now *shodan*, it is like you are—how you say? Like kind of beginner carpenter?"

"Apprentice."

Beyond Spirit of the Empty Hand

"Yes, apprentice. You have made good tools. Your *uke, zuki, geri,* and *uchi* (striking) are strong. And you can do some kata and formal sparring."

"Yes, *Sensei*. It's been a long road, these past five years."

"You think so, Stan! Five years very short time in karate. Same as learning a language. It take baby seven years to speak. Karate same. Like baby, must grow up and use language in good way. You must now begin to find more real meaning in your *kihon,* kata, and *kumite*. Each day of hard training you learn more about what?" He waited for my answer.

"About being faster, stronger, and better."

"Yes, Stan, but more than this. Up to now you do karate like parrot speak."

I laughed and agreed with him.

"Later, you will get high *dan* if you begin to speak karate like poet."

"*Osu!*" I said. "Very interesting."

"*Sandan* very hard, very important *dan*. If cannot get *sandan,* then you stay like amateur. *Sandan* like professional."

"Why, *Sensei*?"

"Because very hard and very dangerous test. Like real life. If someone get JKA *sandan*, then very strong. Very dangerous. Now, no foreigner take *sandan* yet. Very difficult. Okay? You understand?"

"*Osu*, Sensei!" This was all far above me and more than a little frightening at the time. Yet, I knew deep down that I was not going to be one of those who dropped out and took the easy way out, nor was I going to stay doing karate like a parrot.

As it turned out, each time I reached the summit of my new mountain, a new and higher mountain would appear, complete with its ravines, valleys, canyons, and its mysteries. Its unique character would be there challenging me.

After achieving fifth *dan* at one of the first international *dan* gradings held at the 1973 JKA World Championships at the Nihon Budokan, I didn't really think too much about progressing further. After all, Grand Master Gichin Funakoshi, the father of Shotokan Karate, had never promoted anyone higher than fifth dan.

Shortly after his death, the ranking system was changed to the 10-*dan* system, but I felt that fifth *dan* was *it!* Though I had passed, I resolved I would train harder to become a worthy fifth degree holder.

Meeting Myself

Seto had watched my examination and over dinner commented on my kata performance.

"Your *Chinte* kata is like good beef steak, but you need a little more salt and pepper."

I took his advice seriously, reflecting upon it often. It caused me to conduct the Early Birds training less mechanically. Creativity and the meaning of *shu-ha-ri* became my daily quest. *Shu-ha-ri* is a martial art term that describes the nature of human progress in the art. *Shu* means obedience; *ha* means divergence; and *ri* means transcendence. Thus, *shu-ha-ri* means that one learns from tradition, breaks the chains of tradition, and, finally, transcends tradition. For example trying to visualize actual opponents when doing a kata was a new challenge to my students as well as to myself.

We found our minds able to visualize an imaginary attacker now and then, but to achieve this all the way through the kata was another story. To be able to do this is a commendable achievement in gaining meaningful mental focus and in exercising that often unused quality, imagination. To this day I find it challenging to express my kata in this three dimensional way. The one who can achieve this regularly is an extremely powerful person. One transcends the mere physical techniques we see performed by even kata champions, some of whom would get the fright of their lives should they actually be confronted by a real assailant or, worse still, more than one. But, of course, "this won't happen to me," I say. So on I go like a trained circus monkey, doing my moves exactly, every day, to the cue of the ringmaster, the sensei. I allow him to do my thinking for me. I become kata champion. I've done it all, so I think: "Champion means I am the best!" I sometimes go back to the *dojo* and train. Everybody bows a little deeper to me. I live in a false sense of security. The sensei used to be my idol. Now the gold medal is my idol. I gain more energy from it, rather than from training. In fact, training becomes a bit of a drag. The sensei's getting on my nerves, telling me, "More spirit."

"I'm better than him," I tell myself. "The medal proves it."

I begin to worship the idea of the medal. But you and I both know that idolizing a dead thing doesn't give life.

Breaking the Chains

Going back to what Seto had said to me, I realized that I wasn't achieving *shu-ha-ri*. I figured that I had done well with *shu*

Beyond Spirit of the Empty Hand

(training in traditional ways). But now I needed to do *ha* (break the chains of tradition) to get *ri* (spontaneous creative expression).

In my early days of book-learned karate, I was—in a way—pure *ri*—creative and with good spirit, but very little good technique. Now I had tried to mold my long arms and legs and narrow hips into the typical Japanese mold: toes turned in in *kiba dachi*, deeply bent knees, and high side snap kicks. I was the squarish peg trying my utmost to fit into a very round hole. That hole was called Japanese perfection.

I have since come to learn that every human is built differently and that there are even some excellent Japanese karate instructors who cannot get their legs higher than waist height. Not being much of a student of history, I recognized late in my career that high kicks were almost non-existent in the very traditional kata from Okinawa. It was only in modern Japan that certain gifted exponents like Okazaki *Sensei* could elevate their legs without any strain to their frames. But even Okazaki will agree that karate does not expect its practitioners to go beyond the natural range of movement of their given body parts. This is detrimental to one's health and ill-advised. Of course, through systematic and sensible stretching and strengthening programs, a considerable improvement in flexibility and strength can be achieved.

What Seto had told me after my fifth *dan* examination caused me to look deeper. However, having a thick skull, it took me time, for example, to allow my toes to point slightly outwards as they were meant to do, and not worry about forcing them to point straight in *kiba dachi*. But then every time I trained with people like Osaka, Ochi, or Ueki, my limitations would bother me again, and I would sometimes over-stress my poor body and force it into the splits, or carry a heavy partner on my back, trying to get my ankles more flexible. But I have paid a price for trying to force myself into certain positions that even Funakoshi Sensei and Nakayama Sensei would probably not have done in their later years.

13

TANAKA MADE AN IMPACT

Meeting Myself

It was through Takahashi Sensei that I first made personal contact with Tanaka Sensei. This was way back in the mid-1960s. Takahashi had invited me to visit and train at his Shokukan *dojo*, an hour and a half train ride from central Tokyo. Takahashi and Tanaka were partners in this *dojo,* which Tanaka still runs today.

After training, I went with Takahashi, Baba, Tanaka, and all the students to a Chinese restaurant and disco. At this stage I had not yet been formally introduced to Tanaka. Even in those early days his reputation had preceded him. He was talked about as being a modern day *samurai*, who could literally cause the toughest black belts to succumb like sacrificial lambs under his unpredictable techniques. Although young, he was respected as a karate master who truly possessed the power to kill with his empty hands. Yet, they said, he would always deal with his opponents in a relatively gentle fashion.

Tanaka was viewed as a deadly specialist. "Beware of stepping on that panther's tail," was the type of advice I was given long before I ever confronted him.

But, of course, what one person views as being vicious may be seen as compassionate by another.

Anyhow, Takahashi's *dojo* party got into full swing. The beat was on and everybody danced with anybody—men, women, whatever. You just moved and added in a kick or a punch just for the hell of it. As I rested and sipped at a can of Kirin beer, Tanaka walked up, stopped about six inches from me, and gave me a friendly punch in the stomach, saying, "You strong man, *neh?*"

His first-time greeting nearly floored me, but I was able to disguise the fact that he had winded me slightly, saying, "*Osu!*, Sensei! Me not so strong."

"Why you not speak Japanese?" His gaze seemed to penetrate my soul as he waited for my reply.

"Every day training at *honbu dojo*—no time to study Japanese." My voice petered out.

"Good answer," he said.

It was shortly after this that Tanaka *Sensei* began inviting me to spar with him after instructor training at *Honbu dojo*.

Takahashi and a Gemstone

In 1974, the same year that JKA moved from Suidobashi to their new headquarters in Ebisu, Takahashi *Sensei* was tragically

Beyond Spirit of the Empty Hand

killed. One of his students after a class showed him his new motor bike. Takahashi took it for a ride around the block. It had been raining, and on a corner the back wheel slipped away. Although he was not traveling at a high speed, he fell, striking his head on a curbstone. He was in a coma for a time, yet his heart, I am told, beat strongly until he passed away, at far too young an age.

I wrote this poem and sent a recorded tape to his wife. Tanaka, Baba and his students played the tape at a funeral ceremony held at the temple next to Shokukan *dojo*. (The words were spoken onto a recording tape with the song "The Sounds of Silence" being strummed and hummed in the background).

> Where's our Sensei, where's our friend,
> Has he really reached the end?
> Will we never see him train, again
> Nor hear his words, with which he turned us, into men?
> But the vision, that he planted, in our brains—still
>   remains—
> Although our hearts are grieving!
>   ---O---
> For our Sensei we cry—
> Young fighting—Samurai
> On a day in July seventy four,
> He took a ride, upon a bike, of war
> And though fate struck him down—and left him—lying
>   still—upon the ground—
> His heart kept strongly beating
>   ---O---
> He helped and taught us to the end;
> His skills and thoughts,
> He was our friend.
> Now his spirit lives within, the walls,
> Of the Shokukan and Honbu halls;
> In South Africa, his memory, lingers on—although he's
>   gone
> Our hearts are with his beating!
>   ---O---
> He was a warrior and a fighter
> His smile would make a dull day brighter;
> And though his Sun has sunk and left the sky,
> What he left for us, will never die,

Meeting Myself

For a new sun—soon will rise—and as we gaze—into
the skies
We'll know that he—is part of it.

Strangely enough, just prior to his death, I approached Takahashi for advice. He had been away from training for about one week. But on his return he was glowing with radiant energy. His head was clean-shaven. When I asked him where he had been, he said, "To the mountains—to do meditation."

"Sensei, please give me advice about myself."

"What kind?"

"Just what you feel I need, Sensei."

"Okay, Stan. We go for lunch. We speak."

We sipped thick noodle soup and talked. Then, taking a pen from his pocket, Takahashi drew a little picture on a paper napkin and handed it to me.

"For you," he smiled.

On the subway back to the Asia Center, I scrutinized the drawing. It was simply a man standing, looking into the distance. In the distance were what looked like a pile of rocks. At the feet of the man was what looked like a small stone that sparkled. Back at the Asia Center I placed the drawing on my desk.

Sometime during the night it came to me. Takahashi had given me the advice I had asked for. But I hadn't expected to receive it in the form of a cartoon.

The man was me. My eyes were focused on a pile of rocks, or something similar, vague and distant to me. Yet, at my very feet lay a diamond which I was not perceiving. I thought about what Dr. David Berson had said to me a few years before, and his words now made sense: "You may very well travel the whole world, only to find that what you're looking for lies in your very own back yard."

Takahashi, I concluded, was pointing me back to the source, to my roots, to the treasure that ultimately lies within.

Nakayama Sensei Visits My New House Dojo

Since childhood, I have lived in three different houses, and in all three I always built a *dojo*. The first two were very small, makeshift studios.

Beyond Spirit of the Empty Hand

In 1975, three exciting events occurred. First, we moved into our present residence in Morningside, Sandton (near Johannesburg), complete with a new *dojo*. Second, our new home coincided with the arrival of our fourth and final daughter, Lisa. Third, Nakayama Sensei, Chief Instructor of the Japan Karate Association, came for the first time to instruct in South Africa. It was he who had guided me with regard to the ideal size and shape of my new *dojo,* and here he was present for the "floor wetting."

"This *dojo* has good atmosphere, near river and trees. I want to bring my Japanese instructors to train here," he said.

During his stay we took him to the Kruger National Park. As we were approaching the Numbi gate, he spoke, "You South African karate-ka are so big." He was perched comfortably on the front seat of the Volkswagen minibus. "My name so big, but I am so small," continued the voice of Masatoshi Nakayama.

There was an undisguised sense of humor in this statement. The head master of Japan Karate Association had been enthusiastically questioning us about the wild life we were soon to be seeing. On reaching the mountainous country, somebody had coincidentally asked him what his name, Nakayama, meant.

"Nakayama means middle mountain," he replied, gazing across a nearby precipice, which commanded a panoramic view of a never-ending stretch of mountains and hillocks.

He was close to 60 years of age, certainly the most prominent "mountain" at the center of the world of karate—one of a handful of students under Gichin Funakoshi (the father of karate-*do*). Under his leadership the Japan Karate Association had grown into an international organization with millions of members. He authored more than 20 comprehensive works, the leading one being *Dynamic Karate*.

Although Nakayama was the inventor of championship (sport) karate (the first championship was held in Tokyo in 1957 under rules formulated by him) he said, "I often worry that Master Gichin Funakoshi will reprimand me in the next life for doing this, but the university students wanted more than kata and *ippon kumite;* they wanted combat. So I was forced to research and develop a workable set of rules; otherwise, it would have come in a disorganized, dangerous way."

Nakayama was still not totally happy about the sport side of karate.

"The one good thing is that it has helped spread the art all over the world," he said. However, he still believed that in sport the emphasis is on the body, while in true karate the emphasis is on the mind.

"Everything begins and ends with the mind," he claimed, "and this gives the karate-ka qualities that he can carry over into his daily life and use to his benefit."

Master Nakayama was most certainly a living embodiment of the mind/body ethic. On a tour of the USA, where he was demonstrating and teaching, he took off the top of his karate suit to show the students which muscles they should use. One of the students, a nurse, was amazed and said afterwards, "I've seen a lot of 70-year-old bodies, but this is the first one I have seen that looks like 35."

The highest stage of karate-do, he said, was where the mind and body move freely and smoothly regardless of age or physical condition. For proof of his capability he was also a master ski instructor (in his capacity as chairman of the Physical Education Department at Takudai University). In 1971 he was crushed by an avalanche in the Japanese Alps. The doctors gave him up for dead. Rather than die, Nakayama woke up after a few days in a coma and announced that he was hungry. He ignored the seven shattered ribs and punctured lungs, and within six months was back on the floor of JKA headquarters, training and teaching again.

"There is something special about him," said his doctor. "It is a miracle."

But Nakayama played himself down. He said: "Karate-do is attained one step at a time, and so is life. Just train every day and try your best; the truth will come to you."

Only The Color Of One's Spirit Matters

South Africa became isolated from world sport because of the Government's *apartheid* policies. While some of the *dojo* heads would not accept blacks into their *dojos*, most of the senior instructors of the South African JKA never saw color as being a criteria for being accepted into karate training. But, sadly, the police did. I was told on a number of occasions that they would close me down if I taught any more blacks.

Despite these enforced bans, we were still able to secretly teach and develop the likes of Edward Mtshali, who at the time of this writing holds a fifth *dan*. He is today a leading figure in the development of underprivileged karate-ka. Sixth *dans* Derrick and Keith Geyer had a lot to do with Edward's early development, and so did

Brian Phillips, who used to illegally enter the black townships. They would get him to lie down on the floor of a battered old Volkswagen. Edward and his students would cover him with a blanket and they would drive him into the township where he would secretly train them.

After Edward became a first *dan*, he trained every morning in our Early Birds instructor's class, and he progressed rapidly. Then, in the evenings, he would run classes, mostly in secret, in the various townships around South Africa.

"They Will Shoot You...."

The South African JKA karate team was banned from competing in the IAKF World Championships held in Los Angeles in 1975. We were the first team to arrive in Los Angeles, about 10 days before the tournament. We trained with Nishiyama Sensei.

I heard that Nishiyama had said that our team was expected to reach the finals against Japan. But our hopes and dedicated training were short-circuited two days before the tournament. Nishiyama came to our hotel and told us that the Mayor of Los Angeles had received a number of anonymous letters and telephone calls, stating that the South African team would all be shot and killed if they took part in the championships. After a short discussion, our team unanimously voted to enter the tournament despite the death threats. We felt we were not racists, so, "Why this unfairness? After all, this is America."

But the next day, a day before the tournament, we were asked nicely, *"Please* withdraw. They're now threatening to also shoot the organizers."

We withdrew. We didn't want Sensei Nishiyama harmed. He was far too precious. The one good thing that came out of the tournament was that Tanaka, my hero, became world champion.

South Africa was increasingly becoming the black sheep of world karate and sport in general, with 15 years of almost total isolation in the sporting sense of karate. But despite being banned from international competitions, we were given something else far more valuable. We concentrated on karate as a martial art, and the Japan Karate Association allowed us to visit Japan and train at the *Honbu dojo* as often as we wished, as long as we didn't take part in any public demonstrations, tournaments, or allow ourselves to be featured in any of the media.

Meeting Myself

We were repeating history in a sense. In the fifteenth through nineteenth centuries, Okinawan karate-ka had to practice in secret for fear of being jailed, killed, or punished by their overlords. We were now going through a similar scenario. We visited and trained in Japan whenever possible. But we went as tourists, wearing no badges, no national tracksuits, no publicity, no sport karate. We brought back *budo*, the way of the warrior, to South African karate enthusiasts.

We had been forced into doing the real thing.

I remember my friend and colleague, Terry O'Neill, karate expert and publisher of *Fighting Arts International*, the famous English magazine, saying to me at the time, "In a way I envy you South Africans. They way you train. You do it all. Real *gashukus* and everything. We tend to specialize in championships. In Europe it's one week fighting in Germany, then the next week in Italy, and so on. I miss the solid basics and the all round *dojo* training."

14

UNFORGETTABLE EXPERIENCES

Kill Or Be Killed

The years between 1976 and 1980 came alive with a collection of unforgettable learning experiences.

I visited Japan as normal. Then Tanaka, for the second time, captured the world *kumite* title at the IAKF World Championships in Japan, in 1977.

A rebel German team, headed by Ochi Sensei and Fritz Wendland, visited South Africa, trained and competed in a friendly event.

Toru Yamaguchi Sensei was sent to us, and through him I learned that karate is not only being tough all the time. After teaching us his "tricky tactics" in the *dojo*, like dropping under an attacker's *mae-geri* and kicking him in the butt from behind, he would ease out on the lounge floor afterwards, and my young children and their friends would gravitate to his lap. He played with them, acted the fool, and all you would hear when entering my house was laughter most of the time that Yamaguchi stayed with us. On the way back from visiting the Kruger National Park, he was telling us, "Micro bird very small but very dangerous."

We couldn't make out what he meant. But, later, when the penny dropped, we packed up laughing. "Micro bird" meant "mosquito."

That same year a local film company asked my colleague, Norman Robinson, and I to act in and supply karate fighters to take part in a film, *Karate Olympia*. We were so keen that we did it all for less than 500 Rand each. We had to do some very complicated sequences and stunts. Locally, the film did reasonably well. A couple of years later an American entrepreneur, Ed Montoro, bought the rights of *Karate Olympia* from South Africa for a small sum. He re-edited the film, changed the name to *Kill or be Killed*, and, according to *Variety* magazine, the film turned over nearly 30 million dollars.

Close Down That Dojo

After six years of study, I was finally awarded my Bachelor of Arts Degree by the University of South Africa. That same year, the local government asked me to close down the *dojo* at my house in Sandton, because my members driving along the narrow sand road

Beyond Spirit of the Empty Hand

leading to my home were "kicking up a dust storm." I had to agree with them.

I was terribly depressed, but then came an unexpected blessing in disguise. I was worrying about where I was going to teach my 150 students, when a real estate agent telephoned me out of the blue. He had no idea I was having a problem.

"Mr. Schmidt, I'm just calling on the off-chance that you may know of someone who wants to buy or rent premises. It's in Melrose north, off the M1 motorway."

"I don't mind having a look." I tried to sound disinterested.

"Melrose North's a good area," I reflected, as I drove my car in that direction. I nearly fell over when I entered the expansive driveway of the three-and-a-half-acre property. Although the grass had not been cut in three months, I could see that this was a gem of a property.

"This was a *shul*, Temple Bet El, but with the violence in the country, they wanted to get rid of it," the agent told me.

"How much?" I was biting my lip, hoping but never believing that the price of this place was anywhere near my ball park.

"They want 300,000, but I reckon you could get it for two hundred and fifty, if you put in a firm offer." This was 1978, and two hundred and fifty was big bucks, especially for a small time operator like myself.

Ray Joffe told me to find three partners and let him make an offer on the property on our behalf. In the end, he clinched the deal for 118,000 Rand, the best buy of the year, a local newspaper reported.

I borrowed 20,000 on my house bond for Judy and I. The other three partners put in 10,000 each, for a total of 50,000, which was the deposit on the bond for 80,000.

Over the next 15 years we expanded the premises to include facilities for aerobics, weight training, tap and modern dancing, and physiotherapy. Melrose became the location for all national gradings and seminars, and my karate membership increased steadily over the next few years.

That same year, Yamaguchi Sensei visited South Africa with Tanaka. This was Tanaka's first of many visits.

Besides some very instructive training sessions, we did a great deal of traveling, and one of the recreational highlights was the first-time experience for me of deep sea fishing off a ski boat near Plettenberg Bay, a resort on the Southeast coast of South Africa. We had a lucky run on Bonita, a lively game fish, and between

Tanaka, Keith and Derrick Geyer, Nigel Jackson, and myself, we pulled in about 19 Bonita.

Sashimi, Tanaka Style

That afternoon, basking in the sunset, we were entertained by Tanaka and Yamaguchi, who switched easily to the role of chefs. They scaled and cleaned the fish, prepared it, and seared the slivers of Bonita steak for a second or two over the glowing coals of a wood fire. Next, they cut the fish into thin slices, rare, which we dipped into a special sauce Tanaka Sensei had magically concocted. It was pure heaven, sitting under the clean Cape twilight sky, eating fresh *sashimi* washed down by cool Nederburg grand cru white wine, together with our two Japanese friends. It was in this type of setting that Tanaka would on the rare occasion open up and talk.

"I have always been a loner," he said. "In my boyhood I lived in Tokyo, but we moved house at least 15 times. I never had a chance to make friends. Also, I had three sisters and no brothers. I had a problem discovering my manhood. So I would pack my little knapsack and go hiking into the mountains alone."

As a boy, Tanaka felt he needed pressure to prove he was a man, so he chose the roughest sport at school—rugby. He had four years of it as a lock forward, and felt unhappy if he wasn't scraped and bleeding when he left the field.

"We had no rugby seasons at our school—we just played all year round," he said.

Tanaka is extraordinarily agile and fast. At the Wits sports center he had onlookers gasping as he moved across the long floor, delivering an assortment of machine-gun-like techniques down a row of 30 lined-up karate black belts.

No one came near to emulating his amazingly quick performance.

An astonished audience watched him sprint forward and backward on his haunches at an alarming pace, like a supersonic frog, from one end of the large arena to the other.

"This is where I get 90 percent of my striking power," he said, pointing to his legs. "From my ankles, knees, and hips. Rugby—pushing in the scrum—helped me to mold my legs in those early days.

"At university I was studying economics in the footsteps of my father. He died when I was 19, and my life changed direction. I switched courses and did what I felt was calling me—to study to become an animal doctor and an expert at forestry. I wanted to farm in South America.

"One day, a university friend took me to a karate *dojo*. I joined immediately, but trained secretly, not telling my other university friends. Then, one day, someone saw me training. I was a wild fighter at the time, and he invited me to fight for the university team.

After university, Tanaka didn't go farming in South America. He had become a third *dan,* and he badly wanted to become a student instructor at the Japan Karate Association.

They refused him because their funds weren't sufficient to support a learner instructor—but if he could support himself, they would allow him the honor of training in "the hornets' nest."

"I worked at everything from being a riverman to selling real estate," he said. "For a year I transported logs along canals. It improved my balance. I fell into the water less and less. All through these different jobs, I trained when I could in the instructors' class.

"And from 1962, I entered every year in the All Japan Karate Championship. From nowhere, I gradually worked my way up, and my first break came in 1973, when I came in third in the JKA international competition.

"The world championships were held every two years. I won in the USA in 1975 and again in Tokyo in 1977."

Unexpected Dan

I often reflected upon Tanaka Sensei's achievements and the long hard road that led to them.

When I was suddenly given my sixth *dan* in 1979, I had mixed feelings. I was happy, but I also felt that I should have done a test. Little did I realize that I had already done the test in many ways.

Why did they just give it to me? I learned later that Senseis Asai and Yamaguchi had recommended to the Masters Union that I be awarded the sixth degree. I was told that the panel's decision was unanimous. But why this way? Why not a test? For my seventh *dan*, nine years later, I certainly had to undergo some tough physical and psychological trials, challenges, and a little disillusionment. That was at the age of 52. But more about that later.

Meeting Myself

Why a sixth *dan* without a test? I always wanted to do it the hard way, by the sweat of my brow. The idea of grace and its underlying power hadn't gotten into me yet. I will probably never know the exact reason for being given sixth *dan*. However, karate historian, Randall Hassell, claims he can shed some light on this issue:

"Prior to 1957, the JKA was a very close-knit, fraternal organization. In that year, however, two significant events changed the face of the JKA and, consequently, its ranking system, forever. First was the death of Gichin Funakoshi, which enabled the young JKA men to move forward with competition karate, unimpeded by the disapproval of the great master. Second, they sent Takayuki Mikami abroad, to the Philippines, to start spreading the JKA gospel worldwide.

"As soon as they started sending people abroad, it became clear to them that it would be necessary to fall in line with the vast majority of other karate organizations around the world. It was time, they believed, to fully adopt judo's 10-*dan* system, to bring the ranks of their instructors more in line with the rankings of other instructors being exported from Japan and Okinawa.

"In 1960, Hidetaka Nishiyama was awarded the fifth dan, and Masatoshi Nakayama and Minoru Miyata were promoted to sixth dan by nomination and vote of the JKA *shihankai*.

"It was not thought that examinations for rankings above fifth degree black belt were necessary because there appeared to be no chance that anyone outside of the JKA hierarchy in Japan could ever aspire to that level.

"In fact, it was not until Stan Schmidt tested for and received the *sandan* ranking in Japan that the JKA hierarchy even considered the idea that a Westerner might reach that level. In no case did they believe that a Westerner could ever go beyond *sandan*.

"However, Stan Schmidt woke them up. His unparalleled achievement finally showed them that, indeed, Westerners were capable of rising higher in karate than the Japanese had ever imagined.

"Once Stan Schmidt had broken down the barriers, Westerners from all over the world started reaching the *sandan* level, and as he moved up to fourth and fifth *dan*

Beyond Spirit of the Empty Hand

levels, he made it possible for other non-Japanese to move up, also. At the same time, the JKA more carefully formalized the examination requirements for fourth and fifth *dan*, and they increased the physical testing requirements.

"When Stan Schmidt received his sixth *dan* from the JKA, there still was no testing protocol in place for that ranking. Ranks above fifth *dan* still were awarded by nomination and vote of the JKA *shihankai*, and that is how Stan's sixth *dan* was awarded.

"By that time, however, there were other non-Japanese *fifth* dans around the world, and it became apparent to the JKA hierarchy that they simply were not going to be able to keep track of all of them and nominate and vote on their promotions in a fair way. So they created an examination standard for the sixth and seventh *dan* levels, and every candidate for sixth degree, after Stan Schmidt, was required to take an examination, which also explains why he was required to take a test for seventh *dan*, but not for sixth."

Communications and all of its multi-faceted ramifications fascinated me. For example, to begin with I pored over the full spectrum of the impact communications and technology was having upon our contemporary society—the good, the bad, and the ugly of it. The subject ranged from intra- to inter-communication. On the one extreme there was intercommunication, epitomized by advanced technology and what I will call "State of the Art Hardware." On the other extreme there was intra-communication, what goes on between you and you, or between you and your Maker, "State of the Heart Software."

The scope and effects of mass media and advertising upon our often vulnerable human minds interested me, especially when it came to TV, which is able to intrude upon the privacy and harmony in our homes and can captivate us in this passive and receptive condition.

Furthermore, it dealt with the transmitting of propaganda and the manipulation of human psyches. This horrified and fascinated me. What concerned me most about super technology in communication was just how powerful the various media are. These, of course, range from the simple telephone to newspapers, radio, movies, TV, and the electronic age, heralded by the introduction of the computer and all of its vast possibilities, such as the internet with its instant universal information potential—fast progressing from the written word to auditory and any number of visual possibilities.

What Marshall McLuhan pointed out was that communication technology, while being a superb tool for disseminating great and much needed information for the betterment of mankind, also carried with it the awesome potential to destroy mankind by dehumanizing him through feeding him with biased, untrue, or soul-destroying information and images.

McLuhan claimed that the numerous technological media are simply extensions of our senses. For example, the telephone becomes an extension of our voice and of our ear. He even saw transport as a medium of changing the way humans communicate. For instance, he claimed that the wheel of the car is an extension of the human foot. It largely takes away the human quality of walking. So while we are getting to a destination faster and maybe communicating more and far quicker, we are, in a sense, allowing our God-given legs to become somewhat redundant. Thus, he asserted that any technological extension of our senses, limbs, body, or brain "numbs that sense" to some or other degree, depending upon how dependent we become upon that "lever." The more the lever does it for us, so does our personal strength in that faculty begin to disappear.

What became clearer to me was this: while humanity was beginning to connect and interact in the 20th Century on a global scale, to a degree unimagined in the 19th Century, so was each human being in danger of losing his or her humanity and individuality, becoming passive onlookers rather than dynamic participants in life.

In The Empty Hand, The Cure

During my studies I had been interacting with a man I respect immensely, Professor Philip Tobias, Master Anatomist and Anthropologist. In 1997 he was awarded the most significant accolade, "Fellow of the Royal Society of London" (FRS). He is the first South African to be made an FRS in more than 40 years. His honor-laden career includes three Nobel Prize nominations.

It was my good fortune to demonstrate karate to him and the University of the Witwatersrand Medical Faculty way back in the early 1970s. Professor Tobias was so impressed with karate as an excellent human art, that he included demonstrations of it in his

Beyond Spirit of the Empty Hand

end of year lectures to second year medical students on the subject of human poise and neuromuscular dexterity. Traditional karate and classical ballet were the human arts that Professor Tobias referred to as "Crowing Achievements of Human Skilled Activity".

After attending certain lectures by Professor Tobias and reading Marshall McLuhan, I was prompted to write "The Empty Hand."

THE EMPTY HAND

Five million years ago we're told, man got up and stood.
Was it 'cause he knew he should, or was it 'cause he could?
Did he stand up intentionally
Or was it a reflex of *anatomy?*

Groping 'round in dust and dirt for food was his direction
Quite often there the search was bare and so was the selection
What made him struggle to his feet
That unhappy clumsy brute
Were perhaps the leaves of some strange tree
He reached for—that bore fruit.

From a crawling state of dejection
An upward look and inspection
Caused a physical erection
A change—a new direction.

In greed his hands moved to and fro
Apprentices of wealth and woe
In clutching, touching, feeling around unknowingly
He was doing a form of training in neuromuscular dexterity.

He then no doubt began to grasp and grab at many things
To fight the pull of gravity in his early wanderings
Like rocks and trees and even straws
Hooray for those prehensile paws.

An empty hand to build a home
To swing a stick, or throw a stone
To make or break, to feel and shake
To push and pull, to give and take.

But modern man's become a dunce

Meeting Myself

He's trying to grab it all at once
By holding and keeping, he's losing his touch
He's filled to the brim, he's grasping too much
Like his hand—his mind stores up troubles a-plenty
If he wants to find peace he should make them both empty.

Take a look all around you, at what mankind has done
This most intelligent animal under the sun
With his computer-like mind and his dexterous hand
He's polluted the air and congested the land.

Don't forget his achievements—all his gadgets scientific
He's touching the stars—he's really terrific
All the answers he has—knows the secrets of life
But this Samson is shorn at a glance, by his wife.

He's continually striving to add to his treasures
By his rags and his riches his status he measures
He'll take all he can, and not stop till the sound
Of the clods, hit the lid of his box in the ground!

Maybe it's only a stage he's going through
This grabbing for me and never for you
But a special kind of man is always there
Ready, waiting, wanting to share.

With Empty Hands
He touches our world of strife
With Empty Hands, He died.
He rose. He gives us life.

"We Kill the Jet Lag"

What Nakayama Sensei wished for in 1975 came to pass in 1980—A Japanese team came to train at my house *dojo* in Morningside. The arrival of Tanaka, Shimoda, Kawawada, Omura, and Kagawa in South Africa at a time when our karate-*ka* had been starved of any international competition, caused more than a stir throughout our *dojos*. These men were out of the top drawer of karate-*do* and amazing athletes with awesome skills.

Beyond Spirit of the Empty Hand

They were hardly off the 20-hour plane journey when Tanaka had them on the floor of my house *dojo* training full pace.

"This way we kill jet lag," he told us afterwards. The Japanese team fought our team as well as teams from other styles in a fully packed stadium. Dynamic demonstrations were given, and one and all came away excited and motivated.

Their visit was the tonic South African karate needed in those lonely years of isolation from the rest of the world.

A day after the tournament, our team took the Japanese team to a smart formal Chinese restaurant for dinner. The place was packed with guests who quietly conversed. We filed in and filled the long table that had been reserved for our group. As we waited for the drinks to arrive, there was an uncomfortable silence at our table. No one was quite sure of how to break the ice and start communication with our Japanese guests.

Hardly had the drinks been poured when an ear splitting shock wave filled the entire restaurant.

Kagawa had stood up, raised his beer glass and shouted, "*Kampai!* Cheers!" The loudest I've ever heard it uttered. A second later he had downed the draught in one full sweep. We all followed suit. In one instant the reserved atmosphere in the restaurant changed. People laughed and waved at us, and the entire evening was alive with jollity.

Like Dying And Coming To Life Again

Because of the impressive and exciting Japanese team that had visited our country, a big group of black belts decided they wanted to visit Japan for the 1981 All Japan Championships.

Rob Schmidt, a third *dan*, was one of the team who had trained and saved up to go.

On the very first day of training at *Honbu dojo,* Tokyo, Robert was the fortunate guy who Tanaka selected to do *kumite* with, just prior to the class commencing.

As they started, Tanaka executed a *kani-basami* (crab claws throw) on Robert. Robert was taken by surprise, and he fell heavily on the wooden floor. Thinking he must get up quickly, he collided with Tanaka's follow-up downward stamp kick, which propelled Robert directly back to the floor, against which his already confused head collided, concussing him.

Meeting Myself

He sat on the sidelines for the rest of the trip, nursing one jumbo headache.

"Hard luck," we all told him. "Just keep your spirit."

After we returned to South Africa, Robert came to me one day and told me he was working on a special technique. He would surprise me by showing it to me at his fourth *dan* grading, soon to come.

The grading was held at my house *dojo,* with Tanaka Sensei heading the grading panel.

Five tough young instructors were attempting fourth *dan.* Among these were two *kumite* champions. They first did *kihon* combinations, then kata and finally *kumite.*

Robert Schmidt was called up to fight each of the other four candidates attempting fourth *dan.* In his first fight, he dropped his opponent three times with the crab claws throw and went on to throw the others with the same technique at least once each.

As he finished, he turned to the panel, and before he bowed, he looked into Tanaka's eyes. Tanaka took up his gaze and then returned Robert's very respectful bow.

Tanaka turned to me and said, "Just like demonstration. Robert good spirit."

"Do you remember him, Sensei?"

"Yes. I gave him a present in Japan." He winked at me. "You understand, Stan?"

"Yes, Sensei. I understand very well indeed. You have given me many such presents. Thank you."

He drew a very large circle next to the *kumite* section of Robert's grading card. If a circle indicates "good," a big circle, I assumed, meant "excellent!"

Later, Robert Schmidt confided to me that he had not slept for many a night after Tanaka had helped put him into dreamland with his uncanny scissors move. And when Robert finally did achieve sleep, he told me he kept re-living a recurrent nightmare.

"It was like a spiritual octopus was enveloping me—tying me up and smothering me."

Out of this pit of darkness and confusion was born Robert's own special technique—his equally potent version of *kani-basami.* He said it was like dying for a time and then coming to life again.

I told Robert what Tanaka Sensei had said about giving him a present back in Japan. Robert was grateful and overjoyed when I explained exactly what Tanaka had said about him, and he hasn't had one of those nightmares since then.

Beyond Spirit of the Empty Hand

Soul of Karate

The documentary film, *Soul of Karate*, came out of my concern that I needed to rise up and get going, and take responsibility for my own well-being and face up to life without fear. Dave Friend and I raised enough money to produce this documentary.

I chose only real karate-ka to play roles in *Soul of* Karate. In essence, I gave them two instructions: "Play yourselves and play karate as it should be played."

All but one of the main karate-ka featured in the film are still actively involved in the art at the time of this writing, 18 years after its production. All of them are experts who carry high *dan* rankings achieved in Japan. They are Derrick Geyer, Keith Geyer, Dave Friend, Gordon Richardson, Johan Roets, Ray Joffe, Norman Robinson, Malcolm Dorfman, Ed Dorey, Robert Ferriere, Nigel Jackson, and others.

In scripting the film I wanted to show what I, at that stage, believed was the ideal way of training. The film followed the training of five people from white belt through black belt—first *dan*.

By 1981, *Soul of* Karate was shown on TV throughout South Africa and it attracted thousands of new students—children, adults, and even senior citizens—into taking it up. Chief Instructor, Nakayama, showed the film to his instructors throughout Japan saying, "*Soul of Karate* like the old days, has real fighting spirit."

In order to appear in the documentary, the karate-ka I chose agreed that they needed to be 100 percent honed in. They were to develop the finest cutting edge they could achieve.

One of the challenges we undertook was a 24-hour *gashuku*. About 50 black belts took part. Repetition blocking, punching, and kicking was the cornerstone of our training. Every two or three hours we would collapse on the order, "*Yame!*" falling to the *dojo* floor. We would swallow some water and rest right where we were, until yours truly shouted, "*Yoi!* Pair-off, *kumite!*"

Kumite, (*gohon, ippon,* or *jiyu-ippon*) would go on for at least one hour. Then it would be kata like *Bassai Dai* done 30 times (one soft, one hard, and one free) always in that order.

Then a drink and a rest, only to be alerted again by yours truly. I'd be up and join in with each move, trying to lead by example into the next drill, which may have been bag work, reflex blocking training, or ground wrestling—all very challenging to the body, mind, and emotions.

Meeting Myself

During the 24 hours, there was not one person who wasn't humbled by something, at least some of the time. For instance, me, when it came to doing front, side, and back kicks on one leg. There was one count for three kicks, and on the night of this particular *gashuku* I had challenged the group, "How many must we do?"

"Fifty," someone answered.

"One hundred!"

"One hundred and fifty!" offered a third.

I stopped any more "offers," and we did the 150 on each leg. Side kick always drew my energy more than any other technique. I suffered but pretended to have spirit, although a lot of my kicks went no higher than hip height.

We started the *gashuku* on a Friday morning and it ended on top of a little mountain the next morning. I admit that we took about three hours sleep after the semi-final session at about two o'clock in the morning. At about 5:30, I told the group to follow me up Sylvia Pass. It was only a 20-minute run, but the slope was continuous and steep.

I had set the challenge, so I led the bunch of stiff, sore, bleary-eyed karate-ka up the hill. I have to admit that I suffered. It was the most painfully tiring run I have ever attempted.

"I'm crazy," I groaned to myself about halfway up the hill. "What did I do this for? I must be nuts doing this after 12 hours of hard physical training and only three hours sleep."

The karate group was great. They didn't complain once, only urged each other to greater heights.

At the top of Sylvia Pass was a little park. We ended our training there with *jiyu kumite*—free fighting.

Going back was like a joyride, with wobbly thighs, but a rekindled spirit. Oh, so sweet. It was all over. We had done it. The *gashuku* had flushed out our city minds. We were free spirits, and the camaraderie within our group had strengthened considerably.

It was out of this background that *Soul of* Karate was created.

Select Your Heroes Carefully

Among the Japanese with whom I trained for over 30 years I always found heroes whom I strived to emulate. When I think of them now, these images appear: Nakayama Sensei's perfect blocking and striking techniques; Enoeda's sheer power; Shoji's simplicity of movement; Kase's mystique; Sugiura's grace; Yam-

Beyond Spirit of the Empty Hand

aguchi's tricky tactics; Ochi's all-roundedness; Ueki's clarity in action; Tabata's gentlemanly strength; Oishi's courageous timing; Imamura's snappy and flowing actions; Osaka's pure technique; Yahara's dynamism; Iida's gentle strength; Kagawa's long, devastating kicks; Yamamoto's explosive take-off speed; Tanaka's deadly fighting tactics.

But it is their quality of character for which I most remember and admire the great masters under whom I trained—their attitude of concern, their compassion, their strength of spirit, their humor, their mastery not only of karate but of everyday life relationships, and their trustworthiness. These are people you would like to have living with you and your family in your home.

Nakayama—a living dictionary of karate theory, always ready to discuss technique; Okazaki—a master who sincerely propagates the Funakoshi, Nakayama, and Sugiura line; Enoeda—he has the fearless attitude of a hero, with the loving heart of a child; Ochi—he brings a smile into the darkest day; Yamaguchi—as he sat down on the floor of my lounge, my young children gravitated into his lap; Shirai—there he was cooking breakfast again, always with a song on his lips; Kase—a fascinating magnet of a man guiding others in his special, quaint way; M. Higaonna (of Goju-ryu)—the *makiwara* man with callused hand and a gentle heart; Chinen—warm and open, always ready to share his skills and learn from others; Tomiyama (Shito)—a communicator; Mikami—the active doer; Sugiura—the quiet gentleman of karate-*do*, affectionately nicknamed "The Encyclopedia of Kata;" Ueki—an inspiring teacher and ideal role model; Tanaka—unpredictable yet reliable, an artist and a *samurai* who penetrates the deepest resources of his art, a deadly gentleman, and a great personal friend.

Heroes, yes, and this is a good thing. Without heroes we have nothing with which to measure ourselves or upon which to base our aspirations. Heroes are healthy, provided they are healthy heroes, because even heroes have weaknesses. All humans have weaknesses. But there comes a time in life when one has to allow one's own creative spirit to emerge, flow, and become properly focused. A time to be yourself—nothing more, nothing less. A time to not act out different roles like the Hollywood stars have to do—the good doctor yesterday, the politician today, the madman tomorrow.

How can we expect these poor stars to actually know who they really are, outside of the studio world? Some do, of course, and they are special cases. When you are applying the majority of your daily hours to acting out parts in an unreal world, and maybe assuming the character of someone you don't really admire, it's hard. I'm not saying it's impossible. I'm saying it must be hard to readjust, to be, in essence, your natural self. I believe, as a long time participant in my art, that the truth sets one free. Facing the truth may at times be painful or disillusioning, but facing the truth over time leads to inner strength.

The Movies vs. The Truth

I am no movie star, but I have been intimately involved in the production of a few movies.

After *Kill or be Killed*, the follow up, *Kill and Kill Again*, was the second full feature movie in which our karate-*ka* starred or performed. I could never quite come to terms with the awful titles that were given to these two movies. But then, who can argue with Hollywood? This second film was produced by Ed Montoro of Hollywood in 1980. For this one I was paid a more satisfactory sum of money than I was for the first one.

Around 1986, Norman Robinson and I supplied karate-ka to act as *ninjas* and stunt persons in the Hollywood production, *American Ninja 2*, which was being filmed in Cape Town. We also helped with some choreography and took small parts in the film.

In one part I had to jump out from behind some rocks on the Boulders Beach near Simonstown. I was dressed in a black *ninja* outfit, and I had to try to cut the heroes head off with my *samurai* sword. But the hero, being a hero, stepped back and lifted his wooden stick to block the cut. My sword cut his stick in two neat pieces (all faked, of course). Then the hero had to write me off with three blows to the head, using the two freshly cut batons.

Blow number one and number two seemed to work for the director, but he kept asking us to repeat blow number three, which was a final strike to my right temple. The actor had to feather his blow and make it look like it was real.

"It's not close enough," the director kept saying to the actor and to me. "You're not reacting enough, Stan."

This went on for about six takes. Finally the hero, losing his cool or his control, I'm not sure which, lashed out and hit me full force an inch above my temple. Blood poured out of my head and soaked my *ninja* mask. Although I dropped to one knee, I wasn't knocked out, only stunned that he could have been so reckless.

Beyond Spirit of the Empty Hand

I jumped up and wanted to hit him, but the crew subdued me and took me to the hospital for stitches and observation. I had a splitting headache for three days, but soon recovered.

Now, here is the punch line. Ten years after this little incident, I met and befriended a movie scriptwriter from Hollywood who is still a friend as I write this. The conversation got around to which country I was from and what I did.

"Oh, South Africa. I teach karate."

"You've got good karate guys there, I'm told."

"Who told you this?"

"I heard it through the film industry."

"Oh, I was involved in a couple of films," I told him.

"Which ones?"

"*Kill and Kill Again, Kill or be Killed,* and *American Ninja 2*."

"Funny, Michael Dudikoff told me that the guys there are quite tough and that he had a bit of a rub up with one of the top exponents. He settled him evidently with a stick."

"Ha! Ha!" I laughed, tickled by this story from the past. "That idiot was me!"

"You're serious?" He couldn't believe what I was telling him. "Why do you call yourself an idiot?"

"For putting myself in that situation in the first place. I chose to be the fall guy. My whole life I have trained to be a real fighter. Now I chose to play funny games in movies, an unreal world of make believe. I deserved to get hit."

He laughed. "I'm glad to hear your side of the story. The way Michael put it, it sounded like he had landed himself in a real serious confrontation."

"He's right. It nearly got very serious."

What I learned from that lesson was that if you become too involved in fantasy, you're likely to get a hard, unexpected knock from reality.

15

BACK TO BASICS, THEN...

Meeting Myself

What I now wanted more than anything was to discover how to let my true nature emerge, and to find "the zone," as some top pro golfers call it when everything goes right in their game.

Trying, or expecting to be zoned in can be a dicey game of hide and seek.

My student, friend, and instructor, Wayne Westner, (he teaches me golf), who is one of the longest drivers in international golf, told me, "I always return to basics; otherwise I find it difficult to become tuned in to the zone." He carries a golf club wherever he goes and is forever "doing kata," as he calls it, swinging the club at an imaginary ball.

Anton Geesink, after winning the judo Heavyweight Gold Medal at the Olympics in 1964, in Japan, said, "I won because I trained in judo as a way of life, as Dr. Kano taught. While the Japanese were devising competitive strategies, I was in the *dojo* practicing basics and kata. I defeated the Japanese because my 'secret' was to train every day in the basics. This will make you unbeatable."

Thus, the ongoing cycle of *shu-ha-ri* is completed through diligent practice of the basics, and then having the faith to allow your deepest spirit to do *it* for you and to trust *Him*. Good, simple daily habits are the path to excellence and success.

My school friend, Gary Player, the master golfer, has always said, "I love adversity. It makes me practice hard. And the harder I practice (the basics), the luckier I get." Gary does not have the word "fear" in his vocabulary.

"Faith," he says, "rules out that other nasty word."

Prepare Properly

Researching and writing a dissertation for my Master's Degree gradually revealed to me a few of my inherent weaknesses, weaknesses which sometimes got me into trouble both on the karate floor as well as out in that great marketplace called life.

When my supervisor, Professor van Schoor, agreed in principle that I may do a thesis in which I could relate the art of karate to the science of communication, I was ecstatic and was about to rush out of his office and immediately launch myself full-scale into the task.

"Whoa, Stan!" he chided. This is January, nineteen hundred and eighty. You have got at least 24 months to get this important publication together. What's the rush?"

"Just keen to get it done with, I suppose."

"You haven't even chosen a title for it yet. Isn't this important?"

"Sorry. You're quite right, Professor." Then, on impulse, I threw in, "What about 'Karate Communicates'?"

"Doesn't everything communicate?"

Professor van Schoor sat opposite me looking like a serious old owl. But his eyes sparkled with traces of humor as he continued.

"It certainly needs more thought. Now go and write your ideas down. See in what direction they take you, in terms of the subject of *communication*, that is. Don't forget this side. We don't just want a thesis on karate, per se. It's got to have ... how shall I put it ...?"

"Balls," I offered.

"Exactly, my man. When you arrive at a title with a few substantial points to show what direction you aim to take, we can talk again."

On the way home in the car I reflected. "He's right. That's me again, always too impetuous, wanting to get going before doing some simple basic planning."

Eventually, with Professor van Schoor facilitating the process, we arrived and agreed upon, "Karate and Communication—A Study in Human Awareness."

Having finally chosen the title for my thesis seemed to give me the focused motivation I needed. My ideas and writing literally flowed. I enjoyed every moment creating it, except for ...

Zanshin

"Stan, the body of your work is good," Professor van Schoor was saying to me nearly two years later, after I had presented him with my "finished" draft. "But you have given no attention to the finishing touches."

I felt let down and dismayed by his frank words.

"It's like a good painting with a cheap frame. There are still a few spelling mistakes. Your use of grammar could do with a little restructuring. And, well, the referencing of your sources is totally inadequate. Just follow the guidelines provided. You've done the hard part. These last few bits are easy. I look forward to reading," he paused and nodded his head as if agreeing with himself, "your well-finished product."

Meeting Myself

These unexpected recommendations of his were, to me, like having sat upon a cactus plant—multiple pains in the butt. I had thought I was at last finished with it all. But now, the hardest part of all loomed over me. Grammar, spelling, and pulling out and accurately recording all of those boring references. This was like having all of my teeth drilled without taking an anesthetic. But with a lot of help from my friends I finally completed the thesis, had it properly covered and bound, and handed it to the professor.

"Thank you, Professor van Schoor, for insisting that I perfect the finished product. I need that kind of discipline. The Japanese have a word for this. It's in my thesis now. It is called *zanshin*, perfect finish."

"*Zanshin*. An interesting sounding word," he repeated as I left his office.

It was shortly after this that I wrote to Tanaka Sensei and told him that I wanted to learn about the deeper meaning of the word *zanshin* when I next visited Japan. He replied to my letter but made no reference to what I had said regarding *zanshin*.

I sent a copy of my Master's thesis to karate instructor Steve Ubl of San Diego, who had expressed interest in it. He, in turn, gave it to Randall Hassell, an accomplished karate historian, instructor, writer, and publisher of books.

Hassell quickly contacted me and, to my pleasant surprise, told me that he wanted to publish it. We re-arranged the text into a smooth-flowing story and published it in book form as *Spirit of the Empty Hand*, the precursor of this book.

Sometime after receiving my Master's Degree in Communication, I visited Japan for my yearly updating and study of technique at JKA headquarters.

A few weeks after my arrival on this particular trip to Japan, Tanaka called me after the class was over and said, "*Kumite.*" We did free fighting for about half an hour. Every time I trained in Japan, Tanaka would invite me to spar with him at least once. It was always both the highlight and most challenging half hour of each visit. Like Miyamoto Musashi, Tanaka changed his approach every time we fought. It was on this occasion, if I remember correctly, that he fought me "floppy octopus" style. After it was over, that was the name I gave it. It was most disrupting and confusing trying to deal with this relaxed, walking, rotating, floppy, slapping octopus way of fighting. Gone was his usual bent knee position and the cutting kick and relaxed-arms-at-his-side posture. All he did now was whirl at me. None of my usual blocks worked. I was

Beyond Spirit of the Empty Hand

being slapped all over with back hands, front hands, wrists, elbows, and unorthodox variations of knees and feet. But always in the near front of my mind was that cutting kick. "Expect it at any moment," a worried little inner voice warned.

Then, out of sheer frustration, I began to fight "octopus-style" in my own way. As we finished, he was smiling.

"Ah, I see you like my new style."

I didn't tell him that I found it extremely disconcerting.

After I had changed and was preparing to go, Tanaka came out of the resident instructors' change room and did something unusual, as usual. He handed me an envelope and said, "You have free time this weekend?"

"Yes, Sensei."

"Okay, tomorrow morning you catch plane at Haneda airport. Take karate-*gi*. Inside envelope is air ticket. You ask the reception at Asia Center. They will explain."

With that he was gone. Simple, clear instructions. That was that; that was Tanaka.

Early the next morning, as I was boarding the plane to Toyama prefecture, I was greeted with a slap on my shoulders, far harder than that of the *Zen* monk's flat stick.

"*Osu*, Stan."

"*Osu*, Sensei."

"Toyama, high mountains, snow, river, good *dojo* and many good friends," he explained.

We were met by an entourage of fans who didn't stop bowing to Tanaka until we had driven away in the smart limousine provided. The big boss, as Tanaka referred to Mr. Yamazaki, drove us to the best hotel in Toyama.

"US President, he stay here before," Yamazaki told us.

My room was palatial compared to my postage stamp-sized room at the Asia Center. I bathed and changed into comfortable clothing, and Tanaka and I were once again received by the big boss, who I later learned was currently building one of the biggest *dojos* in the world, which would be situated right here in Toyama. Yamazaki's son was a member of the instructor training program at *honbu dojo* in Tokyo.

This time Yamazaki was driving a modern 4 x 4 vehicle. With him were three other people, to whom Tanaka introduced me. Although I sat on the back seat, I noticed that the knuckles of Yamazaki's hands were covered in calluses. I tapped Tanaka on the shoulder and indicated to him Yamazaki's knuckles. He turned to

Meeting Myself

me and whispered, "Oh, he top businessman, but he likes karate very much. Before, he had auto accident, and now every day he does *makiwara* training. Cannot move so well but he has very powerful blocking and punching techniques."

Yamazaki stopped at a house just outside of town and a distinguished looking man with neat, spiky gray hair got in next to me. He was not introduced to me.

Within 30 minutes our 4 x 4 was traveling up and along the edges of a snow-covered mountain. Sheer cliffs bordered the narrow mud road which we precariously moved along. We eventually stopped at an outpost, which was a rectangular shack of a building perched on the side of a gorge. It was cold outside. An icy river rushed by. We were quickly ushered into the warm interior of the simple building. A merry fire was crackling away in the grate. One large table occupied the middle of the room. We sat down on simple square cushions, and within seconds, a large bowl of steaming hot *sake* (rice wine) was placed on the table. A stream of tasty snacks followed. The seven of us were the only customers in this little outpost *sake* bar.

"You drink first, Stan," said Tanaka, passing me the heavy bowl. As I took it in my hands, I noticed a large fish floating around in the brew. Ignoring the fish, I took a deep swallow of the fishy *sake* and passed on the bowl. By the third round it began to taste just fine. And it certainly warmed up one's body in this cold, remote part of Japan.

The man who had been sitting next to me in the Landrover now sat opposite me. His calm and serene expression and the way he held his head and shoulders intrigued me.

"Who is this gentleman?" I whispered, turning to the others.

They all smiled in unison, almost as if they had been waiting for me to ask. One of them said, "This is Sensei Wakabayashi, one of the top 20 *shodo* (calligraphy) masters in Japan. Meet Mister Stan Schmidt." He turned to the sensei and introduced us.

On impulse, my question to him literally rolled out of my mouth.

"Sensei, what is *zanshin*?"

His eyes lit up, but he sat unmoved at first. Waited. Then, leaning forward as if wanting to communicate his message more intimately to me, he did the following.

"*Zanshin* is like when a bell rings." He sang out loudly, "Dong-ng-ng-ng-ng!"

Beyond Spirit of the Empty Hand

He stretched out the last part of the "nnnggg" gradually fading it out. Simultaneously, his hand moved away from his mouth and as his arm was becoming fully stretched out, he said, "This part is *zanshin*."

There was still a faint resonance of the sound present in the room as his posture returned to normal.

We all applauded spontaneously.

"What an experience!" I told Tanaka later.

"You understand *zanshin* now, Mister Stan?"

What is Mister Stan?

We returned to Toyama that evening and I was asked to instruct a class, which I did by communicating in a mixture of broken Japanese and English. Later that evening we were entertained by *geisha* with song, a Japanese tea ceremony, and finally a meal, which was presented in stages. It consisted of almost the full spectrum of Japanese cuisine from *sashimi* (raw fish) to *yaki-tori* (broiled chicken), every dish garnished with colorfully carved and shaped adornments. No helping was ever too small or too big, always just right. I did not feel stuffed up by the end of the evening.

Just before we departed, the *shodo* master who had accompanied us on our little mountain excursion produced a neatly wrapped parcel, which he handed to me across the low, purple-lacquered table around which we sat. Everybody became attentive as I opened the present. As I pulled each item out everybody applauded—a number of calligraphy brushes, an indented stone, and a solid black ink stone, which the calligrapher would, with the addition of a little water, rub against the saucer-shaped stone in order to produce the ink or paint used in traditional calligraphy.

Then the final part—a thin square object, wrapped in a burgundy silk scarf. As I untied the scarf, what fell into my lap was a white square of cardboard with four calligraphy characters artfully inscribed upon it.

"Thank you very much, indeed. *Domo arigato gozai masu, Sensei*," I repeated in Japanese, bowing to this fascinating man. "Please tell me, what is the meaning of these characters?"

As he began talking, the room went silent. Everyone hung on his every word.

"Today Mister Stan asked me what is *zanshin*. When I got back home, I placed empty white paper on my easel. Then I prepared my brushes and made good ink. Then I looked at the empty page and asked, 'What is Mister Stan?' I waited. I watched." He paused. "Then, suddenly, my hand painted these characters."

I was stunned. What a wonderful thing to do and for me a *gaijin*, a foreigner! A top master, who no doubt is a busy man, does all of this for me!

"Sensei," I told him, "I am truly grateful and honored by this gift of yours."

He went on, talking in Japanese. As he finished, the guests, even those from other tables, applauded. Then the interpreter said to me: "He says it is very difficult to translate from Japanese to English, but, basically, the four characters mean 'Cow walks 10,000 *ri* (one ri equals four kilometers).

Seven Significant Things

Between 1983 and 1986, seven significant things happened to me.

The first was that Peter Bunkell, one of my long-time students, one day informed me, "We want you to do a weekly column for the Rand Daily Mail." He was the assistant editor of this popular morning newspaper. I couldn't believe my ears, but with plenty of sweat, writing, rubbing out, and sleepless nights, I finally squeezed out my very first of 150 articles over a three-year period.

The second significant thing was my good fortune in being able to visit the original home of karate, Okinawa, and being able to take more than 100 South African karate-ka to the *dojo* of my friend, the famous Morio Higaonna Sensei of the *Goju-ryu* style. He had stayed at my house a year or so before and taught me (using the *makiwara* as well as tree trunks) the art of *makiwara* striking, kicking, blocking, and more.

He told me that in the old days of secrecy in Okinawan karate, one friend would visit another and they would spend a pleasant afternoon chatting while standing side by side, each striking their *makiwara*. Now and then they would pause for tea and then continue with hundreds of repetitions of yet another technique.

"Karate training without *makiwara* training is like winking without smiling," he remarked.

Seniors from our group later trained at his *dojo* at everything from carrying heavy jars to wielding a *chishi* (a stone attached to a stick, used to develop powerful wrists and arms) as well as *maki-*

wara striking. One or two of our black belts, when asked by Higaonna Sensei to demonstrate their punching skill on the *makiwara*, literally hit one or two fresh-air shots, missing the board completely in their enthusiasm to impress him. He was very kind about this, quietly telling them to be more gentle in their approach.

"Out of gentleness stems true strength," he told them. "Strike softly and correctly, and power will come to you naturally."

The next day our group was invited to attend a special martial arts festival especially arranged for our benefit. That was a memorable day for us as we watched demonstrations by masters of every type of Okinawan martial art.

They asked Norman Robinson and I to demonstrate the kata, *Tekki Sandan*, and our entire group did a demonstration of basic Shotokan techniques. It was an exhilarating experience—watching, learning, demonstrating, and finally socializing with these friendly, salt-of-the-earth, Okinawan warriors.

The third significant thing I experienced was a near fatal auto crash.

After training one evening, I was traveling home along the motorway at a slow 50 kilometers per hour, due to heavy bumper-to-bumper traffic ahead of me. I was driving a Volkswagen Golf, and I was hit from behind by a minibus, hurtling down onto the motorway from an on-ramp at all of 120 kilometers per hour. The forceful impact from behind propelled my car directly into the car in front of me, sandwiching me in between the two vehicles.

When I finally extricated myself from the wreck of my car, I was aware of three things. I was alive and intact, thank God; my neck area was both numb and painful; and I felt a distinct stiffness in my hip joint area, which became increasingly painful over the next three years.

After examining x-rays of my hips, top orthopedic surgeon Ian MacRogan told me that I had undergone severe damage to the soft tissue in my hip joints and that I would need bilateral hip replacement surgery in the future. "In about five to 10 years' time," he informed me.

I was shocked to the core by this horrifying news. "Me, the fit karate man, a cripple? No way!" I put the bad news behind me, thinking I could cure myself with things ranging from deep knee squats, homeopathic remedies, stretching, vegetable diets, physiotherapy, and other such approaches. I refused to believe his diagnosis, and I pretended the condition didn't exist. I would simply endure the pain. I was used to facing pain, so I continued with my regular training, becoming more and more uncomfortable in my moves as the months rolled by.

Meanwhile, I carried on as normal, often having to grit my teeth, pretending it didn't hurt when I lifted my knee to do a side kick. Tying my shoe laces and pulling on my socks became increasingly difficult. But strangely, two things relieved the pain in my hips—doing front kicks and back kicks. I suppose this relieved the pressure of bone on bone within the joint. Everyone in my classes had to do plenty of those techniques at that time.

The fourth significant thing was the marriage of my daughter, Debbie, to my student and training partner, Keith Geyer (six times South African All Styles Open Kumite champion), in 1985.

In 1986 the fifth significant thing happened in the form of the arrival of our first grandchild, Dean (now a junior karate champion).

The sixth significant thing was my visit in 1986 to Japan, where I participated in an instructors' *gashuku* in the mountains, run and taught by the doyen himself, Nakayama Sensei. This *gashuku* was significant for me because it heralded the end of a golden era of karate-*do,* and because it was the last time I saw Nakayama Sensei alive.

What I remember most vividly was the Friday night of that *gashuku* because it was different from other previous *gashukus*. Normally, after training had ended for the day, more than 150 black belts would all eat supper together. Then everyone would go their own way. Some would go for a walk, a few would group together in a room or in the foyer to renew friendships, while others would go to bed, preparing for the full Saturday schedule of six hours of training, ending with *dan* gradings for the eligible candidates.

On a number of those *gashukus* I was invited into the inner sanctum, Nakayama's room, where about a dozen of the association's most senior instructors would share experiences. There was always a spirit of harmony and humor surrounding Nakayama Sensei.

During those few unforgettable evenings with Nakayama Sensei and the likes of Tabata, Oishi, Tanaka, Nakamura, Imura, Osaka, Ochi, Iida, Enoeda, Kon, and a few others, Nakayama would turn to me every now and then and talk in English, including me in the conversation, or he would explain to me what the conversation was all about. Although I was miles away, language-wise, I always felt warm and at home with the groups surrounding the Master.

Beyond Spirit of the Empty Hand

The Friday evening of the 1986 *gashuku* was different from other *gashukus* because Nakayama Sensei did something out of the norm. He announced that he wanted to talk to all of us in the dining room after dinner.

This announcement canceled the various plans some of the karate-*ka* had arranged for after dinner. I sensed that some of the younger ones were a little put out by this change in schedule. The Japanese like to stick faithfully to any schedule they are involved in, often becoming more than disgruntled when someone moves the goal-posts. But in retrospect, this spontaneous talk by Nakayama Sensei to the cream of his instructors and students was a highly significant event. For he died just a few days before the 1987 *gashuku*.

I did not understand all of what he said on that Friday night. But somehow, a spirit of wisdom and caring seemed to fill that dining hall. At one point, someone tapped me on the shoulder and whispered: "He now talking about you, Mister Stan, and Minami-Afrika (South Africa). He say you not Japanese but you are like *samurai* and some other South African instructors also have good fighting spirit. Big compliment for you, Mister Stan. Because he also say we Japanese instructors must not forget *samurai* spirit."

That night of our last dinner with Nakayama, he also told us a story about a bird and an egg. As he told this story, it was like a veil was lifted from my eyes. I somehow new exactly what he was saying. His gestures were clear and he used simple language, with a few English words included. The gist of the story was this:

> The small speck on the distant horizon grew larger. And then they saw it had wings. It was a big bird, an old bird, a well-traveled bird, coming home for the last time to roost.
>
> It laid one egg and faithfully warmed the egg with its body and feathers. When it was time, the bird stood aside. The egg split. A scrawny little form determinedly pecked its way out of the confines of the shell.
>
> The big bird nurtured the small form, feeding it, protecting it, keeping it warm until it had grown a fine plumage and was standing upon its own two feet, ready, waiting, watching the big bird fly in and out of the nest.
>
> Then, one fine spring day, the young bird stepped onto the highest branch and flew away toward the blue horizon.

Meeting Myself

"This is *shu-ha-ri*," said Nakayama. "All instructors must try to understand this."

The seventh significant thing happened a year later when, in April, 1987, I flew again to Tokyo, together with Norman Robinson and Kathy Shaw, to attend Nakayama's Sensei's instructors' *gashuku*.

Our usual routine was to arrive in Tokyo, book in at the Asia Center, have noodles or rice pilaf at "Jack and Betty's" in Roppongi, a night life area 20 minutes walk from the Asia Center. The next day we would visit Tokaido Company, the famous martial arts supply store in Iidabashi.

On the morning of 16 April, 1987, we entered the front door of this shop, which was packed with karate-*gi*, *makiwaras*, belts, badges, tracksuits, books, and video tapes. Also displayed were Okinawan weapons such as *nunchaku, sai, tonfa,* and a host of other martial arts gear and equipment. I immediately sensed something was wrong. The usually smiling faces of Mr. Sugiura, the owner, and his son, Taro, were somber.

Mr. Sugiura ushered us into his office and quietly conveyed to us a most devastating message.

"Very sorry," he paused for a time, gathering himself. "Nakayama Sensei ... yesterday die."

It was like a bolt of lightning had struck our small group of three. We went back to the Asia Center in a complete daze. Something very unreal and disturbing was happening to us. We were experiencing a living nightmare—like we would wake up soon to find this was only a bad dream. According to Mr. Sugiura, Okazaki Sensei from the USA was at Nakayama's bedside just before he died. Okazaki Sensei later told me that Nakayama's last wish was for harmony among the many different karate factions.

Tanaka telephoned us at 5:30 that afternoon and told us that the *tsuya* (death watch) would be held at Nakayama Sensei's private home *dojo*, Hoitsugan, at sunset. We borrowed three black arm bands from the Asia Center receptionist and took a fast cab to Ebisu station. Black-tied, black-suited JKA instructors, staff, and students lined the entire roadway from Ebisu station to Hoitsugan *dojo*, each one bowing as we passed.

At the entrance of Hoitsugan, we signed an attendance list presented to us by Mister Osaka and Miss Nomura. They looked as shattered as we must have looked.

After joining Mister Kon, Shunsuke Takahashi, and Tanaka, we filed into the *dojo* and one by one, we sprinkled incense over a flame, which faced a little shrine with a photograph of Nakayama Sensei hung above it.

As we filed out again, we were each given a present consisting of a small bottle of *sake* and a packet of green tea, a token of appreciation from Nakayama Sensei's wife, two sons, and family. Outside we met Tabata, who told us to go to *honbu dojo,* five minutes walk from Hoitsugan. The normally stark, shining wooden floor of the expansive *dojo* was covered with tables laden with drinks and eats.

"He wants us not to be sad at his passing—only to remember him and be of good cheer," said the toastmaster.

We drank, ate, and talked with Seto, Yamaguchi, Yamamoto, Sakata, and so many other loyal followers of Nakayama Sensei.

On Friday, 17 April, we returned again to attend the *sogi* (funeral). This time there were many more people attending a service held on the floor of the Hoitsugan *dojo.* Rows of chairs faced the far wall where Nakayama Sensei's coffin was placed, surrounded by colorful decorations. On Thursday, 23 April, we attended the official funeral in Shinano-machi.

Thousands of people lined the roadway, many holding up high, large, circular wreaths mounted on long sticks. We registered at a long line of tables. Leading into the ceremonial hall were a host of white chrysanthemums with wooden name plates interspersed among the flowers sent by mourners.

We stood at the back of the hall, which was packed with hundreds of people. We looked down onto a wide-spread altar arrayed with an intricate display of color consisting of flowers, carvings, and other artifacts.

A large portrait of the sensei was backed up by a sea of red and white carnations forming the JKA symbol of the red rising sun against a larger white circular moon. A wide expanse of greenery framed this awesome presentation honoring him.

A terraced part of the altar leading up to and to the sides and back of the portrait were filled with bunches of fruit—apples, melons, a golden eagle carving, and other intricate, colorful tapestries adorning the altar—as well as lanterns of stone and wood. To the sides, four fir trees kept vigil over the proceedings. A long table draped in scarlet cloth with "Japan Karate Association" inscribed in black upon it held a central position at the front of the hall.

The chief priest was dressed in a golden robe with a towering head dress which pointed skywards. Subdued, deep throated chanting resonated through the hall. The odor of incense permeated the atmosphere. After the prayers, speeches of praise and honor were given by the FAJKO head, the JKA president, the Takudai (Nakayama Sensei's university) president, and by Sensei Hidetaka Nishiyama.

We approached the Nakayama family and exchanged bows.

Hundreds of people, unable to enter because of the large attendance, still stood outside as we were leaving.

The last thing we did was to throw salt over our shoulders like *sumo* wrestlers. It is a Japanese custom supposed to chase away evil spirits.

"Take It With Your Own Hand"

Before I returned to South Africa, Seto invited me for dinner. We talked for hours about Nakayama Sensei. We felt it was sad that only after a great man like him departs from this world, does one begin to realize just how great he was. We agreed that he developed outstanding instructors who pioneered and fostered Shotokan karate worldwide. Furthermore, he produced a series of books and video tapes at a technical level that is unsurpassed. But most of all, we remembered him for his acceptance, understanding, and sincere interest in all of us.

As we were leaving the restaurant, Seto turned to me.

"What about *nana* (seventh) *dan*? You are now a long time sixth *dan*. How long now, Stan?"

"Eight years, Seto."

"Why do you not take seventh *dan* examination?"

"Because no one asked me to take the exam. Nakayama Sensei always used to tell me when he wanted me to try for the next *dan*."

"Stan, next year you must take seventh *dan* examination."

"Seto, unless they ask me, I'm not going to ask."

"Why not?"

"Because it is a loss of face for me to ask such a thing. When I am good enough, they will see. They will tell me."

"Mister Stan, I know that you admire the old *samurai* way. But now that Nakayama Sensei is gone, things will be different."

"How do you mean, Seto?"

"Okay. Now I tell you, Stan. In JKA I have no power because I am only a business man." He stood there, all five foot of him, staring up into my eyes, his eyes alight with passion. "But you, you train very hard. You always come to Japan. You chose the hard

Beyond Spirit of the Empty Hand

way. But now everything will be different." he repeated. I waited. He continued with strong words.

"You have good spirit and power. So you must take seventh *dan* with your hand."

"How do I do that?"

"I am not seventh *dan,* so I don't know. This is a very special level. You must do something special." Again he repeated, "Take it with your own hand."

16

THE ROAD TO SEVENTH DAN

Meeting Myself

"You think"

"'Take it with your hand,'" I thought. But I couldn't figure out how to go about preparing for such a big step—except for continuing with my regular hard training and visits to Japan. There was no one for me to ask exactly what the criteria were, because no Westerner had ever graded to seventh *dan* with the Japan Karate Association.

Heeding what Seto had told me, I bounced a question off Tanaka Sensei a day or two later.

"Sensei, can you give me some idea how I should go about preparing for *nana-dan*?"

He gave me two words of advice: "You think." And that was that.

Soon after my arrival back in South Africa, I had a sudden inspiration. I looked back through old records and found what Nakayama Sensei had written down regarding the seventh *dan* level:

> "You must have undertaken advanced research through actual application and extensive testing of the general research technique."

For the past 30 years I had been training, testing, and applying a number of techniques—some in very real confrontations.

"Do something," my little inner voice suggested. "Okay," I thought, "I will. I will do a report."

Ushiro-geri (back kick) sprung to mind. My Japanese nickname in the 60s, after all, had been "Mister Back Kick." Why not go back full circle and do a report with *ushiro-geri* as the corner stone? I had practiced thousands of *ushiro-geri* against a mark on the coal shed wall of my mother's house. In March 1963, a few days before my first visit to Japan, I kicked the wall and it fell down.

Finally, after much soul searching, I produced a report and posted it to Tanaka and forgot about it. Some time later, Tanaka contacted me saying that he enjoyed reading it. (I had had it translated into Japanese). He said he would pass it on to the head of the instruction department.

The headings of my report were:

- *Ushiro-geri* and the contemporary state of karate-*do*
- *Ushiro-geri* appears in Shotokan kata as a hidden technique
- Qualities and problems in the application of *ushiro-geri*
- *Ushiro-geri* as *tokui waza*
- *Ushiro-geri* as form and spirit.

I concluded the report with this:

> Like a growing cherry tree
> A technique develops *character* as it moves
> Through many life cycles—taking *form*.
> It first takes root in the mind
> Of the *sincere* karate-*ka*
> Who bows in *reverence* towards the technique
>   And to those who reveal the way.
> He struggles to take hold of the technique,
> He toils with increasing *effort*.
> As the technique becomes an adult tree
>   A measure of *self-control* is achieved.
> It appears complete with sturdy
>   stem and branches.
> But not until the tree bursts
>   into blossom,
> Revealing even momentarily its
>   excellent and unique *spirit* -
>   It is special.

The Golf Drive and the Reverse Punch

Golf seems to be a form of recreation common to quite a number of karate-ka. Nakayama Sensei saw the body rotation in golf as similar to the way a karate-ka generates power through the use of the hips.

Our association holds a golf day, a least four times a year, at Sun City. Some leaders of other styles sometimes participate. Tanaka is often the guest of honor at these highly competitive events arranged by Keith Geyer. Everybody takes this very seriously—all in good fun, of course. And there are usually some attractive money prizes for the winners in various categories. After Tanaka Sensei captured two good wins, I decided I needed to go to a golf pro in order to catch up with him. We both play off the same handicap, and I will not tell you what it is. But more than this, I was becoming frustrated, scratching around in the very thick, thorny rough of the Gary Player Country Club at Sun City. There are poisonous snakes and even the odd crocodile lurking around waiting to terrorize desperate duffers like me.

As fortune would have it, three golf pros came into my life in close succession. Ed Holding, the golf coach-*kung fu* man who liked karate, taught me the basics at the Bobby Verwey Jnr Driving Range. He would tie my arms up with rubber bands, trying to get me to keep my flapping elbows in.

"Like you do in karate," he would chide me. But do you think I could ever get that right? No way. Golf-wise my arms seemed to have a mind of their own. But at least I progressed from slicing and duck-hooking the ball, to just hooking that confounded little white teaser.

Bobby Verwey Jr., a pro on the local circuit and owner of the driving range, would watch me, and in a gentle way eventually coaxed some nice drives out of my painful body. My hips were gradually deteriorating from the auto accident, and even the golf swing produced pain in my lower back, especially when I stupidly attempted to hit the ball onto the M1 motorway, only to reach the 150 meter marker. Bobby and I became good friends, and we would spend hours having little chipping and putting competitions at the range.

Wayne Westner is now an international golf star. In 1996 he and his partner, the famous Ernie Els, walked away with the World Cup of Golf by a record margin of 18 strokes against international teams composed of major winners, such as Steve Jones, Tom Lehman, and many others.

One Friday evening in 1989, I was sparring with various members of my Melrose *dojo* black belt squad. My right hip was quite sore, and I was increasingly finding that the swiveling movements of kata training were hurting me. So I opted for free sparring training, with particular concentration on blocking, keeping a firm shortish stance, and refraining from bouncing around like a lot of all-styles competitors do today. Taking this simple approach improved my blocking abilities considerably and restored some of the confidence I had lost after the auto accident.

On this particular Friday, I noticed a man standing outside the sliding door of the *dojo*, quietly watching the training, which turned out to be a pretty rough session. After the class I ran out pouring with sweat and wanting to take a shower, but the man stopped me.

"I want to be like that," he said.

"Like what?" I was impatient to take a shower.

"I like the way you move. So calmly. My name is Wayne Westner."

"Oh, Wayne Westner!" I recognized him immediately. "Sorry, I was in such a hurry, I didn't realize it was you. What are you doing here?"

Wayne was already well known in South African golfing circles, having won a number of titles including the South African Open. What's more, I had been at high school with his father, Eldred Westner, a golfing buddy of my other school pal, Gary Player.

"I need you to get me disciplined and into shape," said Wayne.

That evening Wayne and I talked for three hours. Wonderful stuff; stuff that penetrated the mind and body of both karate and golf. We got on like lifetime friends, both of us enthusiastically demonstrating and discussing the various parallels of the two arts. This dynamic communication continues today.

The next Monday, Wayne enrolled as a white belt student and gave a full six months of his precious time to taking instruction and sweating it out and learning the dynamics of the art of the empty hand.

"Through training I am learning that minimal effort is required to produce the perfect golf swing," he said. "I've got to stop *trying* to do it. I must allow the club head to do it."

When I asked him how he manages to hit the ball such amazing distances, he said, "It's because I leave the club head behind the moving mass of my body longer than most pros. It must stay linked to my mass—remain poised—relaxed until the final strike, which just happens like cracking a whip. Certain karate moves and the golf swing are very similar. On my own I'll be doing karate/golf katas, as I will not be able to attend regular *dojo* training.

"Like karate, the golf swing is one continuous blow. Like this." He demonstrated the golf/karate kata he had developed. He took a *kiba-dachi* stance and then explained while demonstrating the following.

"The backswing is a block, like this." He rotated his body, and an *uchi*-uke, inside forearm block, materialized next to his right ear. The back of his open right hand formed the block. His right arm had moved because his body had moved. His left arm was straight, like it was reaching out to pluck fruit from a tree to the right of him.

"For the downswing, I drop my weight onto my left leg, like this." He dropped into a back stance, facing away from the target with left leg bent, and his left arm descended with increasing speed like a downward block, with the right arm still attached and bent. As his arms reached the six o'clock position, he literally did a downward reverse punch. His right arm snapped straight like he was punching downwards at an imaginary ball. As his right arm straightened, the left arm folded into a perfect *uchi-uke* There was a distinct, whip-like crack as his arms reversed their original position and his hips smoothly rotated to the left, drawing the arms fluidly up past his left ear. He added a little right front kick.

"Comes out of the flow," he smiled.

His dream was to enter the international scene of golf and go right to the very top, "Where I belong." We both agreed this was his destiny.

We had been hitting balls one day for about 10 minutes when he stopped me. He pointed to the ground where his feet had been while he punched out a series of 400-yard drives. The cropped grass looked neat and unmarked. Then he pointed to where my feet had been doing my "mammoth" 180-yard drives. I had managed to create two ugly *dongas* (ditches) with my feet.

"Stan, you have to learn to be soft-footed. You're destroying the grass and hampering your natural flow."

I felt goose pimples on my neck. It was uncanny. Tanaka had told me the very same thing about my karate a few months before this.

1988

In March, I left for Japan armed with a back kick and a thorough knowledge of the kata, *Tekki Sandan,* or so I thought.

I had been training a lot on this kata due to the fact that my hips did not hurt when I did it. Doing a right back kick also temporarily relieved the steady ache in my right hip area.

Wayne Westner and Masahiko Tanaka had both told me to be more soft-footed. Now I had no option but to be light footed. Hard, tense movements hurt, whereas I didn't feel as much discomfort when I did soft moves.

Beyond Spirit of the Empty Hand

At *honbu dojo*, Tokyo, I practiced back kick every day in many ways—on the stem of the *makiwara*, against various sub-instructors, and on the roof garden of the Asia Center against a towel hanging from a washing line.

With reverse punch, one rotates the hips forward. Back kick requires that the hips rotate quickly in the opposite direction. My main form of training was to assume a kind of back stance fighting *kamae* (set up position), with my left foot forward and both feet in line with the target. Through thousands of repetitions of this kick, I eventually discovered that if my feet were in line, the kick would home directly in on the target (the opponent's stomach). Also, I achieved better balance at the critical halfway stage of the move. I would snap my hips around at a quick rate and easily stop with my right knee raised up, balanced, poised, and ready to release the kick.

If I took up a conventional fighting stance with feet slightly apart, the natural path of my kick would project just past the right side of my opponent, missing him. By placing my feet in a back stance, in line with my opponent's solar plexus, the kick would flow easily in the right direction.

I did a lot of work and soul searching on the roof of the Asia Center, sometimes around midnight with the subdued roar of Tokyo traffic, the winking lights of the Tokyo Tower ever present, and the intermittent police car sirens sounding off in the distance.

It was only after I had arrived at the *gashuku* camp venue (again with Norman Robinson and Kathy Shaw), that the possibility of taking a grading examination became a reality.

On the Friday after training, one of the instructors happened to ask me if I would be taking a *dan* grading examination.

"I don't know," I answered.

"Tomorrow afternoon is *dan* grading examinations. You want try?"

Norman urged me, "Go on, Stan. Do it!"

I filled in the necessary registration forms and didn't get much sleep that night, working out how I should approach the test. Luckily, a Japanese karate-ka whom I didn't recognize and who was also registering alongside me, gave me a vague idea of what was going to happen on the morrow. But he, too, seemed to be somewhat in the dark regarding the required procedure. All he told me was, "*Nana-dan* test—you demonstrate *tokui* (favorite) *waza* and do *tokui* kata."

Meeting Myself

"Nice to be so filled in on what's going on," I thought. The upper echelons of JKA karate are men of few words. You're just expected to know what's going on. If, by some remote chance, you actually get to find out what is going on, it seems like it happened by pure accident—like the way I had found out at the last minute that I was now entitled to attempt a higher grading.

That night, lying awake, my mind worked overtime. The back kick: variations of approach, like first leading in with a jab punch and following with the kick. Or switching back as my imaginary attacker started his attack, to create an opening and good distance, and the kick homing in on the target. Variation after variation flooded my mind. I thought of the *samurai* axiom, "I have no limbs; I make promptitude my limbs."

I would show the panel that the back kick was a unique, unusual, and powerful technique, often neglected in basic training, and that it was therapeutically necessary as a counter-balance to front kick training. In other words, "If you work the front, then work the back, too."

I would show them that *ushiro geri* subtly existed as a "hidden technique" in some of the 15 Shotokan kata. For example, a back kick was just asking to be executed when entering the third move of *Heian Shodan* (A straight line kick from $0°$ to $180°$). Then in kata number two, it lay there waiting to be done on move number 12, after the spear hand thrust (a $270°$ turning back kick before the knife hand block). Furthermore, in kata number three, its most obvious application was in move number nine, after the spear hand thrust (to be done with a full $360°$ turn as the opponent grabs one's hand and twists it).

Already there were three angular variations of the back kick in the first three kata. My mind rushed on, creating, discarding, reshaping, and finally arriving at the simple clarity of three important points.

Three Important Points

Three tables lined the main wall of the grading hall. At the first table, fourth *dan* examinations were already taking place. The second table was for fifth *dan*. Behind the third table, sat the Masters grading panel for sixth and seventh *dan*. Assisting them with the paperwork was the young instructor, Naka, with whom I had

Beyond Spirit of the Empty Hand

trained a lot and who I respected for his quick techniques and friendly attitude. Only three of us were attempting seventh *dan*. There were bigger groups attempting fourth and fifth *dan* at the other tables.

It took close to one hour of waiting and watching, never sure when my name would be called. As it was, my name was called last.

The chairman of the grading panel asked if I needed an interpreter, and someone stepped forward to assist me with the first part of the examination, which, after watching the others, was confirmed to be a presentation and demonstration of one's special technique, *tokui waza*. I felt confident now as my previous soul searching had been on the right track.

"You have five minutes," he said.

As I bowed to the seven *Shihans* of the grading panel and announced my topic, "*Ushiro Kekomi Geri*," I noticed that grading activities at the other two tables had stopped, and everybody in the grading hall was watching my presentation. Unusual, I thought, and commenced by raising three fingers and saying, "I have three important points to demonstrate to all of you! Number one, back kick is unusual. Number two, it is powerful and yet therapeutic. Number three, it is a hidden technique in some of our Shotokan kata."

A couple of the members of the panel sat forward, looking interested. I demonstrated each of my three points against an opponent. Not once did the panel question me. Normally they would call up a tough opponent to see whether one is able to make one's *tokui waza* work in a real *kumite* situation. But the whole hall watched in rapt silence.

In conclusion, I told them that because back kick requires that you turn, losing sight of your opponent, I had found that a closed stance (back stance) shortened the rotating and turning time of the technique. With that, I spun around in mid-sentence and stopped dead, balancing on one leg, looking directly at the panel.

"Speed and balance are very important!" I continued. It was about the best turn I had ever done. Maybe it was because I wasn't thinking too hard. It just seemed to happen spontaneously.

The entire hall, including the other grading candidates and examiners, erupted in applause. I was astounded.

As the examiners wrote down my result, Naka bounced out of his seat, grinning and holding his arm up. His finger and thumb formed a circle meaning "good pass." Immediately one of the panel pulled him back onto his chair, admonishing him with a frown for letting the cat out of the bag. I must admit that this was a heartwarming momemt.

About 15 minutes later, when I presented my kata, *Tekki Sandan*, things didn't feel quite right. I did the kata at a frantic pace, trying so hard to be faster than fast in my hand movements, in order to make up for the fear of having to protect my hip.

No results were given. As we walked out of the hall, one of the examiners said something to me that I will never forget. And it wasn't so much *what* he said, but the *way* he said it that made me want to kill. His face contorted as if I had just committed some unforgivable sin, and with an unmistakable expression of contempt, he said just this, "Why you do *Tekki Sandan?*" As he turned to go, pure anger flooded my entire being. His attitude made me feel like a wild animal—most vicious when wounded. I wanted to punch him hard, right in the teeth, and tell him, "Didn't you know I was crazy with pain and worry over my sore hip?"

Instead, I bit my lip, looked directly into his eyes, and uttered a gruff, *"Osu!"*

Today, I thank him for being so direct and hard on me. He made me angry, and anger, I believe, can be a great motivator, provided you don't allow it to become hate, in which case it will devour you. This did not happen, thank God.

A day later, when I heard from one of the karate-ka that I had not passed, I loudly announced to Norman and Kathy, and whoever else was in hearing distance, "I'll show them! You watch me!"

Too Sharp!

Norman suggested that we make an appointment with Asai Sensei and ask him what went wrong.

"Stan, your *tokui waza* was excellent. Everybody applauded, and I thought your hand movements were very crisp in your kata," Norman said.

Two days later, we sat facing Asai. Norman spoke. He was doing things the Japanese way—a go-between for delicate matters. He got to the point immediately.

"Sensei," he asked, "Why did Stan not pass?"

"His *tokui waza* okay, but kata, ummmm...," he paused, looking down.

Beyond Spirit of the Empty Hand

"Sensei, I thought that his hand movements were fast. What did he do wrong?"

"Too sharp!" he said. "Maybe better he do other kata next time."

"Thank you, Sensei. When can Stan do this?"

"Maybe six month's time. Kata only. Not necessary he do *kumite* again."

I left Japan re-motivated. Norman had suggested I go back to my original favorite kata, *Chinte,* and that I dedicate 100 percent of my training purely to *Chinte*. This was about the best bit of practical advice I had received in a long time.

Specialized Training

For a solid six months, I trained nearly every day exclusively on *Chinte* kata. It was an amazing experience. This focused training changed me. And change is what reaching a higher *dan* level is all about. Over this period, I did *Chinte* an average of 15 times a day. It doesn't sound like much, but if you count it up over a six-month period, it is one big sackful of kata. Two thousand, seven hundred, to be exact.

What about my hips? Well, right after returning from Japan I visited Frans Weber, one of the world's foremost orthopedic surgeons, who's *tokui waza*—special expertise—is hip joint replacement surgery.

"You're going to need a hip replacement within the next couple of years," he told me.

"When must I have it done?"

"When it gets too painful to bear any longer."

"And what about my karate training until then?" I wanted to know. "Will I hurt myself? I have a grading to do."

"Go at it hammer and tongs." He was serious. "It is not going to make that much difference in the end. So enjoy your training, while you still can. Go for your goal."

"Why? Will I not be able to do karate with a new hip?"

"Of course you will, but you will have to approach your training with circumspection. You don't want to do silly things."

"Such as?"

"Flying kicks over garden walls," he joked.

Frans Weber's words had given me new life. I would do just that. Go hammer and tongs at *Chinte* kata. Of course, I would not do anything stupid to put unnecessary strain on my body. But I would not worry anymore about over-protecting my hip like I did in Japan when I chose to do *Tekki Sandan* because of feeling insecure.

The insecurity I carried inside of me must have transmitted itself to the grading panel. A true grading is where strength is supposed to manifest itself—strength of character, strength of technique, and strength of spirit. All human beings have some weakness, but whatever it is, it should not be entertained or revealed to one's opponent, and a good grading panel is most certainly one's opponent—a formidable opponent. At last I understood Seto's words: "Take it with your hand!" Now I was learning that if you show even one weakness, they'll stand on you. Set weakness aside. Reveal your excellence. Conquer their doubts with your strength of spirit.

Now I was choosing to do *Chinte*, which was always my special kata, with a strength of purpose that surprised even me. I had always wanted to do everything in my training. Now I was actually enjoying the challenge of doing one thing properly.

Some of the Early Bird trainers must have thought I was crazy. They would be doing their normal training under Derrick or Keith Geyer, and there I was outside, striking a horizontal *makiwara* with hundreds of repetitions of *nakadaka ippon ken uchi otoshi* (dropping one-knuckle-fist strike). I had placed a *makiwara* board across two sturdy tree branches and would hit downward with the heel of my palm, like a cricket bowler delivering a fast ball. This overhead strike, as well as other moves from *Chinte* kata, changed the way I did free fighting. I was later able to catch various opponents with some of these unusual techniques, many of which are extremely effective.

Not only did I do free fighting and *makiwara* work using moves from *Chinte*, I also did a lot of *bunkai* (application of kata movements), every day, against my students, coming from all directions at me.

Because of the discomfort in my neck and hips, I had not performed a demonstration in public since my accident. Even before the accident, I was reluctant to do a kata for a demonstration as I felt kata wasn't really my *forte*. Now I planned to revisit Japan in September 1988, to train and to re-perform my kata for the grading panel. In order to prepare for this challenge, I decided to do a demonstration at our South African Championships. I would perform *Chinte* kata—with a difference. This was quite a big challenge for me, performing the kata in front of all of my students and colleagues after being out in the cold for the past four years.

On the day of the championships, I performed the kata. Then I did it again, surrounded by opponents. Some of them held pieces of wood, while others attacked me. Thus, I performed the kata, but this time, wood breaking and *bunkai* were integrated into the sequence.

I don't know how good it looked, but doing it in front of more than 1,000 people gave me renewed confidence.

"Okay, You Change Flight"

I arrived in Japan for the second time that year. I went through the instructor training, and judged at the All Japan Championships, but I said nothing about grading. I felt, as usual, that someone would approach me about it. With a few days to go before I was due to return to South Africa, I approached Asai Sensei after training one day and asked him if he could look at and correct my *Chinte* kata.

"Oh, me now very busy with championships and many visitors from overseas," he said.

"Sensei, I need you to look at my kata. I will be available at any time you choose."

"Okay, Mister Stan. Thursday I train very early at *honbu dojo*. My own training. You come after I finish training at 8 a.m."

I arrived early and what I saw from the doorway impressed me. Asai was traversing the length and breadth of the *dojo* floor, executing an exciting array of circular moves, dropping and rising, changing direction with ridge-hand strikes, knife-hand strikes, and all kinds of punches and kicks. I concluded he was doing his own, spontaneous, free-movement kata, which was extremely creative, and which was exhilarating to watch. I subsequently have seen Tanaka Sensei do a similar thing.

As Asai finished, he walked up to me. Perspiration was pouring from his brow.

"You show me *Chinte*."

For the next 20 minutes, Asai was onto my every move.

"Again, Stan. Drop more. Again. Relax shoulders. Next two moves quickly. Once more, smooth. Legs more fast." And so on, non-stop.

Meeting Myself

As he said, "*Yame!* Now better!" I nearly kissed him. I was so stressed out from the training, my legs wobbled as I descended the stairs.

He told me, "You try seven *dan* grading on Monday."

"Sensei, my flight leaves on Monday morning."

"Okay, you change flight."

"Okay, Sensei. Thank you!" I changed my flight.

Monday arrived far too slowly.

There was a group of about 16 black belt karate-ka from all over the world, ready to grade. We lined up in front of a very large panel that included Asai, Ueki, Tanaka, Enoeda, and four or five other members of the *shihankai*.

I kept doing warming up exercises each time a candidate went on to grade. There was an assortment of first *dans* up to fifth *dan*. I was the only one going for seventh *dan*. After warming up and cooling down about 10 times, I was finally called up, last again. It had taken about an hour and a half. No water, and I had sweat profusely during those false-start warm-ups.

I strode across the wide *dojo* floor toward my opponent, the grading panel. I looked straight into their eyes and walked like a *samurai* warrior. I was about to do *Chinte* kata, but my entire being was keyed up to do *kumite*.

I stopped on the designated mark and bowed slowly but surely. I took up a ready position, waited, and looked ahead, my gaze looking right through and way past the people on the panel.

I announced, *"Chinte!"* in a voice that would wake the dead. Every one of my previous pent-up emotions was coming out now, and I literally exploded into the kata after smoothly completing the first two, slow bottom fist strikes. The rest I do not remember. The kata performed itself. It was only as I made the final turn and executed the scissors punch toward the front, that I clearly saw three members of the panel nodding their heads and handing their marks to the panel chief.

17

UPS AND DOWNS

Meeting Myself

After receiving seventh *dan* in 1988, my life up to the mid-1990s was like a mammoth roller-coaster ride, filled with a variety of traumatic lows, which were contrasted with wonderfully uplifting highs. But never was there one dull moment.

Tanaka Sensei's visit in 1989 coincided with serious hospitalization for my training partner and son-in-law, Keith, who, having undergone a routine knee operation, suffered the near loss of his leg because of a serious infection in the knee joint. As a result of surgical incompetence and incorrect aftercare, he suffered months of indescribable agony, lying in bed on his back, which left him with a frozen knee joint. This was a heavy blow for such a champion of champions. But, champion that he is, he rose above his hardship and again trains daily with the Early Birds. He continues to produce world class competitors.

When I took Tanaka to visit him in the hospital, Tanaka's face was grave.

"Keith now face biggest challenge of life. Not easy for young champion, this."

And then later addressing me he said: "Stan, I see you limping. Why?" I didn't think anybody had noticed, but nothing escaped Tanaka's canny eyes.

"Soon I will need a hip operation, Sensei."

"What about your karate?"

"I'll be okay, Sensei."

Leading into the 1990s I was totally golf mad. My hip didn't allow me to express myself fully in karate, so with the help of Wayne Westner and Bobby Verwey Jr., I studied the art of golf. I spent at least two hours a day trying to master the basic swing. Wayne showed me a way of striking the ball in a type of back stance facing away from the target, so that I didn't place pressure on my right hip joint. It worked quite well, with my handicap dropping from 26 to 18.

The arrival of four new grandchildren—Jessica Geyer, Sean Hildyard, Tatum Geyer, and Christy Hildyard—brought welcome light into all of our lives. In keeping with the family tradition, Jessica (Debbie and Keith Geyer's daughter), became the Under 9 World WKF Kata Champion in 1996.

In 1990, Judy and my other son-in-law, Mark Hildyard, had plans of opening a new health club at Melrose next to my karate school. The additions and alterations, including a half Olympic size pool, would cost over one million Rand, it was estimated.

"These kind of bucks are way out of my ballpark," I thought. But later during a golf game with a prominent banker, I joked with him as we stepped onto a green.

"Peter, how about a two million Rand loan?"

"What for?"

"For additions to my Melrose property."

"You mean that property with your karate on it, just off the M1 motorway?"

"Yes."

"Shouldn't be a problem," he said, lining up for a putt that rattled into the back of the cup. "Come and see me Monday."

My putt rocketed way past the hole. Was I hearing right?

Five years ago, this same bank had refused me a loan of 18,000 Rand for a piece of land I had wanted to buy at Plettenberg Bay, the popular coastal town where we had enjoyed *sashimi* with Tanaka and Yamaguchi.

The next week, my fellow shareholders and I had meetings with the architects. "The building alterations will cost you R636,000; the new pool, over R100,000; other improvements and costs, R100,000; and then you will need to service your loan as building operations progress. To be safe, borrow an extra R200,000 for this. All in all you will need to get a bond for about 1.1 million Rand."

The thought of borrowing extra money to pay interest on interest made me shudder. I wasn't used to such high-powered transactions. My fellow shareholders agreed that it was a good idea to expand the premises. "More rent in our pockets from the new health club," they said. But when the bank finally approved the loan, my fellow shareholders were not prepared to sign the bank papers, accepting even partial responsibility for the loan.

"Your signature will be sufficient," said the man from the bank. "You have a good name."

I wasn't sure whether this was a good thing or a bad thing at the time. Nevertheless, I signed for the loan on my own.

"Promises, Promises ...

Before I signed the actual building contract, the builder, who happened to be a student of mine, assured me that he would be able to complete the work for the agreed amount, if not for less, because I finally decided to do away with extra stairways and other items in the plan in order to save on costs. But like an impatient fool, I had not made any effort to have my lawyer friend and student, Ray Joffe, read the contract before signing it.

As the building operations progressed, so an escalating living nightmare began to haunt me almost daily. My karate was making me a living, but I personally did not have much money in the bank—only a share in the Melrose property. And large properties, I came to learn, are like financial black holes, swallowing up money at an alarming rate. Not long after building operations commenced, the builder began telling me, "Oh, it's going to cost a little more," and as the weeks sped by, he became the bearer of further bad news. "It's going to cost a little more." And, "a little more," and so it went. In desperation I went to Ray, who asked me why I hadn't shown him the contract sooner.

"It all favors the builder," he told me.

To make things worse, the pain in my hip had gotten so bad that I needed to have the hip replacement operation that I had been putting off for such a long time. It would cost in excess of 20,000 Rand, and this didn't include the instructors I would have to pay while I was convalescing. I didn't have any medical insurance, and my personal banking account was overdrawn.

The building was nearing completion, and the building contractor was already informing us that it was going to cost over 200,000 Rand more than the original contract price.

I kept kicking myself for going into a deal with people who couldn't keep their word. Not only did my hip cause me sleepless nights but the horror of this escalating financial monster—and how I could defeat it—ate at my heart and disturbed the lives of my entire family, who stood by me during this trying time.

Despite our fears of financial ruin, there remained some remote hope. Eighteen months before this building disaster, Ray Joffe had filed a claim with third party insurance regarding my auto accident. But these things take time and often come to nothing. So I wasn't banking on any extra money coming my way.

Deep Depression, Then ...

I entered the hospital in November 1990, and went through considerable mental, physical, and emotional traumas, which were aggravated by the builder's latest information that the amount due to the contractor would now be more than 300,000 Rand over the

Beyond Spirit of the Empty Hand

original agreed price. All of this, plus the physical pain of the operation and an embolism caused by a clot in my thigh, which developed during the long operation, dragged me down into the deepest depression I had ever experienced. I had hit rock bottom. Lying flat on my back on the fifth night after the operation, I refused to take any more pain killers.

"I've never seen this before," the nurse told me. But I did not want to escape into a drug induced haze where I had little control over myself.

Late that night I lay there watching the rain falling outside my window, which overlooked the hospital car park.

"Help me, God. I don't know where to turn," I pleaded aloud. "I cannot take all of this any longer." I felt powerless and sorry for myself. As a last resort, I challenged God—aloud.

"If you are there, God, come and speak to me. Help me! Otherwise, please let me die right now." I lay there, my head to one side, crying my eyes out. This was around midnight. The door of my ward opened and I sensed somebody standing next to my bed. As she spoke, I turned my head and saw that my visitor was a Black nurse.

"What's wrong?"

"I feel useless," I told her. "Maybe it's better I die."

"Where is your spirit, Mister Karate Man? Aren't karate champions supposed to have fighting spirit?" Her voice was soft and caring, yet challenging. I had to smile.

"You're right, but everything seems so bleak."

"Well, let me tell you a little story. I once felt like you do now, and my mother told me that if I counted my blessings, I would never stop."

"You're right," I repeated. "I do have plenty to live for. Thank you for caring."

Her reassuring hand touched my forehead. Then, as she left, she said, "Trust God."

Some little spark of strength was re-kindled in me. I would stand up and fight against the unfairness that was depressing me, and I would win by doing the right thing. I would fight the builder's unfair claim, and I would also fight to get myself fit and well again. I felt I had been bullied by too many things and too many people, and lying there on my back, with nothing to do, I thought about many things.

The bully pushes you around. You are puny and you know he is going to really hurt you. Or, maybe the bully has already hurt you. And, of course, the bully can hurt you physically, or psychologically, or both. The bully can be anything: A guy at the *dojo* or a sadistic husband. The bully can be a situation you are in, or a bodily ailment, or even a builder. The bully may even be you, when you are punishing yourself or attracting punishment from others. Run away from this truth, and in the end game you may be losing more than your teeth or your dignity.

To give in, I realized, was not the answer. Instead, I would let the bully be my motivation for healthy change. Did I want to be psychologically and physically stronger than *him* or *it?* Then I had to take the first step in conquering my fear of the bully. I would face the truth. Where wrong, I would make right. And when right, I would wipe out wrong, ruthlessly! I would plan, act, and be strong with the help of God.

Also, I remembered the words in that first karate book: "The karate man never stops training."

I reached into my kitbag and pulled out a flat river stone that had lain there dormant for too long. I held it in the palm of my hand and began to strike it with the other hand. The next morning a nurse came into my ward.

"Mr. Schmidt, what in heaven's name are you doing?"

"This is my new painkiller, a *makiwara,*" I replied.

"Nutcases, that's what you karate people are. Nutcases."

Later that day Ray Joffe popped his head into my ward.

"You're looking a little brighter than yesterday," he said. Then he pulled a small bottle of champagne and two small glasses out of his pocket. He filled the glasses, gave me one, raised his glass and called out: "*Lechaim,* Stan."

"*Lechaim,* Ray! Thanks, but why the champagne?"

"For two good things: For your speedy return to good health and ..." he paused.

"And what else?" I was curious because, judging by the impish expression on his face, I knew he was about to break some good news to me. I knew him too well. Good news and blessings were his regular way. "Come on, Ray, you've really got me going. What is it?"

"We got you 260."

"Two hundred and sixty what?"

"Two hundred and sixty thousand for you—for pain, suffering, and expenses. Two hundred and sixty thousand *Rand.* Is this all right by you, Stan?"

His eyes and mouth had spread into a wide, Cheshire cat smile.

Beyond Spirit of the Empty Hand

"What? Ray! I don't believe it! Two hundred and sixty thousand Rand! Is this true, or am I dreaming? Pinch me, man!"

I polished off the champagne in one shot. My depression had vanished, and as Ray left, I told him, "You're my guardian angel!"

"*Zai gezundt,*" ("Be well") he responded. "See you tomorrow. Is your hand strong enough to sign a few papers?"

"Never been stronger," I laughed a little too loudly.

"Thank you, Ray. Thank you, God," I said out loud to myself, as I started re-counting all of my blessings.

Back To White Belt

My friends, karate colleagues, and family were wonderfully supportive during my extended stay in hospital. Extended because of the seven-centimeter clot lodged in a vein in my thigh. Wayne Westner arrived one night with a full five-course meal prepared by himself, complete with expensive cutlery, crockery, and Guinness stout to wash down the meal and "to boost your red blood cell count," he claimed.

While I was in the hospital, a team of physiotherapists gave me an exercise schedule to do every two hours—first breathing exercises, then stomach, leg, back, and thigh routines. I had to learn to walk again with crutches, a few extra steps each day. And, of course, there was my stone-striking routine. So I kept pretty busy each day.

"The patients who follow the designated exercise routines from day one usually progress quickly," said the physiotherapists.

"The breathing exercises are boring," I told them. "How about me blowing a trumpet instead?" I told them that I had played the horn 30 years ago.

"That will be quite okay in place of your breathing exercises. You can go right ahead, but not here in the hospital, please!"

Funny how the Master arrives when the student is keen and ready. It was around that time that I met Robin Finlay, a brown belt karate-ka from another *dojo* who happened to play the trumpet in the South African Broadcasting Corporation National Orchestra. After leaving the hospital, we made a deal.

"You let me train in the Early Birds class, and I will teach you trumpet," he offered. The deal was on. He trained regularly and eventually made black belt, while I re-learned the rudiments of the horn.

Meeting Myself

"The correct breathing for trumpet is the same as for karate," he claimed. "Your lips don't blow the note. They have to be soft and pliable. The pure note comes from control of the lower abdomen and a good upright posture, which allows the free passage of air."

This was great. In learning the horn with a master concert performer, I was getting a fresh viewpoint about the functions of different types of breathing. This related directly to my karate and the better performance thereof.

Mike McLoughlin, a black belt from my club, took me under his wing and nurtured my music by inviting me once a week to play with him at his house garage music studio. Mike, director of an insurance brokerage, was previously a professional jazz pianist-keyboard player. I found that playing with him, Robin, and Johnny Maritz, a second *dan* percussion man from the SABC Orchestra, gave me immense inspiration and joy. When you interact with lions, you either become a lion or get devoured. In my case, I am still a musical cub, but who knows what the future holds. I enjoy nothing more than spending an entire Sunday evening jamming with Mike. Hours pass like shooting stars.

Rebuilding my physical strength took a long time, but right from the day I was permitted to walk with one crutch, about eight weeks after the operation, I left for Japan with a couple of my karate colleagues. South African Airways arranged a special seat for me on the plane, and in Japan I was kindly treated by all of the instructors. I attended JKA Chief Instructor Sugiura Sensei's training courses. Complete with crutch, I did as many hand techniques as I could manage. The leg movements I sat out for. But this training, despite my handicap, helped me recover quickly. It took more than one year to even approach full recovery. It was a step-by-step, daily, gentle progression. I felt like I was a white belt again, having to systematically go through all of the basic steps, but this time more thoroughly and sensibly.

When I heard the occasional report that someone had said, "Stan is finished, he's got a plastic hip," it motivated me all the more. I would prove them wrong. Sometimes it would get to me, but in the end, the negative rumors had a positive effect on me.

After the operation, I studied things concerning the body through Mark Hildyard, my son-in-law, a strength and conditioning expert and karate instructor. I re-examined karate technique, and many exciting concepts became more clear to me, like soft-footedness, the development of stable emotions, and the importance of maintaining a calm physical state to generate positive energy flow.

Mark stressed the importance of training, regaining and maintaining, as far as possible, a full range of motion of all of the joints in the body. He pointed out that many physical trainers concentrate purely upon aerobic fitness, while neglecting suppleness and range of motion.

"When people allow themselves to grow stiff and stick-like, they lose their youth," he said. "Suppleness and youthfulness go together. I devote at least 30 minutes of each 60-minute workout to slow stretching exercises for my older clients."

Some well-meaning people advised me to call it a day. "You've done it all. Sit back and enjoy the rest of your life," they advised. "Why do you stress yourself like you do?" It made me think about stress and what place it had in my world.

Stress

Stress in today's world has become a dirty word. The popular notion is that stress is responsible for heart attacks, ulcers, emotional breakdowns, divorces, and a host of diseases. Society increasingly tells us that we need new techniques, new instruments, new drugs, and new miracle methods to reduce or eliminate this so-called malady, stress. Many of the instant cures ("We'll do it for you; you lie back.") are exactly what *increase* stress or sickness. I believe that modern technological people need stress, but in the right doses and of the right kind. The word, stress, in essence, means state of physical or mental tension, or something inducing it.

Let us look at physical stress and see whether it is harmful or whether it can be beneficial to a person's well-being. I know of two "grannies," both in their early 80s. Both suffered falls that resulted in fractures in their hip joint area. Both had total hip replacements, but while their age and misfortune was similar, their respective resultant states of well-being were diametrically opposite. Granny A (I will call her) landed up bed-ridden and unable to move without the aid of others and, of course, suffered terrible emotional stress as a result of her physical state of degeneration. Granny A had never believed in exercise. "That's for the plebs," she always said. "A waste of good reading time." When she had pain, she popped a pill. She never put herself under much physical stress in her 80 years, living a typical, educated, urbane life. She was diagnosed as having advanced osteoporosis, another term for soft, de-mineralized bones. They had degenerated beyond repair and could just not support her overweight body anymore, nor could these crumbling bones adequately support the prosthesis that the surgeon inserted. It became loose and useless as a walking or supportive aid. She forever complained of being overweight and in pain, always stressed out, but she always put full trust in the most advanced medicines, gadgets, and treatments.

Granny B recovered quickly. She is back doing her regular daily walks with her family and dogs. She bowls twice a week, still goes to the gym, does light workouts and stretching regularly, and eats balanced meals. Her orthopedic surgeon, Frans Weber, told me that her post-operative recovery had been quick and successful.

"Why?" I asked, thinking of Granny A's predicament.

"Because her old bones were like young bones."

I knew why, but I asked him anyway. "Why is she different from those others?"

"Well, Stan, bones and muscles remain strong and pliable and healthy if they are put under regular stress. Overload, we call it. Bone and muscle cells die off and regenerate all the time. But they do so more effectively when they are made to work, made to move. Movement is life. Being static and resting is death. Mrs. B has always led an active life."

"She's quite sexy for 80," I added.

"Take care now, Stan," he smiled. Then, returning to my case, he advised me, "Be sensibly active, but not over-active!"

"How do I do that?"

"That's for you to find out."

It was good advice from Dr. Frans Weber, who had performed the operation on my hip.

He told me something similar to what he had said about Granny B. When I complained how much pain I was experiencing a few days after the operation, he just laughed, turned to the nurse, and said, "What does he expect?" And then he looked down from where he stood and in his mother tongue said, "Jy is so taai soos 'n ou ram (You are as tough as an old ram). I had to use an electronic scalpel and saw to get through those karate muscles and bones of yours. It was difficult to get into your hip area. That's why it's sore. But that's also why you have a good prognosis."

"But those old ladies in the other wards don't seem to be in pain like me. I feel like a sissy."

"Stan, when I operated on some of them I hardly needed a scalpel. Their muscles were so weak. Not good. They'll be okay for a little walking, but not for doing karate like you. Stan, *you* know about the human body. Just do your exercises gently and build your strength up again. Go to a good physio and then to an expert physical trainer, and be sure to gradually increase the work load in your training. Only do what your body and limbs are made to do and will allow you to do. If you go beyond your natural range of motion, especially with vigorous or jerky movements, you may harm not only your new hip, but other parts of your anatomy. And then of what use were all those hours of effort? Be wise. Train, but keep a watchful eye on every move you make, and you'll be fit for a long time still."

This little talk by Frans Weber was like gold. And it clearly put the role of *stress* into perspective.

After all the negative things I have said about modern technology, I now say, "Yes." We do need advanced technology. Frans Weber's technical expertise not only gave me new hips, it also gave me new life. But that was not the end of it. I, too, had my part to play, which I am still playing to this day. I keep reminding myself to remember this:

"One can only progress with a little healthy stress."

While most of the modern communication media want to lure you into sitting down on your butt, to vegetate and watch, while they do their little thing, karate does quite the opposite. It invites you to be active, to participate with every limb, sense, faculty, and brain cell you have.

Injury To The Body Of JKA, But The Soul Stays Healthy

At the same time that I was going through testing times, physical and financial, in South Africa, so was Japan JKA going through a major upheaval. Nakayama Sensei, the great leader, had passed away, and the inevitable happened. An instructor communicated the distressing news to me.

"I am sorry to tell you, Stan, but JKA have bad accident."

Although they tried to run the Association with eight or nine senior people at the helm, it took but a few short years for disagreement on the operation of the association to develop into a conflict of interests. The result was that a number of instructors split away from the main JKA organization. I will not go into the legal battle surrounding this split, as it detracts form the theme of this particular book. Suffice it to say that I chose to remain with the JKA, with Mr. Nakahara as President.

The instructors and staff of JKA had all moved out of Ebisu headquarters by 1994. The rent there had always been impossibly high, forever stretching the association's funds to the limit. In Tokyo, all rentals are ridiculously expensive. The JKA Association to which I belong moved a few blocks down the road into a new *honbu dojo,* which I will call Ebisu II. Ebisu II was more affordable and perfectly adequate for the association's training of instructors and administration of affairs.

My colleagues and I train at Ebisu II, and there is a fresh and dynamic spirit in the instructors' class. All instructors and student instructors are intimately involved, not only in the training, but also in the administration and running of the organization. A healthy division of labor has been created that trains, prepares, and educates the instructors both physically and mentally, and welcomes visitors from overseas.

-----oOo-----

Back in South Africa, the battle over the excess of over 300,000 Rand on the building contract raged on for more than a year. It was finally resolved when, in order to get rid of the dark cloud hanging over our lives, we reluctantly agreed to pay approximately 200,000 Rand above the contract price. The end of the saga was that the 260,000 Rand insurance payment from my auto accident was gobbled up in two swift swallows. Two hundred to the builder and about 60,000 for medical expenses and other losses incurred during my convalescence.

Back to Square One Again

I was back to square one again with one new hip, a bond of 1.1 million Rand over the property, which never ceased to be a source of aggravation, and my other hip starting to act up, as Dr. Weber had predicted.

Training, teaching, and visits to Japan and from Japanese instructors went on as normal. But by the end of 1992, my left hip became so bad that I booked a second operation with Dr. Weber. I had taken out a hospital plan with my old school friend, Neville

Beyond Spirit of the Empty Hand

Nathan, of Liberty Life Insurance Company, and I had prepared properly, both physically and psychologically, for the ordeal of the operation and post-operative months of stress and rehabilitation.

Suffice it to say that the second operation and recovery was more bearable than the first one. Although it still took more than one year for me to feel anywhere near normal, I suffered no further blood clots, and at least the insurance company paid for all of my medical expenses. Besides having to be very careful not to injure myself while training and instructing, two further burdens weighed down upon me.

My wife had to undergo a serious operation which, thank God, she recovered from totally. This was largely due, I believe, to her superb level of fitness from her 30 years as an aerobics instructor.

I had not managed to reduce the bond of 1.1 million Rand by one cent. Over four years we had literally scraped up just enough money to pay the bank about one million Rand, but this had merely covered the interest factor on the loan. The principal debt remained.

Furthermore, the Johannesburg City Council had been escalating their monthly water bills, electricity bills, and taxes at an alarming rate. Thus I had steadily crept deeper into the red. I tried to initiate different schemes for the property, such as the idea of adding a townhouse development, but this never materialized due to insufficient capital. I even went as far as putting my house up for sale, in an effort to reduce the heavy debt. I would either rent a house or build a small house on the *dojo* property at Melrose.

But South Africa was going through political upheaval at the time. People were leaving the country. Managing to sell a house for a reasonable price in Johannesburg at that time was as hard as trying to sell a pair of spectacles to a blind man.

I managed to keep a good, positive spirit because of three main factors: training every morning with the Early Birds, associating with loving friends and family, and being guided through some very testing spiritual battles by my friends, Pastors Ray McCauley (an ex-Mr. Universe), and Joe Peter.

"Love conquers fear," Ray had said, "but make sure it is the Godly kind of love that you seek, receive, and give out."

Through being humbled by certain experiences, I came to realize that I had been leading largely a selfish type of existence.

"You have to be careful that the object of your desire is of a beneficial nature; otherwise you may just get what you want," said Joe Peter.

Meeting Myself

Desire and faith are close friends. If one possesses enough of these two factors, one has the means of entering the gates of Heaven or the pits of hell. It's a matter of free choice as to which path we decide to take.

For example, I can say, "I want one million Rand. One million Rand is the object of my desire." Then I can say, "I have the faith to achieve this. I believe I will acquire one million Rand." Good. Nothing wrong with this so far. But *how* you gain the money and *what* you do with it will determine where you eventually end up.

One has to be strong because the path that leads to peace and joy is often precarious, like walking a high tightrope. You need courage to walk this road.

The Man With Spirit

I may have felt depressed at times but there was one person whose "long walk to freedom," gave me strength and inspiration—Nelson Mandela. This great man was jailed unjustly for twenty seven years. Then he was released from prison on the 11th of February, 1990, and lauded by the very same regime that had branded him a traitor. He emerged from prison as a shining light to hundreds of millions of human beings, worldwide.

His life is a superb example of a man with purpose, patience, and fortitude who, after a lifetime in chains, rose meteorically to the greatest heights of glory. He and his party had tried for decades to pursue their cause peacefully. They forever made applications and appeals through the correct channels, only to be shunned, ignored, and scorned. All he was asking for was liberty, equality, and human dignity for his people.

After years of being condemned for his efforts, Nelson Mandela and his African National Congress finally were forced to put on the gloves and fight for their freedom. The regime speedily clamped down upon his efforts.

As the famous Rivonia Trial drew to its end, people were expecting the death penalty to be imposed on Mandela. When, in fact, the verdict was life imprisonment, his people actually rejoiced. They cheered. They danced. They sang.

"He has received life. Mandela has life!"

His living example, his attitude, his spirit, both during imprisonment and after his release, has caused me to look at and examine my own life and what it stands for. Here I was moping and worrying about my physical and financial problems. How paltry. How self-centered. How pathetic, when compared with Nelson Mandela's interminable struggle. He must have experienced the very depths of despondency, yet during his 27 years of being shackled, he maintained his dignity and never wavered once from his cause, despite attacks on what he stood for from every quarter.

Like a floating cork, he rose time and again. They punished him; his purpose stayed intact. They tried to crush him; his faith grew. They tried to sway him; he focused in all the more. They tried to weaken his resolve; his fortitude grew. They struggled to change him; he struggled back in his quiet way. They offered him "half the world" if he did it their way; he refused to compromise his people and his principles. He remained patient. When they finally released him on 11 February, 1990, he owned the whole world. But above all, after such unjust persecution, he came out actually loving the world and its people. Amazing. Just amazing.

The prime part of his destiny was fulfilled on 27 April, 1994, when nearly every South African of every creed, race, and religion voted in peace and celebration, with little or no violence to speak of. Nelson Mandela was inaugurated as President of the Interim Government of the new, free South Africa. His fall and rise had a great positive impact upon me. I learned I must appreciate every day and make the best of it—to be purposeful and keep going for my goals, no matter what!

Beyond Spirit of the Empty Hand

18

NEW ATTITUDE, NEW LIFE

Meeting Myself

During the *apartheid* years of worldwide sanctions against South Africa, I had gradually grown used to behaving like a third-class citizen of the world, while traveling abroad. I was forever on the defensive about South Africa. My attitude was apologetic, and on one or two occasions, I lied that I was Australian or British, just to keep the peace. I wasn't proud of my country, but to be honest, I also hadn't done much about changing the desperate plight of the suppressed people. I thought that if I treated people of all races with dignity and fairness and voted for the Progressive Party, I was doing enough. Also, I tried to run JKA on non-racial lines, from its inception in 1963. But that monster, racism, forever poked its ugly head into karate events, when least expected.

On one *gashuku*, all had been going well, or so I thought, until someone pointed out to me that two white fourth *dans* were intimidating a group of young black instructors.

"Watch when they enter the training hall."

The black instructors had arrived early and were warming up prior to me taking the class. I watched from a distance and was flabbergasted as I saw the two "heavies" (both in weight and attitude), call the young black instructors off from the floor, to outside where they proceeded to insult them, using foul language, while pushing them on the chest. Their "crime" was having entered the *dojo* before they had. It jarred my spirit to witness this wrongdoing.

I called everybody together inside and spoke to them.

"There is only one color that counts in karate. Not the color of your belt! Not the color of your skin! Only the color of your spirit counts in our association!"

I told the two heavies that if they were so keen to express their unwelcome and uncontrolled emotions, they were very welcome to express them against the likes of Derrick and Keith Geyer, who enjoy free fighting even more than Castle beer. The heavies came out of the free fighting looking extremely light. Sometime later they joined a rival association, much to my joy. I don't normally like to kick people out of our organization. I am forever hopeful that the prejudiced ones may just change and become more civilized. But when one of these destructive characters chooses to leave our association, I have to admit, we celebrate. And that is one thing we are very good at.

After the *gashuku* two of our senior black instructors came up to me at dinner.

"Thank you, Sensei," was all they said.

Beyond Spirit of the Empty Hand

Once, when I visited Okazaki Sensei's *dojo* in the USA, he invited me to teach a class of instructors. Many of them were black, and being a South African in the US at the time was nearly as bad as someone from the Gestapo visiting Israel. After the class was over, a dignified, smartly dressed black man approached me.

"Sensei Stan, my son just trained in your class. I have been watching you with great interest. I have read your book, *Spirit of the Empty Hand*. I loved your words, but to be honest, I still had my reservations about you, a white South African, you know."

"I don't blame you. All I can say is things are not right in my country yet, and I am sorry."

"Don't be sorry, Sensei. I have watched you closely and I have to tell you this. I could follow you around the world, Sensei. And I like the way you look into my eyes."

My eyes were wet as I left the *dojo*. In harmony with the rebirth of South Africa, I wanted harmony, health, and prosperity in my now very large family. I wanted to be a good friend to my friends, not so much the other way around. I wanted to become a real karate master. (I am still working on that one.) I wanted to give good and uplifting instruction to my students. I wanted to keep training sensibly and be open to learning so that I could communicate and share with karate-ka and other people worldwide, the value and unlimited scope of my chosen art. I wanted to settle all of my debts and have enough means to pursue a constructive and meaningful life.

I wanted to experience the love of God and man. And lastly, I wanted to blow sweet, blue and bright notes out of my jazz trumpet.

Self-Defense Through The Spirit

South Africa, especially Gauteng Province where I live, is a dynamic place in many respects. It is a melting pot of scores of cultures. Our humor, music, rhythm, sport, and dance are great. But if Al Capone's Chicago was rated fifth *dan* in terms of violence and crime, then greater Johannesburg is a seventh *dan*. We need to change this, and I believe we can. In my club alone there are at least a dozen of my members or their families who have been mugged, shot at, car-jacked, or assaulted in their very ownhomes.

High walls, electrified fences, barbed wire, barred windows, car alarms, security guard services, knives, guns, and AK47 automatic weapons are as common to South Africa as talk shows are to the USA.

In the past 30 years, nobody ever attempted to assault or mug me personally. But just when I was at my weakest, two months after my second hip operation, it happened.

They say that sharks prefer to attack a weak and floundering prey. Well, there I was out on the street, on one crutch, pale, and far too thin for my liking, carrying a canvas bank bag. I had just stepped out of a drug store near my *dojo* when two thugs approached me. I was fair game. As the one was edging in close, and the other started reaching out for the canvas bank bag, I did something I would never have thought of ever doing. In fact, I surprised myself as I suddenly pointed to behind the two men, shouting, "Hello, Johnny! How are you?" like somebody I knew was there, right behind them. They both fell for it. Their heads turned involuntarily to see who was behind them. There was no one there. But during that brief moment, the traffic light changed and I moved, crutch and all, across the intersection, waving them good-bye. They stood there looking dumbfounded but made no attempt to follow me. If they had managed to get the bank bag, they would have been quite upset as there was no money in that bag.

That same evening, when I related the incident to my students, one of them commented, "Sensei, you really used your head there."

"I didn't have time to use my head," I responded. "It was like it was done for me. Like I had nothing to do with it."

"How do you mean, Sensei?" another student wanted to know.

"Well, I am still trying to understand it all myself. Do you agree that when you have trained the body and the mind through kata, *kihon*, and *kumite* properly, and your techniques have become highly skilled, you can be quite lethal. Do you agree?" They nodded in agreement.

"But," I continued, "the interesting thing is that I never once ever practiced the move I did out there on the street this evening."

"Then shouldn't we be practicing that sort of thing?"

"There is no way of practicing every type of scenario. Practice your basic techniques and katas correctly, and your confidence should grow. And confidence has to do with faith in yourself. But having faith in yourself *only* is not enough. You may well become a lethal fighting machine when you achieve peak fitness. But should you fall off that shaky physical pedestal like I have done recently, then faith in your ability to perform demanding physical

Beyond Spirit of the Empty Hand

feats is simply phony faith. That's why faith in yourself, *only,* is limiting."

"What are you saying, Sensei?" someone wanted to know.

"All I am saying is that somehow it seemed to me that some greater power than me acted on my behalf out there tonight."

Keith Geyer nodded. The others looked quizzical. I turned to Keith.

"Maybe I'm putting it badly. How do you understand it, Keith?"

"Sensei, I think you are trying to say, 'Greater is He that is in me, than he who is in the world' and that *He* protected you when you were at your most vulnerable."

I bowed once to Keith.

"Thank you, my friend." Then to the group I said, "I think he's right. We cannot always rely on our mortal flesh and bones to solve problems of the spirit. The human predator comes like a thief in the night to steal, kill or destroy. He attacks when you are least ready to cope with him—when you are asleep, weak, proud or vulnerable. Why? Because in him dwells an evil spirit, the spirit of the vampire that has to operate in the darkness. It cannot face the truth. When a robber or killer confronts you in the shape of a man, or a group of men intent on destroying you, it is their spirit you have to deal with more than their weapons. It is the spirit of the *full* hand that wields their weapons. Capture, conquer, or change their spirit and they are lost, or won over. But to achieve this, we have to have the right kind of spirit dwelling within us. For in the end, any serious warfare that we may be forced to engage in is, in essence, spiritual warfare, namely, good versus evil. The *open,* giving hand, against the *closed* selfish hand.

"Of course, you must do everything you can—study, learn evaluate, and apply your learning. But when a problem that is above you arises, you have to learn to let go. To have enough faith to allow *Him* to do it."

"Who is *Him,* Sensei?" asked a young brown belt.

"Well, my son, my job is to teach you practical self-defense. If you really want to know who *He* is, then go to your pastor, your rabbi, your priest, your spiritual advisor, and tell them this story. Ask them who *He* is."

As I drove home later I began to realize how, having been humbled and hospitalized, I had begun to see that I needed to expand my faith beyond my own physical strength and carefully cultivated ego. It was now quite clear to me that it was not *my* mind, not *my* body that rescued me from the muggers. It was pure spirit that did it. I remembered what Pastor John Stegmann had told me years ago.

"My strength is made perfect in your weakness." That was it. I had managed to let go, for once in my life, and by grace I was directed by none other than the power of all powers, the spirit of God.

I just wish I could be like that all of the time. This, in essence, is "beyond the spirit of the empty hand."

Milk and Honey

In 1994 there was a great spirit of revival in South Africa. As I have said, the first non-racial general elections took place in an unexpected atmosphere of peace and joyful celebration. Nelson Mandela became the new President, his countenance shining over all of Africa, reaching around the entire globe.

That same year a big consortium bought the Melrose property from me at a price I couldn't refuse. All of my debilitating debts were settled in one day, and I had enough put aside to buy another property and build the *dojo* that I had always wanted. I was now a tenant at the Melrose property, with the huge responsibility of being the proprietor off my shoulders.

Even though it was two years since my second hip operation, I was still not yet able to perform the traditional katas smoothly and without experiencing twinges of pain or losing balance. My body had changed radically, and it would need time to heal and adjust to its modified state. At the end of 1993 my family and I took a month's vacation. I spent 30 days on a mountain overlooking the idyllic Hout Bay near Cape Town. There I trained outside on a lawn for a couple of hours every morning, developing a kata that enabled me to move smoothly without any hitches. Furthermore, there were moves (many I had learned from Master Claude Chanu) that had been percolating in the back of my mind, and were crying out to be expressed. These I included in the new kata.

"Sensei, I would like to learn that kata," a student requested after seeing me practicing it back at the *dojo*.

"First try to master the traditional Shotokan katas," I told him. "This kata is not for anybody else. I am still busy developing it. It isn't complete yet."

Beyond Spirit of the Empty Hand

On a trip to the USA, I met my publisher, Randall Hassell, of Focus Publications, for the first time. We had, of course, been communicating for many years. But meeting him in person was wonderful. I found him to be a sensei with a great depth of understanding of karate, its history, and philosophy. From our first handshake we got on well. He arranged some clinics for me throughout the United States and introduced me to Master Osamu Ozawa, the famous Japanese karate man and ex-*kamikaze* pilot, who survived when his plane crashed. Randy was busy writing Ozawa's biography at the time.

Later in 1994 I returned to the USA to Philadelphia together with my wife, family, and a South African contingent of more than 300 karate-ka supporting our team, which took part in the Fifth Shoto Cup, the world championship of JKA Shotokan karate. The championship turned out to be an event to beat all events. It was staged by Master Teruyuki Okazaki and his International Shotokan Karate Federation.

South Africa, having been out in the cold for so long, experienced great and unexpected fortune at this well-run and well-attended tournament. No Westerner had ever managed to capture the title, "All Japan Champion" or "JKA World Champion," but somehow, Pavlo Protopapa, a student of Keith Geyer, systematically worked his way through the numerous rounds, past the likes of the powerful Shina from Japan, up to the final match against the six-foot-three Mulolo of Belgium.

I have never experienced a more exciting tournament in my life. A greater part of the audience was yelling and cheering, "Pavlo! Pavlo!" He won. Sensei Sugiura was the referee. I shouted and jumped out of my seat, cheering so loudly that the two Japanese officials sitting next to me must have come close to having a heart attack. Colin Smith, another student of Keith Geyer, reached joint third place with Shina.

Furthermore, a young black student of mine, Jason Khumalo, who was part of our development program, managed to win the junior *kumite* world title. When he returned to South Africa, Steve Tshwete, Minister of Sport, said to the press, "This is good for the underprivileged youth of our country. Jason, you are my hero. You are a role model for South African youth. You have shown them that it can be done."

Another great highlight was renewing friendships with a number of famous Japanese senseis based in the United States—

Meeting Myself

Teruyuki Okazaki, Takayuki Mikami, Yutaka Yaguchi, Shojiro Koyama, Shigeru Takashina, and Masataka Mori.

A touching part of the World Shoto Cup was a little incident that remains forever in my heart, as an example of what the spirit of karate is all about. After Pavlo had won, Shina, the powerful Japanese who was the favorite to win, walked over to me. He bowed and extended his hand.

"Congratulations, Mistah Stan. Pavlo good world champion."

Shina's sincerity brought a tear to my eye. I bowed to Shina.

"Shina, in my mind you are also a good world champion *and* gentleman. I admire you."

In 1995 I was invited by Ozawa Sensei to do a demonstration and give a clinic at his famous annual International Tournament at Bally's Hotel, Las Vegas. Although I was a little unsure, I accepted this challenge. I had not done a demonstration since before my first hip operation in 1990.

One of the first people I ran into at the tournament was none other than Gary Friedrich, that tough little American I first trained with in Yotsuya in 1963. Clearly a popular man, he was surrounded by a group of friends and students who hung on his every word, words which were garnished with an irresistible sense of humor.

About 100 karate-ka attended my clinic. It was the first I had had the honor of giving in the USA for a long time. The tournament was held in a large auditorium, one of those that stars like Barbara Streisand, Frank Sinatra, and Tom Jones appear in.

On the final day of Ozawa's tournament I grew quite apprehensive about appearing on stage after other experts like Senseis Takayuki Mikami, Fumio Demura, Teruo Chinen, John McClary, and John Daniel had performed flawless demonstrations in front of a large audience consisting of a mass of black belt karate-ka and martial arts senseis. For my demonstration I had been practicing *Tekki Sandan* kata together with my team of Mark Hildyard, Colin Smith, and Joel Proskewitz as well as the *bunkai* of the kata. The three *Tekki* katas had been perfect for training during my rehabilitation.

As I was about to mount the stage, I decided at the last moment to do the demonstration a little differently. I asked my team to wait until I called them on.

It occurred to me that I now had the perfect opportunity to communicate an uplifting message. I would not be able to get it through to this audience by merely doing *Tekki Sandan* and its application against three attackers.

Before being hospitalized, I would never have thought of actually speaking as part of a karate demonstration. But the hospital had somehow caused me to be less inhibited. I had no fear. I would just do it.

As they called me on stage, I placed a chair in the center of the stage and sat down on it. I started telling the story of a man who was hospitalized and who, from being left powerless on his back, raised himself up. I acted out each part. I even pulled out a flat stone and struck it while lying half propped up. I progressed to sitting on the edge of the chair, to doing *Tekki Shodan* sitting, to standing up, doing the same kata on the spot, to doing it in a small *kiba-dachi* stance. All of this I demonstrated with soft and delicate moves while talking into the microphone. I told them it took me nearly two years before I could once more interact again freely with my fellow karate-ka. It had been a lonely, yet fulfilling road, back to good health. It was then that I called on my team.

After me talking and showing the audience very deliberate, slow, soft, tentative movements, my team and I exploded into *Tekki Sandan* with a dynamism that had been absent during the first part of the demo. I completed the demo by fighting off three attackers using moves from *Tekki Sandan*.

I suppose that the audience enjoyed the demonstration, but more than that, the experience had done something for me. I experienced a sense of satisfaction that money cannot buy when my family, friends, and senseis like Chinen, Gary Friedrichs, and Keith Geyer told me the demo was nice.

I was humbled when *Black Belt* magazine later reported on the demonstration and said, "Stan Schmidt is the type of man you would want to have teaching your children karate."

Reunion

A highlight in my karate life was my visit to Japan in 1995. Seto had arranged a reunion between us and Nick (C.W. Nicol), our mutual friend from 1963.

The journey by train with Seto to Kurohime, was a special trip for me in many ways. I learned things from Seto that are not easy to express in words. He told me that Nick owned a forest of his own in the mountains of Kurohime and that he couldn't wait to see me. I felt the same way. Thirty-two years had passed, and this was like returning full circle, into one's past, but through the present.

It was dusk when we arrived at Kurohime station, a quaint siding over which a range of tree clad mountains kept watch. Seto made a telephone call, and while we waited outside the front entrance of the station, I saw in the deepening shadows, a tall rock, artistically set in a small garden. On looking more closely, I noticed that there was a haiku poem in Japanese characters, neatly carved into it. Just below the characters was the English translation, with the notation, "Translated by C. W. Nicol."

"Yes," smiled Seto, "our Nick very famous in all of Japan."

We were transported in a 4 x 4 to a spacious, modern, wood-and-glass-type country residence set at the foot of the mountain, on a glade surrounded by a dense forest of trees. The pathway leading to the front door was well-lit and welcoming.

As we entered the expansive lounge, dining room, and kitchen combined, two people rose from their chairs next to a wood fire to greet us. One, a huge bearded man with a bush of curly hair and naughty, twinkling eyes, Nick.

"Welcome, Stan. Welcome, Seto," Nick said, handing me a glass of dry white wine.

The other man, a Japanese, I recognized but couldn't remember who he was.

"Ikeda!" he beamed.

"Oh, yes! You are the *kendo* man and sculptor in Nick's book, *Moving Zen.*"

"Long time no see."

Soon we were hugging each other, laughing, and swallowing cool crisp wine, drinking to each other's health and good fortune. We settled down and talked animatedly. Nick was the perfect host—mature, charming, wise, and humorous, all in one. Three of Nick's friends, who ran a restaurant in the village—a man, his wife, and his daughter—were present, laying out an exquisitely prepared meal, the aroma of which had my mouth watering. This meal was prepared "in honor of the reunion of Nick, Seto, Ikeda, and Stan," declared the cook.

We ate heartily. Then we settled ourselves, wine in hand, in the lounge.

"Ikeda Sensei, show us your art of the sword," Nick requested.

Ikeda performed a series of moves first on his knees, moving like the wind across the polished wooden floor. My heart was

Beyond Spirit of the Empty Hand

beating at twice its normal speed as he completed his short but superb demonstration with a gladiatorial shout, "I-ya!"

"Stan, that is why he is an eighth *dan* in his art," said Nick.

I had known Ikeda as a first *kyu*, brown belt. What a change. He had demonstrated such outstanding technique and expression.

"Okay, Stan, now it's your turn. Show us *your* art of karate," Nick challenged.

"What?" I exclaimed, totally surprised by this unexpected request. When I appealed to Seto for help out of this predicament, all he did was support Nick, saying, "Stan, please show them your new kata, the one you told me about on the train."

There was no way I could refuse. Refusing the request would be a total loss of face for me under these circumstances.

I walked into the center of the lounge, bowed to the small group of Nick, Seto, Ikeda, and the three hosts, and performed my kata. My two *kiais* resounded through the house, crystal clear. I liked the sound.

Nick and Ikeda jumped to their feet, applauding my effort. Nick was already talking into his walkie-talkie.

"Come to the house, now. Yes, right now." He turned to me. "Stan, I like your kata. I want to learn it. It's nice and circular. It would suit my body."

"What is the kata called?" Ikeda wanted to know.

"No name. It's just for me," I said.

About three or four of Nick's rangers arrived together with Kensuke, Seto's younger brother, who was recently promoted to seventh *dan*. They greeted me and sat down on the floor, waiting.

"Please do it again for us, Stan."

As I finished the kata for the second time, more rangers arrived. The lounge was now full. Nick asked me to do it for a third time, for the benefit of the new arrivals.

"Before you do, Stan, please give your kata a name," pleaded Ikeda.

"Will you name it for me?" I asked him. "I would consider that an honor."

Ikeda and the group huddled together, and there was a lot of animated discussion. Ikeda drew something on a piece of cardboard. At last there was a resounding cheer from the group.

"We have a name for your kata, Stan!"

"What is it, Ikeda Sensei?"

"*Uki!*" he solemnly announced. Everybody in the room applauded. "It is a perfect name," he proudly told me, handing me his pen drawing of a man balancing on a rock and pushing down with a stick onto a log which was partially immersed in a lake of water.

"*Uki*," I repeated. "What does it mean, Sensei?"

"It means 'floating log'. *Uki; the floating log* kata," he repeated. I was intrigued. He explained how he arrived at the name.

"I listened to you at dinner telling us about your down time in hospital. And now we all see you doing this kata. Like a floating log, you push one side down, and the other side comes up. This is your spirit, Stan san. Like a floating log. Can never keep you down."

Nick led me into the center of the lounge.

"Stan, please perform *Uki* for us, just once more."

"*Uki!*" I announced. The word echoed through the house. This was a very special and proud moment for me, far more meaningful than doing a seventh *dan* test or winning a gold medal. It was a moment in time every artist and sportsperson strives for—one of those extraordinary moments when one has the rare fortune of briefly touching heaven.

And right there, in that Japanese lounge, in the midst of the forest and mountains of Kurohime, reunited with my special friends, Seto, Nick, and Ikeda, I experienced for one fleeting moment, ecstasy.

Appendix 1

General Standards for Black Belt Rankings of the Japan Karate Association

Shodan (1st *Dan*)	This level necessitates the motivation of all basic body movements and techniques, including hand and leg techniques to be applied with extended force and proper application in basic combinations.
Nidan (2nd *Dan*)	This stage requires the personal assimilation and performance of all basic body movements and techniques to such a degree that their application is in accord with the individual's own unique body demands.
Sandan (3rd *Dan*)	Has acquired the understanding of the underlying principles in all basic body movements and techniques. This understanding must be demonstrated in the application of techniques under varied circumstances and conditions.
Yondan (4th *Dan*)	Has excellent knowledge of the principle body movements and techniques and their application under varied conditions to such a degree that the ability to instruct others has been gained.
Godan (5th *Dan*)	Research has been completed in some limited area. This research includes its application in a manner that is both relevant and applicable to the individual's particular physique.
Rokudan (6th *Dan*)	Has completed research in an area that by its nature has a universal benefit to be derived by its application.
Shichidan (7th *Dan*)	Must have undertaken advanced research through actual application and

Beyond Spirit of the Empty Hand

	extensive testing of the general research technique.
Hachidan (8th *Dan*)	Research completed in a new and previously unknown area.
Kudan (9th *Dan*)	This level calls for an extended period of time to the areas of individual achievement, research and technique. This dedication must have culminated in *karate* achievement and development of the highest and most extraordinary order. Moreover, this accumulated knowledge and expertise must have been utilized in the general service of *karate-do* development.
Judan (10th *Dan*)	This is the stage where the individual has finally neared the highest ideal of *karate* development which has been brought about by the continuous practice and pursuit of truth that is to be found in the highest degree of human excellence possible.

Appendix 2

The Early Birds Past and Present

Meeting Myself

Affleck, Jimmy
Almeida, Gilbert
Beckenstrater, Charles
Becker, Mike
Belnick, Brian
Bilchik, Anton
Bilchik, Brian
Boltina, John
Brick, Laurence
Brits, Pierre
Bunkell, Peter
Crane, Alan
Devine, Robin
Diavastos, Costa
Dix, Neale
Dorey, Eddie
Dorfman, Malcolm
Drakoulas, Spiro
Duncan, Ian
Efstratiou, Elena
England, Mike
Evian, Cyril
Faiga, Roy
Fasoli, Gino
Ferreira, Jose
Ferriere, Robert
Finlay, Robin
Fisher, Des
Fourie, Allen
Foyn, Peter
Fracchiolla, M.
Friend, Dave
George, Alan
Geyer, Derrick
Geyer, Keith
Gibson, Buddy
Gigante, Pino
Gillespie, Bob
Godorr, Sven
Greenblatt, Laurence
Grevler, Basil

Groess, Hans
Hauptfleish, Chris
Herold, Arthur
Hertz, Arnold
Hertz, Roleen
Higginson, John
Hildyard, Mark
Hlobo, Paul
Holton, Alan
Jankes, Phil
Joffee, Raymond
Karamitis, Tony
Kerrane, Pat
Khumalo, Jason
Kornberger, Carl
Krug, Jeff
Kruger, Mark
Kruger, Percy
Lambrechts, Al
Legrange, Johan
Leiman, Michelle
Lentin, Mark
LeRoux, Piet
Leiman, Darryl
Lester, Mike
Levinrad, Ivan
Levy, Neil
Lubner, Tony
Macfarlane, Vic
Macintosh, Al
Makete, Hanley
Malusi (Kwatsha), Stanley
Mance, Chris
Mann, Gary
Mantovan, Mirco
Marques, Mario
Maritz, Johnny
Mennen, Nardo
Meyer, Fanie
Miller, Mike
Mokgoro, Theo

Beyond Spirit of the Empty Hand

Mosedi, Dan
Mothusi, Badu
Mtshali, Edward
Nteso, David
Ogura, Sami
Oosthuizen, Coen
Palm, Bev
Parvis, Philip
Polovin, Peter
Pretorius, Koos
Proskewitz, Joel
Protopapa, Panico
Protopapa, Pavlo
Rabinowitz, Garry
Regtien, Rene
Richardson, Gordon
Robertshaw, Dave
Robinson, Norman
Rodriques, Jose
Roets, Eugene
Roets, Johan
Roos, Fanie
Ross, Arthur
Ruehl, E.
Sacks, Robert
Sangweni, Gibson
Schmidt, Robert
Seabelo, Chris
Shadwell, Rodney
Sham, Les
Shandler, Mike
Shaw, Kathy
Sherman, Les
Smith, Bruce
Smith, Colin
Soloway, Maish
Steinburg, Coert
Stevens, Les
Sullivan, Terry
Theron, Steven
Toulouras, Angela
Van den Bergh, Lutie

Van Rensburg, Piet
Van Tonder, Giel
Venter, Willem
Wanenberg, Wendy
Webber, Ronnie
West, Norman
Wittstock, Ken
Wolov, Cecil

LOOK FOR THESE FINE BOOKS AT YOUR BOOKSTORE
or Order Directly From

Focus Publications
P O BOX 15853
ST LOUIS MO 63114 USA

Phone: 314-426-3328 • Fax: 314-426-3610
Order Line: 1-800-56-FOCUS

Samurai Journey
by Randall G. Hassell & Osamu Ozawa

The biography of Osamu Ozawa, the most senior Shotokan instructor in the Western world! Follow Ozawa's remarkable story, from his *samurai* upbringing, to crashing as a *kamikaze* pilot, to his run as the most successful TV director in Japan; from his rise to riches and decline into poverty, to his final triumph as a karate master. Features Ozawa's remembrances of the many influential people he's encountered including the world's greatest karate masters like Gichin Funakoshi and Kenwa Mabuni and Hollywood stars like Frank Sinatra and Rita Moreno, plus much more!
 "A fascinating, honest look at a true karate master."
— *Bugeisha Magazine*.
 Illustrated. ISBN 0-911921-24-9

Zen, Pen, and Sword:
The Karate Experience
by Randall G. Hassell

In the spirit of his bestseller *The Karate Experience, A Way of Life*, Hassell brings to life the essence of traditional martial arts: "For me," he says, "Zen symbolizes the spiritual dimension of the martial arts, pen the intellectual dimension, and sword the physical dimension."
 ISBN 0-911921-13-3

FOCUS PUBLICATIONS
P O BOX 15853
ST LOUIS MO 63114 USA

Phone: 314-426-3328 • Fax: 314-426-3610
Order Line: 1-800-56-FOCUS

Meeting Myself: Beyond Spirit of the Empty Hand
by Stan Schmidt

The autobiography of the world's highest-ranking, non-Japanese, JKA master! Re-live with Stan Schmidt almost 40 years of karate training—much of it in Japan! Share the insights he has gained from his experiences in the famous JKA Instructors' Class in Tokyo, competing against Japan's elite competitors, teaching in his native South Africa, and more! Also—read about his experiences performing in several famous martial arts movies and see remarkable photos from Schmidt's personal collection!

"Incredibly inspiring...A definitive representation of the true spirit of traditional karate." — *Rick Brewer, Inside Karate*

"A story of struggle, tragedy, and triumph...Inspiring!"
— *Karate-do Times*

Illustrated. ISBN 0-911921-25-7

Conversations With the Master: Masatoshi Nakayama
by Randall G. Hassell

The author was the only Western journalist to whom the late headmaster of the Japan Karate Association granted extensive, in-depth interviews for the specific purpose of writing a book. Nakayama describes his early training under the founder of modern karate, Gichin Funakoshi, and talks extensively about modern karate—where it was, where it is, and where it is going. Must reading for all serious martial artists!

Illustrated. ISBN 0-911921-00-1

FOCUS PUBLICATIONS
P O BOX 15853
ST LOUIS MO 63114 USA

Phone: 314-426-3328 • Fax: 314-426-3610
Order Line: 1-800-56-FOCUS

Spirit of the Empty Hand
by Stan Schmidt
The fascinating true story of the author's journey from the first day of karate training to achieving 3rd degree black belt in Japan. Written by the world's highest-ranking, non-Japanese, JKA master instructor.
  "Stan Schmidt is the best example of what dedication to karate can do for a man. A martial gentleman."
— *C.W.Nicol, Author, Moving Zen.*
  ISBN 0-911921-02-8

Shotokan Karate: Its History and Evolution— Revised & Illustrated Edition
by Randall G. Hassell
The first comprehensive written history of Shotokan karate in any language! In this completely revised edition of the classic bestseller, Randall G. Hassell covers recent developments in the art of Shotokan karate-do. Rare and never-before-published photos complement everything from the Okinawan roots of karate to the JKA in Japan and the United States, American karate organizations, and the current state of karate. Also in this edition: A chronology of Shotokan Karate, the origins of all Shotokan kata, a genealogy of traditional karate, and much more.
  "A masterful portrait of modern karate's development."
— *The Fighter Magazine.*
  Illustrated. ISBN 0-911921-20-6

FOCUS PUBLICATIONS
P O BOX 15853
ST LOUIS MO 63114 USA

Phone: 314-426-3328 • Fax: 314-426-3610
Order Line: 1-800-56-FOCUS

Karate Ideals
by Randall G. Hassell
A serious, thought-provoking book that examines the philosophical, historical, and societal influences on the martial arts of the *samurai,* and how these influences are reflected in modern-day karate training.
 ISBN 0911921-18-4

Karate Training Guide Volume 1: Foundations of Training
by Randall G. Hassell
An illustrated guide to the basic techniques and philosophy of karate training. Clear line drawings and move-by-move instructions make this an invaluable sourcebook for beginners and advanced alike. Includes kata *Heian Shodan* and *Nidan.*
 Illustrated. ISBN 0-911921-22-2

Karate Training Guide Volume 2:: Kata—Heian, Tekki, Bassai Dai
by Randall G. Hassell
Complete, simple, move-by-move instructions of Beginner through Brown Belt Shotokan-style kata:*Heian Shodan through Godan, Tekki Shodan through Sandan, and Bassai Dai,* plus detailed analysis of selected moves
 Illustrated. ISBN 0-911921-23-0

FOCUS PUBLICATIONS
P O BOX 15853
ST LOUIS MO 63114 USA
Phone: 314-426-3328 • Fax: 314-426-3610
Order Line: 1-800-56-FOCUS

The Karate Spirit
by Randall G. Hassell
A revised, selected collection of the author's popular column that originally appeared in *Black Belt* magazine for more than three years.
    ISBN 0-911921-19-2

Modern Karate:Scientific Approach to Conditioning and Training
by Milorad Stricevic; Dusan Dacic; Toyotaro Miyazaki; George Anderson
Learn how to acheive peak conditioning and unbeatable competition skills—regardless of style! Over 750 photos, charts, graphs, and illustrations.
    "Authoritative...Excellent..."
    — Hidy Ochiai, 8th Dan, Washin-ryu
        •Hardcover• Illustrated. ISBN 0-9622012-0-0

New Students in Karate: The First 3 Months
by Merlin T. Taylor, Jr.
Answers the most commonly asked questions about traditional karate training and offers advice on everything from bowing to ranking to prevention and treatment of injuries. Also a great reference for instructors. Required reading in many *dojos* around the world.
    Illustrated. ISBN 0-911921-21-4

FOCUS PUBLICATIONS
P O BOX 15853
ST LOUIS MO 63114 USA

Phone: 314-426-3328 • Fax: 314-426-3610
Order Line: 1-800-56-FOCUS

Advanced Karate-Do: Concepts, Techniques, and Training Methods
by Elmar T. Schmeisser, Ph.D.

A technical book that clearly and concisely analyzes, in detail, the advanced concepts of Shotokan-style karate. Includes a large section devoted to in-breath forms of kata. The author, a Doctor of Medical Physiology, combines his scientific background and three decades of karate experience for the benefit of instructors and students alike.

"Refreshing...Compelling...Unique..."
– *John Cheetham, Shotokan Karate Magazine.*
"...Breaks new ground...I highly recommend this book."
– *Howard High, Founder, Cyber Dojo.*
Illustrated. ISBN 0-911921-16-8

Recognition (A Novel)
**by Stan Schmidt
with Randall G. Hassell**

Promising young athlete, Jonathan Walker, is felled by serious injury and thrust into a strange environment fraught with conflict and loneliness. While painfully struggling to come to terms with his solitude, self-worth, emerging sexuality, and physical limitations, Jonathan unexpectedly falls under the guidance of a mysterious karate master from another land. By secretly observing this enigmatic man, Jonathan begins to see deeper into his own nature and the true nature of those around him. A truly inspiring story!
ISBN 0-911921-17-6

Focus Publications
P O BOX 15853
ST LOUIS MO 63114 USA

Phone: 314-426-3328 • Fax: 314-426-3610
Order Line: 1-800-56-FOCUS

EXCITING VIDEOTAPES

Soul of Karate Original Director's Cut
Featuring Stan Schmidt
Live the essence of traditional karate training the rugged South African way. Contains some of the most exciting karate footage ever shot! The intriguing story never lets up in this completely restored masterpiece documentary!
   "This tape shows what the true karate spirit is about. Every instructor must see it."
   — *Masatoshi Nakayama, late Headmaster, Japan Karate Association.*
      VHS ISBN 0-911921-27-3

The Winning Blow
Showcasing Tanaka, Yahara, Osaka, Oishi, Kagawa, and many others!
See the world's most famous karate-ka like you've never seen them before! This fast-paced, half-hour TV program features over two dozen Japanese karate masters in footage from the *All-Japan* and *World Championships,* the JKA HQ in Tokyo, and much more! **Narrated by Stan Schmidt.**
      VHS ISBN 0-911921-28-1

FOCUS PUBLICATIONS
P O BOX 15853
ST LOUIS MO 63114 USA

Phone: 314-426-3328 • Fax: 314-426-3610
Order Line: 1-800-56-FOCUS

Stan Schmidt Instructs SHOTOKAN KARATE

Volume 1: Beginner Level
The world's highest-ranking Western instructor provides easy-to-follow demonstrations of basic techniques, kata *Heian Shodan* and *Nidan*, 5-step sparring, limbering, strengthening, throws, ground immobilization's, and self-defense.
 VHS ISBN 0-911921-29-X

Volume 2: Intermediate
Schmidt teaches, demonstrates, and provides practical applications of kata *Heian Sandan, Yondan,* and *Godan*. Includes 1-step sparring, *makiwara* training, and more. Featuring World Champion Pavlo Protopappa.
 VHS ISBN 0-911921-30-3

Volume 3 Available Soon!